Brian Murgatroyd has worked as a journalist, broadcaster and sports administrator for more than 25 years, in that time attending more than 170 Test matches all over the world. He was the England cricket team's first full-time, travelling media manager in the late 1990s and subsequently had three separate spells in the same role with Cricket Australia. He has filed copy for two of the world's leading news agencies, Reuters and Agence France Presse, and was the International Cricket Council's head of media and communications for almost four years. Brian lives in Dubai with his wife and young daughter and this book is the sixth he has contributed to.

THE JOURNEY
STEVE SMITH

WITH BRIAN MURGATROYD

My story, from backyard cricket to Australian captain

To Hamilton,
Enjoy the Read!
Best wishes

ALLEN&UNWIN
SYDNEY · MELBOURNE · AUCKLAND · LONDON

First published in 2017

Allen & Unwin
83 Alexander Street
Crows Nest NSW 2065
Australia
Phone: (61 2) 8425 0100
Email: info@allenandunwin.com
Web: www.allenandunwin.com

Cataloguing-in-Publication details are available
from the National Library of Australia
www.trove.nla.gov.au

ISBN 978 1 76063 053 9

Internal design by Deb Parry
Set in 12/16.5 pt Sabon by Midland Typesetters, Australia
Printed and bound in Australia by Griffin Press
10 9 8 7 6 5 4 3 2 1

CONTENTS

CHAPTER 1
'Adapt!'

If you want an example of something from my past that explains how I developed into the cricketer I am today, then a good place to start is not a cricket oval but a tennis court.

I was never as good at tennis as I was at cricket but it was still a sport I took seriously and I played it quite a lot when I was younger, especially during winter when it filled the void left by an absence of cricket matches every weekend. There were courts at Menai High School, just up the road from the family home in Alfords Point, about 30 kilometres from the centre of Sydney, and I enjoyed playing tennis there with my friends and my dad.

But on one occasion, when I was 14 and taking part in a tournament in nearby Bangor, there wasn't an awful lot of enjoyment to be had, at least for me, as I was getting beaten and beaten badly.

I was up against a boy four years older, a man really, and while I was relatively slight at that stage of my development he loomed large as someone much bigger, stronger and faster than me.

Despite the age and size difference, my stubborn and competitive outlook ruled my actions and I tried to match him shot for shot, but his power was winning the day and he was blowing me off the court.

I was 4–0 down and heading for a thumping, and although I was relatively calm—something that wasn't always the case when I played—I was also frustrated by my inability to make any impression on the match. I looked up at Dad, watching on from the sidelines.

When I caught his eye, I was looking for inspiration in an apparently hopeless situation. Dad didn't say anything; instead he made a gesture with his hand, pointing to his temple. 'Adapt!' was his message.

Dad's always been a great advocate of thinking through problems in order to try and solve them. He's a very intelligent man and when he bowled to me during our endless hours of practice at nearby Casuarina Oval, he was constantly challenging me to come up with ways of doing things better. His message was always the same: if something wasn't working then try something different because there's more than one way to skin a cat.

2

He was right too. Muscle wasn't going to win me a game, let alone the match, so I had to approach things in a different way. And rather than looking to blast my more powerful opponent off the court, maybe it was time to try and get him moving.

So instead of looking for power down the middle of the court, I changed my game. I mixed up the pace on my shots, hit some balls with slice and some with top-spin, and I looked to use the angles around the court so that suddenly he was scampering about beyond the baseline.

The new tactics worked too and I won the match 6–4. Dad was happy and so was I and it taught me a valuable lesson that I've carried with me ever since. Life—and for me a large part of that is being a professional sportsman— is all about thinking on your feet, and seeing challenges as opportunities rather than roadblocks.

In other words, it is all about being able to adapt. That word sums up what I did that day in Bangor all those years ago and it sums up my life in cricket.

This is my story.

CHAPTER 2
A father's perspective—Peter Smith

I think the first time Steven's mother Gillian and I realised our son might be capable of doing something special on the cricket field was in his second year at under-10A level.

That summer he scored almost 500 runs and proved a prolific wicket-taker for Illawong, form that won him a whole host of awards including the cricketer of the year prize for his age group at Illawong and the under-10 player of the year for the Sutherland Shire Junior Cricket Association.

There were two innings he played that season that stood out and highlighted that he was a real talent. The first was for Illawong against Engadine when we were chasing

160 to win against a side full of good bowlers. In the end Steven scored a hundred to guide us to victory, an innings that made up the lion's share of our total and which was head and shoulders above what all the other batsmen were able to produce. The innings sticks in my mind because he maintained control of the chase throughout, despite the loss of wickets around him. He also kept scoring and showed a lot of patience. He displayed a level of cricketing maturity way beyond his age.

The other innings was in a representative match for Sutherland against Blacktown. It was a 50-over-a-side match at Blacktown in stifling 40-degree heat. We'd bowled first and Blacktown had scored around 180 with Steven fielding for the whole innings and bowling ten overs. Steven then opened the batting and with seven overs to go we still needed around 40 and had plenty of wickets in hand.

It was at this time he was struck on the body by a delivery and went down in pain. I was called on to assess him and could see he was exhausted. I suggested he came off to give himself time to recover but he refused and for the remaining overs he and his partner ground out the runs. There was no scoreboard and so at the end of each over Steven would look over to the area where all the parents, teammates and the scorers were sitting and shout 'How many?' He showed incredible concentration and compos- ure to keep going although he was exhausted. In the end he scored 93 not out, we won with a few balls to spare and when the winning runs were hit he was swamped by excited, shouting teammates and parents. At this point he showed what the victory had cost him and broke into uncontrollable weeping through sheer exhaustion and relief. We carried him into the shade and cooled him down with water and ice and he quickly recovered, and it was during this time as he relaxed that one of the opposition adults came over to congratulate him on his innings. He told Steven he'd watched junior cricket for many years, but never seen such a fine innings from one so young. It was quite something to hear and made me realise that Steven possessed a special talent.

At that time, though, I don't think we ever gave a thought to him progressing to professional cricket, and certainly not going on to captain Australia. All we were thinking about was making sure our son was having fun and making the progress he wanted to. I think as a parent that's all you can ever wish for.

Throughout Steven's progress in cricket and his career, new challenges have come to him at regular intervals and each time we, as parents, did wonder whether those challenges were happening too fast. But for my part I learnt fairly early on that he was able to handle each new challenge and seemed to adapt quickly.

The Australian captaincy was and is a case in point. It was certainly never something I thought of for Steven as he was growing up, as my main focus, and Gillian's too, was to ensure he was enjoying the game. Once he reached that position of leadership there was an element of it being quite surreal, seeing your son in a role like that, but it also made us realise, I think, just how capable he is, how respected he is within the game and also how much more he can achieve if he puts his mind to it. When he called us once his appointment was in the works in December 2014 when Michael Clarke was injured, I don't recall giving him any advice; I think we were just excited for him, very proud, of course, and delighted to see what he had accomplished through the years of hard work he'd put in.

Gillian was the one who introduced Steven to cricket, taking him along at the age of four or five, and at that point he was playing for the under-eights. At that time the program we see today through Cricket Australia's Milo cricket programmes for junior cricket was still very much in its infancy. Steven rapidly developed a passion for cricket and it became his main endeavour from an early age. In fact, in primary school the class was asked what they wanted to be when they grew up. There were the usual responses of doctors, nurses and firemen but Steven said he wanted to be a cricketer. The teacher's reply was that he wouldn't make much of a living out of that! Well, Steven proved that teacher wrong, but not without a lot of hard work.

My first love was rugby league and I played the game as a junior, only taking up cricket as a teenager. There was a park immediately behind our house in Sydney and cricket nets within that park. Most afternoons there would be children of all ages descending on the nets, composite ball in one hand and cricket bat in the other, and while pads and gloves were optional, protectors were encouraged! The games were fun and competitive and they meant I learnt to bowl many different types of deliveries. Whenever there was a new ball I experimented with swinging it both ways and as the ball got older I bowled spin. I became a jack-of-all-trades and a master of none. That didn't help me in the club games I played as an adult but it did assist me when it came to working with Steven because I could go back to my early days and bowl lots of different deliveries.

Steven's sister Kristie is almost three years older than him, and although she never played cricket with him, they were close and did play a lot of ball games together, games that helped them develop good hand–eye coordination, something that served them well as Kristie went on to play competitive netball and Steven started to get serious about his cricket. Steven played a lot of tennis as a junior, although it was mainly something he did in the off-season from cricket. He enjoyed it, it kept him fit and agile and I'd say he was a reasonable player, but it was never something he excelled at like cricket.

Cricket was Steven's passion from an early age, and he was always meticulous about it. I remember that whenever I took him to select a cricket bat at Harry Solomon's store in the Sydney suburb of Kingsgrove it was a lengthy process, something that could last for up to two hours. Brands of bats didn't interest him, but the feel of them was what he looked out for, even then. He would pick them up, fidgeting and fiddling, testing them out for size, and that attitude towards his equipment has prevailed to this day.

Steven loves his rugby league but as a boy he was quite small and Gillian, probably quite rightly, reckoned it wasn't a sport that would suit him. At the same time, we both loved team sports as a means to make friends—Gillian had played netball when she was younger—and cricket seemed like a nice fit for him. And the fact that Steven took to it like a duck to water certainly helped.

Steven's ability to adapt to different circumstances, so apparent now in his professional career, was something I think he developed in junior cricket, both by playing the game and through our sessions together. Those sessions were for fun and if he hadn't been enjoying them then we wouldn't have carried on. But they also had a purpose, even if Steven didn't realise it at the time.

During his junior years I worked from home. The company that employed me had moved to Melbourne and I was the last employee left in Sydney. I had a sales role covering New South Wales, Queensland and New Zealand and when I wasn't travelling I was able to knock off at 4.30 p.m. and go to the park with Steven. Generally we would have at least an hour's session every day when he didn't have organised training. We also often had sessions on Saturday afternoons and again on Sunday. He lapped it up like a cricketing sponge.

The volume of work Steven did in a typical week in the height of the season when he was aged 12 or 13 looked something like this. On Monday he would have an hour's session with me at Casuarina Oval then on Tuesday there would be junior club training. There would be another hour's session with me on Wednesday evening, then on Thursday would come representative training for the Sutherland Shire Junior Cricket Association (SSJCA).

Friday would see another hour-long session with me then a 50-over club game on Saturday, followed by an hour's session afterwards if he wanted it. The week would be rounded off with a SSJCA representative match, another 50-over game. It all added up to around seven hours of training plus another 11 hours of playing every week and it wasn't uncommon for him to become a little bit drowsy over his evening meal on Sunday, but he was doing what he loved and we were happy to support him in whatever way we could.

Steven's schedule in the off-season was different and involved a couple of sessions with me, plus some tennis training, and maybe a couple of games of tennis with me or with his friends. There'd also be indoor cricket at the Bankstown indoor centre every Wednesday night. On Fridays there'd be coaching sessions organised by the SSJCA, run by experienced Level 2 and Level 3 coaches, then on the weekends he would play competition tennis on Saturdays while on Sundays there was cricket training run by Cricket New South Wales that saw the top performers in the representative competition coming together for specialised coaching, something Steven started from about the age of 12. Adding it all up, it came to between 15 and 20 hours of cricket and sports training each week.

Over the course of a year it added up to around 1000 hours of training or playing. It would have been substantially less at the ages of ten or 11, but more at 15 or 16 as grade cricket for Sutherland District Cricket Club was added into the schedule. That's a significant amount of organised cricket and doesn't include backyard cricket.

It was only possible because Steven enjoyed it, wanted to do it and wanted to keep progressing and improving his skills. What this volume of work did was help to hone his skills and provide the necessary foundation to enable adaptation and the flourishing of his talent in his later cricketing career.

The volume of work had nothing to do with us being pushy parents. It was Steven's choice and he enjoyed it. It was really all he wanted to do. When I wasn't around he used to go into our garage at home and hit a ball that I'd suspended from a beam in the ceiling, and he did it so often that in the end I had to place a piece of board over a part of that ceiling that had been pock-marked and worn away by the ball being struck against it. That board is still there today, as are quite a few other stray marks on other parts of the ceiling, the result of Steven's regular garage batting sessions.

Steven's enjoyment of what he was doing was far more important than the volume of work he did, because it was only through that enjoyment that he was able to do the quality of work that was needed to improve. And much of that enjoyment came from the variety of our sessions together, which kept things interesting. If all the work we did was on a bowling machine then Steven would probably have batted like a machine and quickly become bored. If I could only bowl one type of delivery to him he would have become proficient at playing it but the sessions would have become tedious and repetitive. It was the variation we had that created problem-solving opportunities and little games within a game that fostered our enjoyment. In fact, problem solving was the most important part of Steven's training sessions and it was the skill that helped him develop his ability to adapt. By problem solving during practice it became much easier for Steven to adjust to different types of bowling in game situations because he had already started to develop strategies to counter whatever deliveries I sent down at him.

My sessions with Steven would normally begin with me bowling seam-up, as fast as I could, with the newest ball we could find. We'd buy a new ball every two weeks, so we had a good collection of balls in various stages of wear. I'd try to bowl at a speed around or just above his comfort level and as he got older this meant bowling two or three paces down the pitch to simulate faster bowling. I was better at inswing than outswing but could sometimes get my outswinger working. I would try to swing the ball, vary my pace and length and vary the way I tried to get him out. Sometimes I would concentrate on leg stump, sometimes outside off and sometimes I'd use short-pitched bowling.

As I started to tire I would change to medium pace and then spin, and as a spin bowler I would often start with off-breaks, changing my pace and length and throwing in the occasional straight ball and what could be called a leg-cutter. Again it was a match-type situation in the sense that there were many different styles of bowling and so Steven had to watch my hand closely to see what I was bowling. I'd then change to leg-breaks, again bowling with variation and including top-spinners and the occasional googly. I would also vary where I bowled from—sometimes over the wicket, sometimes around the wicket and sometimes very wide of the crease. The aim was always to give Steven as many variations as possible to counter so he could develop strategies against different types of bowling. If he got out then it didn't matter to him or me as long as he was finding ways to counter my bowling, something he did very well.

We always ended our sessions with a game scenario of 20 runs required off 12 balls with an imaginary field set by me. This gave Steven a bit of a challenge at the end of our sessions, a way for him to think on his feet and to improvise to score his runs, and in some ways it was Twenty20 practice in a pre-Twenty20 era! The serious part of it all was to try and replicate match situations where runs needed to be scored quickly. We'd also sometimes use other game scenarios like imagining that Steven's side had lost two early wickets and he would need to bat accordingly or pretending he was surrounded by close-fielders and would have to combat that threat.

Indoor cricket was another form of cricket training. A fast-moving game, it gave Steven a chance to develop an additional set of cricketing skills during the winter months. In indoor cricket a player bats with his partner for four overs. The batting side forfeits five runs for every wicket lost and the batsman dismissed goes to the non-striker's end but keeps batting. The aim of the batting pair is, naturally, to score as many runs as possible by running between shortened wickets. Runs are scored by beating a fieldsman and hitting the side-netting, with the number of runs dependent on where the ball hits those nets. The means of scoring runs saw Steven having to develop strategies to hit the ball into the nets and included playing a lot of shots through the mid-wicket or cover area and beating the fieldsmen. He would hit many flicks to leg or pushes into the off side as well as the occasional big shot. Running between the wickets was also important as it was basically a hit-and-run game. I believe that much of what Steven does now in flicking balls off his stumps into the leg side was developed during his games of indoor cricket.

Finding ways to score runs was one puzzle for batsmen in indoor cricket; another was dealing with the variations of the bowlers. The bowlers knew a batsman was coming after them and had to develop their own strategies to curtail the run-scoring. The balls used in indoor cricket swing more than the outdoor balls so Steven had to learn to cope with that movement. Bowlers also used a lot of pace variations and cutters, much like you see in Twenty20 cricket now. Spinners could also achieve a fair amount of turn and even some swing, depending on what sort of spin they imparted on the lighter balls. Bowlers would often bowl six different balls in an over to keep the batsman guessing and to try to reduce run-scoring options.

The funny thing now, looking back, is that there were plenty of what you might call traditional coaches at the time Steven was playing indoor cricket who believed that this form of cricket could foster a different type of technique to the one usually used by players outdoors, with batsmen often working the ball across the line. But it certainly did Steven no harm at all and when I watch him playing now I can see how he's adapted through trial and error what he learnt in indoor cricket into his traditional game. In particular, his ability to take balls off his stumps and play them into the leg side was partially developed through experimentation at indoor cricket. He then experimented further by taking this particular shot and adapting it to traditional cricket and, in doing so, he has made it very difficult for bowlers to target his stumps. Bowlers using many variations were not new to Steven thanks to indoor cricket, and having to score fast came as second nature, along with running hard between wickets and milking singles. These were all strategies partially developed through indoor cricket, then refined in the nets and mastered in the traditional game. And Steven wasn't alone in learning some of his skills through indoor cricket. Stephen and Mark Waugh—the latter very much a player he looked up to when growing up—also played indoor cricket at Bankstown.

Our backyard cricket games were another way of challenging and developing Steven's cricket skills. The way we played was dictated by the shape of our backyard and developed when it had been raining and it was too wet to play at Casuarina Oval. We had a paved area between our small swimming pool and the pergola, the covered area just outside the patio doors. It was basically a walkway surrounded by flowerbeds around eight metres long. Whoever was bowling—usually me—used a junior composite cricket ball that was red with raised plastic mock stitching. It was smaller than a normal cricket ball but, being plastic rather than leather, it lasted far longer on the paving stones. It was also soft and bounced less than a tennis ball so it was ideal for the game we developed, while the bat was adapted from a traditional one that had a split in the toe. I cut the split out and so it was slightly shorter than usual. It also had the edges shaved off, making it about 4 or 5 centimetres wide.

The bowler stood at the pool fence and flicked the ball to the batsman. The flick was from around shoulder height because if the arm was any higher, then that created too much bounce. Flicking the ball also added to the number of variations possible as leg-spin, off-spin and even top-spin were all achievable using this method. It meant Steven had to watch my hand carefully to see what kind of ball I was bowling. The ball would land on the paved area and depending on where it pitched, it could skid through, spin or even squat. Meanwhile, the batsman was surrounded by Gillian's flowerbeds and any ball that went into a flower-bed on the full was a dismissal.

From a bowling—or flicking—point of view there was variation of spin, of pace and variation off the paving stones. From a batting point of view it was survival by picking the ball out of the hand, using your feet to get to the pitch of the ball or playing back. Runs were scored for each ball survived, so if you batted for 100 deliveries without being dismissed you had 100 runs. Initially scores of 20 or 30 were good but eventually Steven developed strategies to counter the bowling and conditions, and scores of over 100 became normal. These same strategies—playing right back or quickly getting down the pitch and having soft hands—have evolved further to be used now when he faces spin bowling in professional cricket.

The backyard cricket Steven played was fun as there were no consequences to getting out, but it was also competitive, an attitude that Steven has taken into his professional career. Steven and a couple of his mates developed a three-player game in the nets at Casuarina Oval and when he stayed with another friend in Coogee, they developed some backyard games too. There were other games in backyards at Vincentia where we holidayed most years with up to a dozen other families. All of the games had rules developed for the particular circumstances involved—the size of the backyard, the number of players, the equipment and so on—but they were fun and competitive at the same time and Steven revelled in them.

We even developed another game, this time played indoors and often while watching television, that used a wooden ruler and a table tennis ball. As a batsman it was all about surviving against a tiny ball, with a tiny bat, with that ball bouncing a great deal and swinging prodigiously. Steven also played this game with one of his mates, Matt Morgan. The art of batting in the game was playing straight, showing the full face of the ruler to deliveries that could misbehave wickedly.

What all of this reveals is that Steven was mad keen to play cricket whenever he could and when it wasn't possible we invented variations on a theme that would satisfy him. And it wasn't just a question of doing nothing but batting, bowling or flicking as we had fielding games too.

Wherever we went we invariably had some balls with us that we could throw around if we had time. One of the games involved hitting a drink can placed equidistant between us. A game was the first person to three points and you got a point if you hit the can or if your opponent misfielded.

In early 2017 I was gardening in the backyard and found an old cricket ball against the fence under some shrubs. It had completely disintegrated and was probably one we lost while playing this game. It had sat there hidden away for somewhere between ten and 15 years.

We also had a trampoline in the backyard and would play a game bouncing the ball off the trampoline. Points came from the opponent dropping a catch. We also used a rebound net and had an old slips cradle as well. Other games included throwing one or two balls between us at speed and getting points if the opponent dropped a catch. Balls were thrown underarm left, right, high, low and with speed variations or even spin to try to get a point. Again it was the first person to three points who won the game. These were all games that helped with hand–eye coordin- ation and also with Steven's slip and close-in fielding as he played more competitive cricket.

When the weather permitted we worked on fielding and throwing at Casuarina Oval, which is part of the reason that Steven looks such a natural in the field these days. Our games on the outfield usually involved me hitting the ball to Steven either along the ground or in the air for him to field and then throw back to me, catching it in a baseball mitt. We also did a lot of drills catching tennis balls hit with a tennis racquet, balls which required catching with soft hands as hands with no give in them meant a dropped catch. We would simulate close-in fielding and at 15 to 20 metres simulate hard-hit catches at mid-wicket or in the covers. We even had a game for outfield catching. With a number of tennis balls I would hit the first one as high in the air as I could manage. Steven would catch it and as he did so I would hit another in a different direction so he had to work out where it was and get to it quickly. As he caught one ball another one was airborne. I could also hit three in a row in the same direction so he had to catch the first, quickly adjust to catch the second, which was already on the way down, and then adjust again to catch the third.

It may sound like a cricket boot camp but Steven was always the one who wanted to play cricket, and I was his willing accomplice. My role was to create enough variety in our games to ensure he kept enjoying cricket and also kept developing his skills.

Once he'd learnt the basic cricketing skills, it was down to Steven to adapt his skills through experimentation. To begin with, most of Steven's experimenting was through trial and error. He would play a particular type of ball in a number of different ways until he found the best way to deal with it. For example, when he became proficient at facing my leg-spin from over the wicket, I switched to round the wicket and he had to come up with a strategy to deal with that. The first time he faced that style of bowling he may have maintained his stance and played in the same way he'd played me over the wicket but as soon as he realised there were different angles and different amounts of spin from around the wicket, he made adjustments. Through trying different things he increased his comfort against that type of bowling and would then use what he learnt when he faced similar bowling in match situations. As he became more experienced he was able to fall back on successful adjustments he made in the past. It's just one example of how Steven was always adapting his cricket.

To experiment you need the freedom to say that if it doesn't work then it doesn't really matter and try something else. That was Steven's approach during our net sessions together, which always ended with that scenario of 20 runs to win from 12 balls. It was the perfect opportunity to experiment because even if Steven got out, he still faced those 12 balls. He could attempt big hits, clearing his front leg and hitting into the leg side or backing away to try and hit over cover. On occasions he also attempted more subtle ways of getting the 20 runs by trying to place the ball in between my imaginary fielders and scampering two or three runs. Looking back, I can see that these types of games were formative in Steven being able to adapt to the helter-skelter of Twenty20 cricket.

I believe the game scenarios have also helped him in his planning and his mental approach to the game at the highest level. In first-class cricket Steven has to think ahead to the type of game situations he's likely to encounter, plan accordingly and adapt to different conditions. His preparation in Dubai in February 2017 for the tour of India where he put his plans into place during the Test series is one example of what I'm referring to. I always encouraged him to think about what he was doing and, more importantly, his rationale, which serves him well now in international cricket.

What's the result of all the hours and hours of practice Steven's put in since he was a very small child? To me it's best summed up by a delivery he faced from Pakistan's Wahab Riaz during the ICC World Twenty20 (WT20) in 2016 in India. Wahab was all ready to bowl with a predominantly off-side field and, as a result, was more than likely to aim his delivery a long way outside off-stump. Steven could see that strategy—the field setting telegraphed it pretty plainly—and now it was up to Steven to come up with an approach to counter it.

Steven's response was to move across his stumps as Wahab hit delivery stride. That movement is classic Steven, but this time was so pronounced that it actually took him outside off-stump and exposed all three stumps to the bowler. Wahab then had the problem: did he stick with his original plan of operating well outside off-stump or aim at the unprotected stumps and dismiss Steven, but also risk being hit out onto the leg side where there were no fielders? Wahab stuck to his original plan, bowling a full toss outside the off-stump. Steven's response way across his stumps was to whip the ball away with lots of bottom hand to the unguarded leg-side boundary.

The shot was called outrageous by commentators and replayed many times on television. People seemed in awe of Steven's ability to improvise in that manner but he was just using his experience to adapt to the game situation. In Steven's cricket career the adage, who adapts best wins, is very apt.

CHAPTER 3
Australia or England?

For many 17- or 18-year-olds when they finish school the major decision is whether to go on to higher education or enter the world of work.

For me things were slightly different. I had to decide whether I wanted to press on with my ambition to play for New South Wales and, ultimately, Australia, or throw in my lot with English county side Surrey and pursue the possibility of playing international cricket for England. Thanks to my London-born mother Gillian, I have English citizenship as well as Australian citizenship.

If it had been about money then it would have been no

contest. Surrey were offering me a three-year deal worth around £30,000 per year while my first rookie contract with Cricket New South Wales netted me around AU$12,000. But I had my heart set on playing state and international cricket in Australia—that was where I'd grown up and where I'd learnt my cricket—so although the chance to play in, and possibly for, England was an option, it wasn't one I seriously entertained.

My mother Gillian was born in Hackney in London and her father, Walter, served as a fighter pilot at the tail end of World War II. He had outstanding reflexes and was a useful golfer and cricketer, although not professional, while her mother, Irene, worked in telecommunications for the Royal Air Force during the war and then as a telephonist for *The Times* newspaper. Mum's mother did have some passing link to cricket, and her half-sister's family were believed to have been involved in the manufacture of bats, but that was as far as the cricketing connection went on that side of our family.

Mum and Dad met when Dad was in England in late 1980. A qualified chemist, he was working for a company called Technical Waxes Australasia, the sister company to two firms in the United Kingdom, Campbell Techni-cal Waxes and Dussek Brothers. Mum was a secretary at Campbell Technical Waxes and when the chemist who was expected to look after Dad broke his leg, she was deputed to make sure he was taken care of. They hit it off, wrote and called each other regularly when Dad returned to Australia in early 1981, and then Mum flew to Australia on holiday to meet Dad in June and July of that year.

Mum's holiday was set to last for around a month but just a week into it Dad proposed. They got married in England in October 1981 and stayed there for three weeks before heading back to Australia. Although Mum still returns to the country of her birth virtually every year for a holiday, it has been a pretty seamless transition for her from England to Australia. Her parents emigrated and lived in Queensland and, when my grandfather died, my grandmother moved down to join us in Alford's Point before she, too, passed away in 2014.

My dad's side of the family has some British heritage too. One of my middle names, Devereux, is a family name from my grandfather. Dad thinks it was also my great- great-grandfather's name. Dad believes there were Scottish roots there, as part of his father's family were called Cameron. The name Devereux is part of Dad's father's and his uncle's names but although it also features in Dad's brother's name, Dad missed out on inheriting it too. Mum and Dad decided to keep the tradition going by including it in my name, while the idea to make me Steven with a 'v' rather than 'ph' came from Mum. She liked the name Steve and opted for the 'v' so that it would fit better with the shortened form. For quite a while now just about the only person to call me Steven is Dad, and when I was younger it was usually if I'd done something wrong!

Our heritage held a fascination for my sister Kristie, who is two years and nine months older than me. She moved to the UK and settled in Maidstone in Kent after originally being based in London. For me, though, the chance to go and play cricket there was based purely on self-advancement.

There's also a New Zealand connection in our lives, as we moved to Torbay near Auckland when I was one. Dad managed a sales office there for Dussek Campbell, the company created by the merger of Campbell Technical Waxes and Dussek Brothers. You could say that had things turned out differently, I could just as easily have been playing for New Zealand as Australia, or even for England. But by the time I started school we were back in Sydney, having first spent six months at Redland Bay in Queensland when we returned to Australia in October 1983. The first school I attended was Alfords Point Public School near the family home.

I first went to the UK as a 16-year-old with a Cricket New South Wales development squad that included Sam Robson—one of my best friends and someone who actually did make the switch to play cricket in and for England— Phillip Hughes and Jackson Bird among others. We played a few county academy sides and some teams that featured county second XI players, and straight away I fell in love with the lifestyle of travelling around the country by road and playing cricket at some terrific locations. We even went to have a look at The Oval during the trip, and seven years later I would make my maiden Test hundred there.

In early 2007, less than a year after that first cricketing trip to the UK, I found my life was already at a crossroads. I was still a student, attending Menai High School, but hadn't really achieved a great deal there, mainly because my focus was almost completely on cricket to the detriment of everything else. It wasn't that I hated school but my focus was elsewhere, trying to think of ways of progressing my development as a cricketer.

By this stage I was playing in first grade for Sutherland District Cricket Club. When we played Campbelltown I got chatting to fast bowler Mitchell Claydon, who was born in Australia but had a British passport and had been playing first-class cricket for English county side Yorkshire.

I explained my situation to Mitch, said I'd enjoyed playing in the UK the previous year and that I'd like to have another go at it to take my game to the next level. He put me in touch with some contacts in the north-west of England, a traditional hotbed of league cricket, and it was arranged for me to go over to play cricket.

The arrangement brought the issue of whether or not I continued at school to a tipping point, although it had been heading in that direction for some time. During the first semester of Year 12 I'd spent a lot of time playing cricket, both for Cricket New South Wales' age-group sides and in schools tournaments too, which meant that my schoolwork was suffering. Matters came to a head when I failed to hand in a major English assignment that was to count towards my Higher School Certificate (HSC), something that meant I would be given a failure mark in that subject. There was no leniency for me in completing the assignment, even though part of the reason for my failure was that I'd been playing school cricket matches. This prompted a meeting at the school between one of my coaches, Trent Woodhill, and

Cricket New South Wales' Welfare Officer Tony Lewis and the school's deputy principal.

Tony was quite keen for me to stay on until the end of Year 12 but Trent was more supportive of the idea of me leaving school. Trent's message was basically: 'He's not really enjoying it and now he's not going to achieve anything either thanks to this failure mark, so he might as well leave and get on with trying to further his cricketing career.' Given my fail in English and the fact that I would not be awarded my HSC, the reality was that any further attendance was a waste of my time. In all fairness to the deputy principal, he agreed with Trent. He recognised my love of cricket, and with my heart set on playing the game as a career there wasn't anything more I could do at school that could further that ambition. I was given the green light to leave school.

My parents were incredibly supportive of my decision. Of course they were apprehensive about the fact I was leaving school without any qualifications, but at the same time they'd seen the progress I'd made as a cricketer and they knew staying on at Menai High School was a waste of time for me. It would have meant repeating Year 12, and by that stage, if my cricketing career continued to go in an upward direction, there was the potential for exactly the same issues to resurface a year down the line.

Mum and Dad also recognised what a great opportunity I had in front of me to go overseas and play cricket and also cut the apron strings by branching out on my own. With the success I've since had in my career it looks like it must have been a straightforward decision for them to give their approval, but it wasn't. Without their love and support I would have achieved nothing.

So off I set for the UK in April 2007 and, even though I was still a couple of months short of my eighteenth birthday, and had never been away from home on my own before, I remember flying to Manchester with a sense of excitement rather than nervousness. I'd seen overseas players in grade cricket where the teams they played for relied on them to a great extent. If you did well by standing up with bat and ball, then you were Mr Popular, and although the flipside was that if things didn't go well then you ended up carrying the can, it was just the sort of pressure and responsibility I craved. It was going to be a great adventure and at the end of it I was certain I'd emerge a better player and a better person too.

The fact that all my eggs were now in one cricketing basket wasn't something I thought very deeply about. Perhaps that was just the confidence of youth, but it never occurred to me what would happen if I didn't make it as a cricketer and, more immediately, what would happen if my season in England didn't go well. In hindsight, perhaps the fact I put myself in a position where it was cricket or bust actually made me focus more carefully on the game than I might have done if I'd had something else to fall back on.

Having said that, my time in England didn't get off to the best of starts. If I tell you I can't remember the name of the club I was originally contracted to, then that will probably reveal all you need to know about how positive my initial experience was. I went to England with the promise of playing with Lancashire's second XI and an involvement with its academy, and the fact I had a British passport had seemed to make me an even more enticing signing. But when I arrived I was told the arrangements weren't possible after all—although I never found out why—and it was all a tremendous let-down.

Suddenly, from arriving at Manchester airport feeling on top of the world and ready to prove myself as a cricketer, I now felt a pretty lonely 17-year-old, jet-lagged and without any real friends to call upon. It was a tough time and I was all ready to board the first flight home.

It was at that point, however, that things turned around for me in a big way and for that I have to thank a man called Tony Ward. Tony is a good friend of Mum and Dad's and a colleague of Dad's at Darent Wax in Kent, in the south-east of England. He is also a fantastically generous man and he and his wife Julie run a music and entertainment festival every year at their property that raises money for the Teenage Cancer Trust in the UK.

Mum suggested I go down to Kent to stay with Tony and Julie, consider my options and let Tony see if there was any cricket I could play in that part of the world. After all, she said, it would be a shame to have flown 16,000 kilometres only to head home without giving myself every chance of making a success of the trip.

I agreed, caught the train down to Kent and Tony went to work to see if he could find me some cricket to play. One of his first calls was to Gavan Burden, the chairman of the management committee of the Sevenoaks Vine Cricket Club. The club had already contracted an Australian professional for the summer, an all-rounder called Matthew Wallis who played for Randwick–Petersham, but Tony proved himself to be an excellent salesman, explaining that I was Australia's next Shane Warne with the added advantage that I could bat a bit too. Gavan agreed that I could go along to the club so they could see what I was all about and whether I would fit in.

Gavan was very good about it because even with Tony's salesman skills he could have refused straight away, given the club already had Matthew signed and playing with them. Gavan was also conscious that he didn't want his club getting a reputation for flying professionals over from Australia only to ditch them when a better option came up. On that basis he agreed to give me a game for the Old Oaks, the club's over-40s side, in a match against Kent over-50s, to see for himself whether I was as good as Tony claimed.

If it sounds like an odd fit, me as a 17-year-old playing for a team of over-40s against a team of over-50s, then it was, but there was logic to Gavan's decision. Pitching the overseas player—or in my case, the prospective overseas player—into the match was something that had been done by the club in the past not only to add some younger legs to the older playing group but also to give the foreign professional a first, quite gentle, look at local conditions so that when the league season started things wouldn't be such a culture shock.

Gavan tells the story now that having given me the chance to have a bowl and positioning himself at slip to get a better look at what I was all about, he was immediately sold on my bowling ability alone as he heard the sound of the ball fizzing down the pitch when I sent down my first delivery. By imparting lots of spin on the ball it makes a noise as the seam cuts through the air. I was determined to ensure that I made every post a winner and that this first impression really should count by getting as many revolutions on the ball as possible.

Gavan said he hadn't heard a ball fizz like that for many years since he'd played with John Dewes, the former Middlesex and England cricketer and later a master at nearby Tonbridge School and Dulwich College. In fairness he added that although my talent with the ball was clear, so too were the rough edges. 'He'd bowl four absolutely masterly balls, one that was okay and one full-toss or long-hop and that was an over from him at that stage of his career,' he says now, and he's quite right.

When I followed up my spell with the ball with a rapid-fire half-century at better than a run a ball, the Sevenoaks Vine committee rapidly went into discussions about what to do next. They decided to go with Matthew as their first team professional to start the league season, which was fair enough given the commitment they'd already made to him, and they gave me the chance to play, initially at least, in the second team, which is where I made my league debut, in a home game against Blackheath's second XI in the first week of May.

The scorecard plus the captain's match report by Tom Nissen are still online, and looking back more than ten years later they are enough to bring back some great memories and raise a few laughs too. Blackheath's batsmen thumped us everywhere to score 4–366 from their 50 overs—only for us to then knock off the runs with six wickets and more than four overs to spare. For my part with the ball I took 0–72 from my ten overs, but that was par for the course on the day.

It was another chance for me to make a lasting impression and so I made the most of it, especially after I was dropped at square leg on five. Opening the batting I scored 185, including 22 fours and seven sixes, and added 230 for the first wicket with Toby Sheppard at just about eight runs per over, Toby's contribution being 118.

The match report is amusing because it refers not just to our blazing stroke play but also my fussiness, even then, with my equipment—or, to be more accurate, other people's equipment. I didn't have any kit with me as my own equipment, which was in transit, hadn't arrived, and so had to rely on gear borrowed from my new teammates. I used one player's gloves only after he agreed to let me cut some of the foam out of the padding so that it allowed me a better grip on the bat. It was also a case of finding a pair of pads that were worn in enough to allow me to use them in comfort—stiff pads are a common problem at the start of every season at club level as players break in new kit— and a bat that wasn't too heavy. The captain said I left the dressing room floor like a 'scene resembling something out of Armageddon' as I went out to bat.

My efforts were enough to convince the club's officials that I had to get a chance with the first team and, to his credit,

Matthew was the first to agree. He knew of me from grade cricket in Sydney and actually told Gavan that he thought I'd go on to play for Australia even then, so he was happy to swap places with me, giving me the opportunity to slot into the first team while he dropped down to the second XI.

I had a great time. I was doing what I wanted, playing cricket, and although the standard wasn't quite as high as first grade back with Sutherland District Cricket Club, I had the chance to bat, bowl and play in different conditions to those I was used to back home. Many of the grounds we played at were quite small, which was great from a batting perspective, but not quite so good when it came to the bowling side of things. The pitches were for the most part very good and although I didn't pull up any trees, my figures were decent: 523 runs across all matches at an average of just over 50, plus 11 wickets at a shade under 30 and an economy rate of a little over four runs per over. I know the club was very happy with my contribution and I was happy to be there. And although I was living with Tony and his wife Julie and so not quite spreading my wings, it was still a great life experience. While the first team didn't win the Kent Premier League that summer, finishing seventh out of 10 teams, the second XI did top its ladder, something that was clearly due to the early-season momentum gained by that win against Blackheath!

My form with Sevenoaks Vine got me on the radar of Kent, the local county side, and that allowed me to play some second team cricket for them. Paul Farbrace, who has gone on to become assistant coach with England, was in charge but, importantly from my perspective, also there was Matthew Mott, the former Queensland and Victorian batsman and then coach with Cricket New South Wales. Kent and Cricket New South Wales had a connection and Matthew was actually the New South Wales second team coach when I made it through to that level, so his presence certainly made me more comfortable in the environment at Kent. I performed quite well for the county but given I was still learning the game, Kent didn't feel able to offer me anything in the way of regular games so when Surrey contacted me through Gavan, I was happy to take a chance and have some game time for its second team instead.

I loved that experience as it brought me into contact with quite a few senior professionals. I was suddenly enjoying a post-match drink with fast bowler Jimmy Ormond, who'd played Test cricket against Australia at The Oval in 2001, and England one-day international (ODI) batsman Alistair Brown, and it was a culture that, as an 18-year-old, I couldn't get enough of, talking cricket and life with these players who had been there, done that and got the t-shirt. I hadn't been much of a socialiser prior to going to the UK and experiences like that certainly helped bring me out of my shell.

One of my games for Surrey was actually against Kent's second team and when I bowled the side to victory, taking 6–14 off 6.4 overs, I can remember the wry look on Paul Farbrace's face as we shook hands afterwards. It was almost like 'I wish you'd have been doing that for us!' But they had their chance and blew it.

The Surrey club was aware of my status as a British passport holder and so I received a call from Alan Butcher, the former England opening batsman and father of fellow England international Mark Butcher, with the offer of the three-year deal. It was a lot of money to potentially throw at an 18-year-old and I'd never conceived of such a large amount in my life, but once the initial shock passed it wasn't such a tough decision to turn it down. I discussed it with Tony Ward and he summed it up pretty well from my perspective. He said I was Australian, I'd grown up in Australia and I wanted to play for Australia and so, on that basis, I'd be silly to risk all that by taking up Surrey's offer. He was right and so I knocked it back, a decision I've not regretted for a moment. It was another fork in the road, just like when I'd left school, and although the financial security would have been great, the fact I burnt that bridge actually made me work harder when I returned to Australia for the following season.

By that stage I'd also been given a clear indication that I was being thought of by Australia's age-group selectors too, which was another positive indicator that I'd made the right decision.

I had an inkling that I was in their minds but at that point in time I wasn't in the national under-19 side's best eleven and it meant I had to content myself with looking at scorecards of its off-season matches against Pakistan on Tony's computer during my stay with him. But then, out of the blue, I got a call that I was to be included in an Australian Institute of Sport side to tour India for the Buchi Babu Invitational Tournament in Chennai, India.

There was plenty of quality in that squad as it included Phillip Hughes—a reassuring face for me given we were already good friends—Ed Cowan, Luke Pomersbach, Matthew Wade, Ben Cutting and Ryan Harris, and although I spent most of the trip batting down the order, I got plenty of bowling in and, more importantly, more experience of different conditions. I shared a room with Phillip. Although I was a late inclusion in the squad and so had some catching up to do socially as the other players had all been training together back home ahead of the trip, I had a great time and thoroughly enjoyed the cricket as we reached the final of the tournament.

The AIS tour did bring to a premature end my summer in the UK, but it allowed me the chance to press my claims for a place in the national squad for the following year's ICC Under-19 Cricket World Cup in Malaysia. Thanks to my form there *(4 matches, 128 runs at 20.83, 12 wickets at 19.08, 5 catches)* I was able to claim a spot in the squad. I can look back now at that period from April to August 2007 and see what a positive experience it was for me, a decisive one too in terms of the direction my life took, and also another step on the learning curve to progress my game.

CHAPTER 4
Ready?

Looking back now at my debut for Australia, which came in a Twenty20 International (T20I) against Pakistan at the Melbourne Cricket Ground (MCG) on 5 February 2010, one inevitable question comes to mind: was I ready?

In reality I probably wasn't ready but throughout my early life my mum always said she felt I was able to quickly master new skills if I set my mind to it and also operate at whatever level I found myself. It was true when it came to riding a bike and even ice-skating, and it was also the case, at first, when it came to international cricket.

The bike riding and ice-skating proved to be instinctive. My sister was able to ride, and despite my parents having training wheels ready for me to use, I set off straight away without any need for them. I think I may have been about four at the time and a year or so later I was able to master the basics of whizzing around on the ice too, at Canterbury ice rink, without any lessons. I did have rollerskates by that stage, so that definitely helped with my balance and coordination but the way I picked up those new skills so quickly certainly stuck in my parents' minds, although I only have the most shadowy recollection of those occasions.

In terms of cricket, once I worked my way into the New South Wales, I did make decent progress and fairly rapidly too. I made my first start for the senior New South Wales side in a rain-affected domestic one-day game against Queensland at The Gabba in December 2007 and the following month took my first steps in both the Twenty20 and first-class sides. I was suddenly on the field with some seriously big names in Australian cricket, up against players including Justin Langer and Jason Gillespie, and although I didn't exactly cause an overnight sensation, I didn't let anyone down, either.

I was quiet, as most young players are in those circumstances, and set my sights on just watching, listening and trying to pick up as much knowledge as I could from the senior players around me. The New South Wales dressing room wasn't quite the star-studded place it had been a few years earlier when it featured the likes of Stephen and Mark Waugh, Mark Taylor, Michael Slater, Michael Bevan,

Glenn McGrath and others. But it still had some players with very impressive CVs, the likes of Simon Katich—who was captain on my first-class debut and scored 189 in that match against Western Australia—Brad Haddin, Michael Clarke and fast bowlers Stuart Clark, Matthew Nicholson—who played a Test in the Ashes series of 1998–99—and Nathan Bracken.

My development continued with the ICC Under-19 Cricket World Cup in Malaysia in February and March of 2008, a tournament in which we finished sixth and one which saw quite a few future Australian internationals take a bow in addition to myself, players such as James Pattinson, Phillip Hughes (who was vice-captain on the trip), Josh Hazlewood, James Faulkner and Marcus Stoinis. I wasn't in the first-choice XI but in the four appearances I made I did a decent job, topping 100 runs *(105 at 28.50, the second highest for the Australians)* and taking seven wickets, with only left-arm spinner Clive Rose, who grabbed nine, capturing more for us. And while sixth was a disappointment, it's worth bearing in mind that there were some players on show who would go on to do pretty decent things at senior level, with Virat Kohli, Ravindra Jadeja, Kane Williamson, Trent Boult, Tim Southee, Corey Anderson and Steven Finn all featuring for their countries.

The tournament was a strange one in that apart from the main venue in Kuala Lumpur, many of the other locations that staged matches were just club grounds, and with the weather playing an increasingly big part in proceedings as time went on, that became a significant source of frustration. All the same, it opened my eyes to what a major event was like with anti-corruption and anti-doping briefings, bat signings, media attention and matches at the Kinrara Academy Oval being televised around the world.

In truth we were always going to struggle to go all the way, because while ten of the Indian squad that won the tournament had first-class experience, there were just two in our squad—Phillip Hughes and me. That's not a criticism of our selection or the Australian system, but simply an illustration of the fact that with just six sides back home, breaking into one of them was then, and remains still, a tough assignment for a young player.

The 2008–09 season was one of consolidation for me at state level with a further four appearances at first-class level, but it was in Twenty20 cricket that I was primarily becoming known and starting to make a name for myself. I was a regular member of the side that won that summer's domestic competition and was seen as a real jack-of-all-trades. I batted a bit (even being pushed up to number three in one match against Victoria, although I made only four before being castled by Dirk Nannes), bowled a bit and put myself about in the field, and that format was what really began to get me noticed.

That was because New South Wales' success catapulted us into the Champions League at the start of the following summer and when we won that tournament suddenly the players who had been involved in such a high-profile victory were the names on the lips of many people within the game.

It was a case of decent timing from my perspective as Australian cricket at international level was starting to experience the dip that almost inevitably followed the retirement of a host of great names in quick succession. Damien Martyn, Glenn McGrath, Shane Warne and Justin Langer had all stepped down from international cricket during the 2006–07 summer, Adam Gilchrist finished the following season and Brett Lee and Matthew Hayden made their final Test appearances in 2009. That was a lot of talent disappearing in a relatively short period of time and those players and others left large holes in the national team that needed to be filled.

Michael Clarke was extremely supportive of me and could see my potential in the shorter formats of the game, and with the ICC WT20 coming up in the Caribbean at the end of our domestic season, he told me he'd lobby for my inclusion in the side for Australia's match against an Australian Cricketers' Association All Star side in Brisbane in November 2009 and, if I kept performing, for that WT20 too.

Sure enough I got the call for the game at The Gabba, and although I didn't bat, I picked up two wickets, including Matthew Hayden, who was stumped off a googly, and that effort was another feather in my cap. I knew my star was rising and what that call-up did was to give me a first look inside the Australian dressing room, something that definitely helped me when I actually became a playing member of the Australian squad in the months that followed. That first dressing room that I was a part of included New South

Wales teammates Brad Haddin and David Warner—who is a couple of years older than me and a player who'd made his international debut in 50-over and Twenty20 cricket the previous summer—plus Cameron White, Adam Voges and Peter Siddle, who were all members of the ICC Champions Trophy-winning squad the previous month, and Shaun Tait, who had been a key performer in the 2007 ICC Cricket World Cup (CWC) squad that won the tournament without coming close to dropping a game. It was quite some experience for me as a 20-year-old without even a decent season of first-class cricket behind me, but although I was in some respects unsure of myself, wondering if I truly belonged, my energy and enthusiasm on the field hid that feeling very effectively.

That element of good timing on my part was emphasised by one look at a spin bowling cupboard that was especially bare and that, again, was to my benefit because it got me into the Test squad as cover for Nathan Hauritz for the Perth and Melbourne Tests in December 2009. My numbers at that stage were eye-catching but for the wrong reasons as I had six wickets at 55 runs apiece for the summer at the time of my Perth call-up and only 11 first-class wickets in my career. It was hardly the sort of stuff that was going to give the Pakistan batsmen sleepless nights if I had ended up playing.

Being in Melbourne meant I was literally like a child at Christmas and the atmosphere around the Boxing Day Test whetted my appetite for higher honours rather than intimidated me. Tim Nielsen, the coach at the time, was terrific for me because he made me feel welcome and valued and that meant a lot to me when I was still finding my feet within the game. And although I missed out on a Test cap at that stage, my time around the squad gave me a chance to work with Shane Warne in Melbourne as I had a session with him on the second morning of that Test.

I'd met him briefly at the All Stars game in Brisbane—he hit me for a straight six in the final over of the match, although by that stage we'd already sealed victory—and the comparisons between us were obvious. They were always going to be made because there was I, a chubby leg-spinner, just like he'd been when starting out in international cricket all those years ago at around the same time as I was starting to pick up a cricket bat and ball for the first time. For the record, although I read those comparisons, I never paid much attention to them. I knew he was a one-off, and even with my belief in my own ability, I knew I was never going to get anywhere near his haul of over 700 Test wickets. In any case, I also knew we were completely different kinds of bowlers: he relied for a fair part of his career on a big-spinning leg-break and the ability to slide the ball on, something that earned him numerous lbw dismissals, and while I also banked on trying to spin my leg-break hard, I used my googly far more than he did, especially at the tail end of his career.

That session in the practice nets at the MCG was fantastic—how could you not enjoy it as a 20-year-old getting one-on-one tuition from the greatest spin bowler of my lifetime, and someone who inspired me as a teenager to start bowling leg-spin rather than medium pace? We worked on slowing down my run-up to the crease to make sure I was more balanced at the crease and therefore able to repeat my action more easily, and also covered the angle of my arm at the point of delivery, as Shane highlighted the fact that the higher my arm was the more bounce and over-spin I could get. But while it was great to get some recognition from the selectors and attention from Shane, I was also realistic enough to know, even then, that it would all count for nothing if I didn't produce decent numbers to back up the buzz around me. That buzz actually helped to inspire me and gave me a focus because the summer as a whole turned into a real breakthrough season for me, with 772 first class runs, the seventh-highest aggregate in that format, including four hundreds, the most by any player that summer. When you threw in the fact I took 21 wickets—albeit at 44 runs apiece—then I was making a compelling case for myself for higher honours.

That was reinforced by another handy return in that summer's domestic Twenty20 tournament as I took seven wickets from just 12 overs in five matches to end as the Blues' leading wicket-taker and it meant that my inclusion in the T20I squad at the end of the summer was not unexpected. I felt confident I could play a role in the side as a spin-bowling all-rounder in that form of the game, which was something Stuart Clark kept on emphasising to me throughout that season: 'Your way into that side is as a number eight batsman who bowls,' he told me whenever he got the chance.

At that time I agreed, but even then, especially off the back of the runs I had scored in the Sheffield Shield that summer, I always had a feeling in the back of my mind that while the all-round package I offered was something that could capture the interest of the selectors, it was going to be my batting that would keep me in the side. And while I felt as ready as I could be to be a part of the Twenty20 International squad, I knew I was there principally because I was a bits-and-pieces cricketer who did something of everything, and that wasn't how I wanted to be viewed.

If I'd been told then that less than a decade later my bowling would virtually disappear from my repertoire, I think I would have been surprised, but back then I was still like a child in the sense that I just wanted to be involved in the action all the time. In the years that followed, that mindset didn't change but what did change was the realisation that to be the best I could be in bowling would mean I'd have to make compromises in the work I did on my batting, and I wasn't prepared to do that.

The expectation of others was never something that weighed me down and even then I found it actually enhanced my performance rather than made me fearful of failure. That was never more evident than by March of 2010 when, having been named in the Test squad for the tour of New Zealand, I followed that announcement with 100 and 7–64 in a Sheffield Shield game against South Australia. I won the Steve Waugh Medal as the New South Wales player of the year and I knew I was close to getting hold of that baggy green cap. Dad even flew to Wellington for the first Test of a two-match series on the basis that it might happen, only for me to miss out, and when we won that Test and one of the players I was vying with for a starting spot, Marcus North, scored a hundred, there was no chance of me getting an opportunity in the second Test in Hamilton either. And at that point I started to focus on the ICC WT20 to come in the Caribbean.

It's not all that common for players with as little international experience as I had at that time to get the chance to feature prominently in a world tournament. I was comfortably the youngest player in our squad, but Michael Clarke quickly made it clear to me that he saw me as having a pivotal role in the starting eleven. He saw leg-spinners in Twenty20 cricket as wicket-takers first and foremost and his attitude was always that the best way to stop a side scoring quickly was to keep taking wickets.

That attacking mindset was never more evident than on my debut in front of more than 60,000 people at the MCG as he had me bowling at the death with Pakistan's batsmen looking to attack me and, at the same time, he gave me a slip, something that was vital in helping me secure my first wicket as the left-handed Fawad Alam edged a ball angled across him to Cameron White. And when Brad Haddin effected a straightforward stumping in my next over to leave me with 2–34, I was satisfied with my evening's work, especially as we went on to win by two runs. Do I remember much about that first wicket or the night as a whole? I remember the emotion I felt when Cameron White held on to that ball, the surge of adrenaline when the crowd roared and afterwards how happy I was for my parents who had come down from Sydney to watch the match.

Michael's approach in using me to take wickets didn't always work as well as that and there were times when I went for runs—our ICC WT20 tournament opener against Pakistan being a case in point as I bowled two overs for 24—but as long as I was looking to get batsmen out then that was enough for him and as a tactic it worked very well.

What helped me, I found, when I was bowling was that I had the ability to think like a batsman. That batting instinct told me when and where the opposition players were trying to hit me and, while I wasn't always able to combat them, it certainly contributed to my success.

I ended up taking 11 wickets in seven matches, which made me the joint second-highest wicket-taker alongside South Africa's Charl Langeveldt and Pakistan spinner Saeed Ajmal and only teammate Dirk Nannes, with 14, took more. It was a return that gave me a lot of satisfaction, not least because I thought I'd bowled pretty well in accordance with what Michael Clarke wanted from me. I took at least one wicket in every match, even managed a maiden over in our win against Sri Lanka *(2–12 off 4 overs)*, and I reckon the delivery I bowled to dismiss Kieron Pollard in St Lucia was the best I ever sent down, a fizzing leg-break that drifted towards leg-stump, luring him into trying to hit through mid-wicket only for the ball to dip, turn sharply and give Brad Haddin a straightforward stumping. In that match I took 3–20 off 4 overs.

I didn't bat very much but that was okay because given I was due to go in at number eight, if I was spending much time at the crease that would have been a pretty good indicator that things weren't going all that well. What was pleasing was that on the one occasion when something significant was needed from me, then I delivered, scoring 27 from 18 balls *(2 sixes, 1 four)* against Bangladesh in Barbados and helping Michael Hussey take us from 6–65 to reach 7–141, a total that gave us a comfortable win.

Michael Hussey provided my best memory of the tournament thanks to his incredible unbeaten 60 from just 24 balls *(6 sixes, 3 fours)* in the semi-final against the defending champion Pakistan in St Lucia as we somehow chased down 192 for victory. When I got out, stumped off Saeed Ajmal's doosra at the start of the eighteenth over, we still needed 48 to win, a mark that was whittled down to 19 off the last over. Incredibly we got home with a ball to spare as Michael went berserk. It was an example of brutal ball-striking and also really clear thinking as, in the final over, he targeted Saeed Ajmal over the leg side, hitting with a pretty strong breeze that was blowing across the oval. I still love to watch the footage of that innings on YouTube and I've even made my fiancée Dani watch it too, something she did with a resigned smile. The way the whole squad can be seen jumping around at the end of the match really sums up the way we felt, that we'd won a match we had no right to win thanks to the efforts of just one man.

We lost the final to England two days later, something that was always on the cards after we'd collapsed early on to 3–8 and 4–45, but I was living the dream and enjoying every minute of it. I then headed to the UK to play in the domestic Twenty20 competition for Worcestershire before linking up with the Australian squad again for limited-overs matches against England and Pakistan and then a two-Test series against Pakistan.

The Worcestershire connection came about during the season back in Australia and was off the back of my efforts in the Champions League and our own Big Bash League. The county wanted an all-rounder and it was former Australian opening batsman Phil Jaques, a teammate of mine at Sutherland District Cricket Club, and someone who was due to be playing for Worcestershire in 2010, who threw my name into the mix. It was a perfect introduction to the rest of the English summer for me, and with Nathan Hauritz then suffering a foot injury during the limited-overs matches against England, it meant I was the last man standing when it came to spin bowling options once the Tests against Pakistan rolled around.

I was realistic enough to know that I was fortunate to be in the frame following what was basically one decent season of first-class cricket, and my chances of playing were certainly helped by the way people like Simon Katich and also Ricky Ponting talked me up in the media. All the same, until Ricky actually gave me my cap on the first morning of the opening Test at Lord's, I was still not sure the opportunity would come my way.

We had played a two-day tour match against Derbyshire to get ready for that Test and although I got some quick runs *(48 off 43 balls)* down the order, batting at number eight, I hadn't bowled especially well *(1–87 off 24 overs)*, with Chris Rogers, who was captaining the opposition, taking a liking to the deliveries I was sending down. That was ironic given the fact we became teammates in the national side three years later but, off the back of that, I still thought the selectors might look at relying on Simon Katich and Marcus North as the spinners for the match and use an extra batsman or seam bowler instead.

I don't remember what Ricky said to me when I made my Test debut or to Tim Paine, who also made his debut in the Test as a replacement for Brad Haddin, sidelined with an elbow injury, but my dad captured the moment with his long lens from the top of the Edrich Stand at the Nursery End of Lord's—those were the days before family members were invited to be part of the cap presentation ceremony— and he continued to take plenty of photos of me during the match, even though I nagged him to stop, relax and just enjoy the cricket. As it turned out I did a reasonable job and although I only made one and 12 with the bat—lbw both times to fellow leg-spinner Danish Kaneria—I did take three wickets for 51 runs—in the Pakistan second innings. Marcus North took six for 55, but that didn't bother me; quite the opposite, in fact, as I was just delighted to get my debut out of the way and end up on the winning side.

It was with the bat that I gave the side a fighting chance of pulling off an unlikely victory after we'd been rolled over for 88 on the first morning of the second Test at Head- ingley. I made 77 in the second innings, batting with the tail, but reflecting on the innings as I write these words I can see that the way I went about it actually had the potential to reinforce a view that here was a limited-overs player operating in Test cricket rather than the Test match batsman I wanted to be regarded as. Alongside Ben Hilfenhaus and Doug Bollinger my instinct took over and I found myself improvising to try and engineer runs, and although it worked well, the 2017 version of me wouldn't go about that innings in that way if I had my time again. I was playing a shot a ball, and perhaps I needed to be a bit more considered with my scoring options.

So leg-spin bowling had been my way into the team, but although I didn't say so publicly, I knew more than ever by that stage that my future lay with the bat. In my heart of hearts I felt my bowling work ethic wasn't as good as it needed to be to make that part of my game the best it could be and, as an example, I was batting far more than bowling during training sessions. It wasn't at that stage that I wanted to drop the bowling completely as I still enjoyed doing everything, but my thoughts were drifting down one path—I wanted to be a batting all-rounder.

As for whether I'd been ready to take that step up to international cricket, the ultimate answer was yes and no. Yes in the sense that I was as ready as I was ever going to be as a bowler, especially in the shortest form of the game, and my results in that ICC WT20 justified my inclusion. But on the other hand, I wasn't yet ready to be a specialist batsman, especially in Test cricket, and that goal was on my mind more and more as time went on.

CHAPTER 5
'I've got to come into the side and be fun'

'I've been told that I've got to come into the side and
be fun. For me, it's about having energy in the field
and making sure I'm having fun and making sure
everyone else around is having fun, whether it be telling
a joke or something like that. It's to make sure we're all
upbeat and we're ready to go. I think that's something
I can bring to this side.'*

I've fronted up to the media many times during the course
of my career, but what I said at the WACA Ground in Perth
on 14 December 2010 ahead of my recall to the Australian
Test side could have come across a lot better than it did.

Reading those words on a page it looks as though I was recalled as much to rush around the field making my teammates laugh as for anything I could bring to the table from a cricketing point of view. And although that's obviously not what I meant, the reality was, to the England players at least, I came across as the team joker. It was something they picked up on whenever I made my way out to bat in the three Tests of the series in which I featured. Lines such as: 'Are you going to tell us a joke?' were commonplace, and given I didn't exactly ram those words back down their throats with a series of big scores in return, and given, in Melbourne and Sydney, we were thumped by an innings on both occasions, I didn't have an awful lot to answer them back with.

I knew what I was trying to say of course, that Andrew Hilditch, the chairman of selectors, and Tim Nielsen, the head coach, had told me my job was to be as upbeat around the squad as I could be, and for good reason too. After all, you have to remember the context of my inclusion. It followed two very sobering matches in Brisbane and Adelaide to start the series.

At The Gabba, England had piled up 1–517 declared in its second innings, comfortably warding off the threat of defeat after conceding a first innings lead of 221, and then, at the Adelaide Oval, Andrew Strauss's side completely overwhelmed us, winning by an innings with more than two sessions in hand, after this time racking up 5–620 declared.

It meant that by the time the squad assembled in Perth for the third Test of the series, there were plenty of footsore players and morale was not exactly off-the-charts positive, so the arrival of a fresh face or two in the dressing room, someone without the baggage of those long hours and days in the field, and the beating that had been received in Adelaide, was no bad thing. And, as history records, in the short term, things turned around for us and we won that Perth Test match as Mitchell Johnson provided a brief glimpse of the sort of form that was to be a regular feature of the corresponding series three years later.

But that bounce wasn't to last, and when England came hard at us over the Christmas and New Year period, we were overwhelmed again, replying with barely a whimper. We lost at the MCG, all out for 98 after winning the toss and batting, and we couldn't even take that match to lunch on day four. And at the Sydney Cricket Ground (SCG) we went down before lunch on day five, as in Melbourne, failing to make the opposition bat a second time.

We used 17 players across the whole series, an indicator of the way the selectors were desperately searching for the right combination, and Ricky Ponting, our captain, senior player and someone we needed to fire in order for us to be competitive, struggled, making just one fifty in eight innings and averaging only 16 for the series before a hand injury meant he missed the final match, with Michael Clarke taking charge for that game.

There was uncertainty around the squad even before a ball was bowled as the selectors named a 17-man group ten days out from the Brisbane Test—which I was a part of—which was pruned to 13 a week later after a round of first-class matches. And while we were playing in India ahead of the series, England had an excellent build-up in Perth, Adelaide and Hobart, so that by the time the first Test in Brisbane came along, its players were very much ready to go.

I guess my place in the set-up pretty much mirrored the uncertainty around the squad as a whole. I saw myself as a batting all-rounder with the emphasis on the batting and I think the selectors probably saw me in those terms too, especially as I came into the Test side in Perth for Marcus North, who'd filled that semi all-rounder role previously. But for all that, I think the media and the wider public, on paper at least, still regarded me as a frontline slow-bowling option. After all, I'd made my Test debut as a spinner who could bat and that was only six months earlier.

I came into the side having scored 59 in a ten-wicket loss for Australia A against England in Hobart before the Test series began—plus a second innings first-ball duck—and so I felt in reasonable touch, and was pleased to get the opportunity to move up the list to number six. But looking back, I can see now that I was nowhere near close enough to being the finished article to fill that batting role adequately.

My presence in the side was certainly a bit of a comfort blanket for the selectors and captain in one sense as I offered, at least in theory, something with the ball. I'd got through 27 overs in that Australia A game in Hobart and picked up two wickets, albeit ones that were pretty much irrelevant in the context of the match as England had already topped 400 by that stage, but you need to remember that at the time our slow bowling cupboard was especially bare, at least in Test terms. Nathan Lyon was yet to debut and as the selectors searched for a reliable spin option after the retirements of Shane Warne and Stuart MacGill, that summer saw Xavier Doherty and Michael Beer, two bowlers who went on to enjoy decent success in limited-overs cricket, both featuring during the Ashes series.

From a bowling standpoint I ended up as a bit of an afterthought as I only got through 31 overs in the three Tests I played, didn't take a wicket and went at well over four runs per over, so that wasn't exactly ideal. I didn't offer the captain control, or the ability to take wickets, but then I wasn't alone in that regard as England had a host of batsmen all in top form, playing on decent pitches and backed up by an excellent bowling attack which, again, was operating at the height of its powers. In the end, Andrew Strauss's side proved way too strong for a team very much in transition.

As a batsman I simply didn't cut it, not at that stage of my career, and I felt a sense of being found out a little bit by the England bowlers. I knew what they were trying to do, to bowl a fourth or fifth stump line and draw me in to playing at the ball away from my body, and that, by and large, was what they succeeded in doing. James Anderson dismissed me three times in succession at one stage, and three of my five dismissals in the series were the result of me driving hard at the ball from that line just outside off-stump with me hitting edges behind the wicket the result. I just didn't have a decent and durable game plan.

There was another technical issue that was highlighted during the series too and that was my back foot play, which was also shown to be substandard. In the second innings in Perth I gloved a ball down the leg side to be caught behind, something that can always happen on a surface that traditionally had more pace and bounce than any other in the country but, more worryingly, in Melbourne, I dragged on an attempted pull shot. The issue, especially with the latter dismissal, was that I was actually trying to play the shot off the front foot. My transfer of weight to the back foot to play a shot like that wasn't as it should be, and it wasn't good enough in terms of my back foot defensive play either. It was something I started to work on with Justin Langer, the side's batting coach at the time, but it was still very much a work in progress and not something that a top-order batsman should have been doing during a Test series.

The memory of the first day in Melbourne is one that will stay with me for a long time, simply because it was just about as dispiriting as it gets. To play in a Boxing Day Test is probably a dream for most Australian children growing up and I was no exception. And although I had experience of the atmosphere of one from the previous year, when I'd been added to the squad against Pakistan but didn't end up playing, this was a different feeling entirely. The series was tied at 1–1, England always brings a massive touring support with it, and there were over 84,000 people in the stadium on that opening day.

So, to collapse in the way we did was soul-destroying, especially as all ten wickets were lost to catches in the arc between the wicketkeeper and gully. It showed we hadn't actually been bowled out as such. England's bowlers had simply maintained their discipline around off-stump and careless batting had done the rest. We didn't even make it to the tea break, and then, by the close of play, England at 0–157 had sprinted away to be 59 ahead in reply without even losing a wicket. The dressing room was a quiet place as we trooped back in after the final ball that evening.

Was it a case of us at that time being a long way under par or of England being very, very good? It was a case of both those factors coming together at the same time as we just couldn't get enough runs on the board to put the England batting line-up under pressure, nor could we maintain any pressure with the ball as its batsmen simply dominated. It was the perfect storm for England as its batsmen put our bowlers under the pump, kept us in the field for long periods and gave its bowlers runs on the board to bowl at so Strauss could continue to set attacking fields. And by bowling us out cheaply time and again, it meant our bowlers were always under pressure and never getting enough of a break between efforts. I think that was probably the high-water mark for that England side, and by the time several of those players arrived in Australia three years later, they were either past their best or close to retirement. But on that trip in 2010–11 they were just too good for us.

I had no problem with either the head coach Tim Nielsen or Ricky Ponting, and I'm not sure, runs from Ricky aside, there was much more they could have done to try and turn our fortunes around in that series. Tim was the coach when I made my debuts in all three formats and I enjoyed working with him. I found him to be honest, straightforward to deal with and hardworking, and given the problems we were having, he maintained a degree of calmness that was impressive. I think any coach would have struggled in the circumstances Tim found himself in, stepping in to the shoes vacated by John Buchanan, but without a host of the legend-ary players that John was able to work with. And as for Ricky, although he struggled for runs, he always seemed to have a positive outlook and his training regime was some-thing I took particular notice of. He would work at 110 per cent, always, and he and Michael Hussey really did set the standard around the group for everyone else to follow. In fact, there was a good work culture in that dressing room and there was no issue within the squad in that regard. It's simply that we weren't good enough, player for player, up against England—and the 3–1 series loss was the result.

My figures in the circumstances were respectable—159 runs at 31.80—but hardly compelling, with an unbeaten 54 in the last innings of the series my only half-century. It meant I was out in the middle when England sealed victory in Sydney and with it the series—they had actually claimed the extra half-hour on the fourth evening to try and win that night—and that wasn't something I found very pleasurable. The Barmy Army, England's travelling fans, made a lot of noise from the area opposite the pavilion, where the old Hill used to be. They had any number of songs—although I don't remember the one they had for me—and its rendition of 'God Save the Queen' was as loud as anything you'll hear from a cricket crowd. England's players were naturally cock-a-hoop and what made it worse was that we had to go back out onto the ground and watch while they were presented with the crystal Ashes trophy while the glitter rockets were fired on the stage. It was rough to watch the opposition do something you'd hoped to be doing yourself, but I stored up the memory as motivation, and it meant when we won three years later, having known what it was like to be on the other side of the result, it made victory even sweeter.

I was part of the limited-overs side that did duty at the Cricket World Cup in Asia and then for a series in Bangladesh in April 2011, but I knew my place was under threat for the next Test assignment, in Sri Lanka in August and September. All the same it still came as a massive disappointment when I got the call from Andrew Hilditch that I'd been dropped. It's never an easy call to receive and, I'd imagine, not an easy call to make from a selector's point of view either, but despite my disappointment I knew in my heart of hearts that I couldn't really complain. I'd had the chance to cement my spot and I hadn't taken it. As Andrew told me, I was still very much part of the selectors' plans for the shorter forms of the game but I had to go away and score more runs and take more wickets at Sheffield Shield level to force my way back into the Test side, which was fair enough.

The call that I took from Andrew came in mid-July in the midst of what was a pretty traumatic time for Australian cricket. The home series loss to England had brought about the commissioning of the *Argus Report* to investigate what had gone wrong with the game and how it could be put right, and the same sort of review was going on in my head over my performance at that time too.

The call caused me to mope around for a couple of days feeling sorry for myself, which is what you might expect from a 21-year-old who'd just been told that his dream of playing Test cricket had been put on hold at least in the short term, but in the longer term it had a very positive effect on me. I realised I couldn't go on being a bits-and-pieces cricketer and expect to make a success of myself at Test level. It might have been the way to go if I'd intended to make myself into a short-form specialist, but playing Test cricket had always been my goal and now, having had a taste, I wanted more of it.

But to do that I knew I would have to concentrate on one skill rather than try to be a jack-of-all-trades, and the decision of the selectors to drop me forced my hand. From that time on, I worked much less on my bowling and much more on my batting, and gradually that switch to focusing on one skill began to pay off.

It was a case of being realistic and seeing the glass as half-full rather than half-empty. Few, if any, players go through their careers without being dropped at least once and the reason for that is simple: the step up from first-class to Test cricket is a big one and it's not one that many players are able to make without putting the odd foot wrong. My initial call-up and my opportunity during the Ashes series, even though I didn't realise it at the time, were a chance to experience cricket at that level and therefore gave me an insight into what I had to do to maintain my place there. When you think about it, people don't get the same opportunity in the non-sporting work arena: you get promoted, struggle with the job and are then either demoted or even sacked. Very few people that I can think of get promoted, find they're not up to the job then get demoted only to have another run at that same job later on.

I'd been given that run at my goal and it was now up to me to do what I needed to in order to get a second chance.

CHAPTER 6

2013—The year the dam broke

The year when I really started to show what I could do at international level was 2013 when I returned to the Test side in India, and made my maiden hundred in that form of the game—138 not out against England at The Oval.

But the start of my march to the top of the batting rankings could have been put on hold almost before it began thanks to a mistake that nearly resulted in me being sent home from the Australia A tour of the UK and Ireland.

The A squad was training in Southampton when Mickey Arthur, the head coach of the senior side, came to visit us and see how everyone was going. The reason for the visit was, I'm sure, to show the players that all of us were in Mickey's sights for the upcoming Ashes series and also the cricket to follow, and on top of that it was also the chance for him to chat to us about contracts.

I'd missed out on a place within Cricket Australia's list of 20 contracted players published at the start of April and that left me more than a little disappointed. I felt I'd played pretty well in the two Tests I'd played in India in March, scoring 92 in my comeback innings in Mohali and then 46 and 18 on a shocking pitch in the series finale in Delhi.

Those were my first Tests for more than two years and I felt I'd acquitted myself as well as I could on what was a pretty tough tour both on and off the pitch. The 4–0 series whitewash also featured four players—Shane Watson, James Pattinson, Usman Khawaja and Mitchell Johnson— suspended for a Test after the so-called 'homework-gate' scandal exploded, as the quartet failed to weigh into the debate about what the side could do to turn things around following defeats in the opening two matches of the series in Chennai and Hyderabad. But the major topic of my discussion with Mickey wasn't my form; it was actually my fitness as he had in front of him the result of my skinfolds test and all wasn't apparently as it should be.

The skinfolds test is one that's used to determine how much body fat a player is carrying. The test uses callipers to pinch fat at specific sites on the body including, as examples, the arms, stomach, legs and back. The measurements are taken in millimetres and the overall score is the sum of the sites.

As I write these words the standard for Cricket Australia players is 60 millimetres across seven sites although the lower the number the better. But my test produced a score in excess of that mark and the result was that I got a rocket from Mickey about my fitness.

I was hauled over the coals and almost sent home, and, if I had been, then that would almost certainly have ended whatever hopes I had of a recall to the squad for the Ashes series that was starting later that northern summer.

What upset me about the dressing down was that I felt the skinfold measurement I'd had taken in the run-up to our meeting was incorrect and, as if to illustrate that point, when I had the test again three days later my score was significantly lower and well within the accepted mark. There was no way my numbers could have dropped to that extent in three days even if I'd eaten and drunk nothing at all, so it made me even more convinced that the first test was wrong.

And what made me even more frustrated was that the telling off came at a time when the penny really had started to drop for me in terms of my fitness and looking after myself. On the tour of India I'd used the time when I was out of the side, both before and during the first two Tests of the series, to work really hard on my fitness and I was beginning to see the results.

We had 17 players in the squad for that India trip, and also Ashton Agar, who was there as something of a project player, and what that meant was that during each day's play of a Test, as long as two players were available to run drinks and gloves out to the middle or act as replacement fielders, then the rest of the non-players were free to work on their skills. For me that involved lunchtime fielding sessions with Steve Rixon, one of the coaches on the tour, as well as running and gym work after the day's play, plus hours in the practice nets with batting coach Michael Di Venuto when he and I developed a close working relationship as he threw me ball after ball.

My desire to get back into the Test set-up had made me change my mindset from viewing gym and fitness work as a chore to actually starting to enjoy it. Previously I'd done all that was required of me and nothing more but now I was putting in extra work, initially at New South Wales and then with the Australian squad on the tour of India, and I felt it was starting to bear some fruit, which made the criticism I received in Southampton so hard to take.

But, take it I had to and rather than sulk about it, especially after that second skinfolds test which showed I was actually fine, it caused me to redouble my efforts off the field.

On the face of it, the A tour could have been a bit of a comfortable ride. It featured matches against Ireland, Scotland and English county side Gloucestershire and could have been viewed by some, including myself, as something of a consolation prize for failing to be selected for the squad for the ICC Champions Trophy.

But the group also included players not in that Champions Trophy squad who'd been selected for the Ashes series to follow that tournament, including A-team captain Brad Haddin, Jackson Bird, Ryan Harris, Phillip Hughes,

Usman Khawaja, Nathan Lyon, James Pattinson and Peter Siddle, and Brad was quick to point out to me that a decent showing on the trip could conceivably result in my promotion to join that group too. I knew he had his finger on the pulse of what was going on around the Ashes squad. His was always a voice I respected through our time together at New South Wales, and encouragement like that was all the incentive I needed to keep working hard.

I'd not considered myself much of a chance to make the Champions Trophy squad and that was how it turned out, but I was pretty disappointed to miss selection for the Ashes series in the first place given I'd played in Australia's most recent Test and had some experience of UK conditions, albeit in second XI cricket for Surrey and Kent a few years earlier. When I wasn't chosen, chief selector John Inverarity called me to deliver the bad news and told me there were concerns within the panel about my ability to deal with England's faster bowlers in conditions that were likely to assist seam and swing bowling. So all I could do in response was to try and make every post a winner on the A tour in an effort to face down my critics, in this case the selectors.

I managed to do that in Ireland by scoring 133 on a tricky surface in Belfast and that was probably the innings that clinched my elevation to the senior squad, although I didn't find out about it until after the third and final match of the trip, against Gloucestershire in Bristol.

It was John Inverarity who again delivered the news, and this time it was much better news to receive, although it was also somewhat overshadowed by other news that came at around the same time, that Mickey Arthur had been relieved of the role of head coach.

That was remarkable, given it was just a couple of weeks before the opening Test of the series against England, but although the timing was surprising, I can't say the decision was one that shocked me.

I liked Mickey as a person. I may not have agreed with his comments about my fitness in Southampton but I found him a really nice guy and the fact he's coached three international sides is impressive by anyone's standards.

But from my perspective I found him hard to play under and I didn't enjoy my time in the dressing room when he was head coach. Under his predecessor Tim Nielsen and his successor Darren Lehmann, the atmosphere in the dressing room was generally relaxed, even if the results weren't always ideal. However, under Mickey I always felt there was an underlying tension.

Mickey was a nervous watcher and when the person who should be something of a calming influence on players is tense then that's just the sort of attitude that can spread to the players themselves. I remember during the Hyderabad Test against India, Mickey actually had to go and stand in the toilets because he was too nervous about the team's performance.

The tension that something like that created wasn't just confined to match days. I also recall on that India tour some players being concerned that the coach might be unhappy with them for having a beer during a High Commission function. There was no suggestion that players were looking to get blind drunk, but the impression I had was that anyone having even a glass of beer ran the risk of being looked down upon by the coach.

The tension on the India trip came to a head with the so-called 'homework-gate' incident and, looking back, I think even Mickey would probably admit that he got that call wrong. I accept something needed to be done to recognise the players had failed to complete an assignment aimed at reversing our slide towards a series whitewash that duly arrived with further losses in both Mohali and Delhi, but suspension was a pretty drastic act. If you look at the ICC Code of Conduct, for example, a player incurs a ban for a serious offence such as abuse of another player, an extreme show of dissent, or racial vilification as three examples. Failing to provide three ideas to stop us from losing doesn't seem to fall into the same category, at least in my book.

In an odd way, I suppose I should actually be grateful for the incident as it gave me a leg-up back into the Test side after more than two years on the outer. And although it would have been nice to have played my way back into the starting eleven, I wasn't—at least at that stage of my career—in any position to turn my nose up at any sort of opportunity.

The truth was that I was fortunate to be on the India tour in the first place as I hadn't exactly set the Sheffield Shield ablaze in the summer of 2012–13, scoring a modest 296 runs in five matches for New South Wales, an effort that produced a steady average of 37. My scores included three half-centuries *(64, 90, 72)* and technically I felt my game was starting to come together as I was focusing more on my batting and less on my bowling, and although the results weren't always apparent, I was much more comfortable with my own game than I had been two years earlier when I'd been dropped from the Test side after the series against England. My back-foot play had improved, I had a better idea of where my off-stump was and I felt the work I was doing was leading me in the right direction.

But despite all those elements, I failed to score a large volume of runs in the matches I played for New South Wales that season and ordinarily I wouldn't have been close to a recall. But sometimes timing is everything and I managed to produce one of my best innings of the summer just as the selectors were considering their options for the India tour, making 72 against Western Australia in Blacktown on a pitch that offered some spin to Stephen O'Keefe and the visitors' Ashton Agar.

That innings, including my ability to handle Ashton, registered with the selectors because chief selector John Inverarity referred to it when I was chosen for the trip to India. 'His score just recently in the Shield match was very good,' he said. 'We see him as a young player of the future (with) enormous potential and one thing in particular in his favour is he uses his feet really well and plays spin bowling really well.'

The news of my return to the Test reckoning was, I have to admit, a surprise to me given my numbers during the summer, although I wasn't complaining. But while that was the positive, John was also realistic when he spoke about where I stood in the pecking order on the trip. 'He will be there as a back-up batsman and certainly to gain experience.' So I flew out under no illusions at all that I was nowhere near the starting line-up and in reality I was actually behind another batsman—Usman Khawaja—in the list of reserve top-order players.

I couldn't even draw a crumb of comfort from thinking my bowling might get me a leg-up either, although that was largely my own fault due to the way I was now concentrating on my batting instead. I'd bowled only 15 overs in those five Shield matches for one wicket and Nathan Lyon, Xavier Doherty and Glenn Maxwell were all ahead of me in the spin bowling stakes—although I knew that, to be fair, and so did John Inverarity, as my bowling credentials weren't even touched upon when he spoke about me as the squad was announced.

I did know that by being in the touring party, I was a lot closer to a recall than someone who was outside it, and thanks to a series of situations that could barely have been conceived of at the start of the trip, I eventually got my chance in the third Test in Mohali. What's more, I was batting at number five.

First of all, the side was beaten and beaten badly in the first two Tests of the series, in Chennai and Hyderabad. We lost by eight wickets in the opening match after India piled up 572 and then we collapsed twice in the second Test, making 237 and 131 while India again topped 500 (503) to win by an innings and 135 runs. That, in itself, produced a clamour for change. Then with Watson, one of the side's frontline batsmen, and Khawaja, the next cab off the batting rank, both out of the reckoning for the third Test in Mohali and wicketkeeper Matthew Wade also ruled out after rolling his ankle on the basketball court, it meant that out of nowhere I had to play. And I thought I played pretty well, too, for that innings of 92, eventually dismissed when I was lured forward by left-arm spinner Pragyan Ojha and stumped by Mahendra Singh Dhoni.

My good fortune was to come back into the side on a pitch that was probably the best of the bunch in terms of the four served up for that series. The surface didn't offer a great deal of assistance to India's slow bowlers, at least in that first innings, and although I didn't go on to make three figures, I felt the innings showed people—and, more importantly, showed me—that I could play at that level. It gave me a lot of confidence.

We still lost the Test, first pummelled by hundreds from Murali Vijay and Shikhar Dhawan and then spun out in the second innings by Ravichandran Ashwin, Ravindra Jadeja and Ojha, and when we lost the next Test too, in Delhi, the series whitewash was confirmed. But I did myself no harm at all in that final match with my two fighting innings, a decent contribution when set against the rest of the side's batting.

The change of head coach was a blessing for me because Darren Lehmann had been involved as one of the backroom staff on the A tour and so had got a look at me, something that meant he knew what I could do for the side if given a chance. He was also someone who'd never really looked all that elegant as a player but he still got the job done, and as I wasn't regarded as a model of orthodoxy myself, I hoped he might see something of himself in me and back me.

From a wider perspective, Darren's appointment was also a blessing for the squad as a whole, because he immediately lightened the mood. Bear in mind he began at a time when not only was the Test side on duty again for the first time since that India tour debacle, but also following a Champions Trophy campaign that saw us fail to reach the semi-finals thanks to losses against England and Sri Lanka and a rained-out game against New Zealand. Off the field captain Michael Clarke had been struggling with his long-standing back condition, while David Warner had been suspended after a late-night bust-up with England batsman Joe Root in a Birmingham bar. Truly, the only way was up.

Darren's approach was to try and get us to play with a smile on our faces again. His message has been a consistent one since that June day in Taunton when he spoke to the staff and players for the first time, that what we're doing is playing cricket for our country, something all of us have wanted to do all our lives. We started playing the game because we enjoyed it so why move away from that philosophy now? As he always tells us: 'We're not trying to cure cancer; we're playing cricket.'

Darren certainly brought the team closer together, using little touches, like stopping players from getting at the mobile phones straight after play in order to encourage us to chat to each other, and even enjoy a beer together if we liked. Make no mistake, if someone had ended up the worse for wear because of drink then Darren would have come down on that player like a ton of bricks but his attitude was that he learnt the game over a post-play beer with the likes of his mentor David Hookes and if that was good enough for Hookesy and him then it was good enough for us. I was no big drinker, especially in the wake of my improved fitness regime, but I was still happy to embrace the new fitness routine given I'd relished just such an approach when I played county second team cricket with Surrey a few years earlier, talking to senior players and picking their brains.

I found out later on that Darren had been impressed by me the previous season when I'd made 90 and 22 against the Queensland side he was coaching at Manuka Oval in Canberra. I got those runs in a low-scoring match and, as was the case with the Blacktown runs I got against Western Australia just before the India tour squad selection meeting. It was a case of impressing someone at just the right time. Of course, neither of us knew then, in late November 2012, how things would pan out just over six months later, but Darren later told me that after watching me bat in that match he said to himself: 'This kid's a gun.' It meant I had him in my corner from the start of his reign and although I didn't repay him with big runs straight away, producing scores of 53 and 17, 17 and 2 and 1 in the first two Tests of the Ashes series, he had enough faith in me to persevere and I rewarded him with 89 in the third Test and 138 not out in the fifth and final Test.

That hundred really did mark my arrival as an international batsman and I haven't looked back since, but

I can now reflect that getting the opportunity to produce an effort like that was something that came down to some good fortune, a happy knack of delivering what turned out to be career-defining innings at just the right time, plus having the feeling that I had no need to be looking over my shoulder. Faith—in my own ability and from those around me—plus a determination to give myself the best chance to succeed was what I needed to allow me to take the step up, and once those factors came together then I was determined to show there was no stopping me.

CHAPTER 7
Technique

'*I find the whole technique thing an interesting question and what I always come back to is, well, what's the perfect technique? Who's got it? The name of the game is to score runs and if you can stay out there (and) do that (then) you must have a pretty decent technique.*'

There aren't too many clearer thinkers on the art of batting than Michael Di Venuto, who worked with me in the Australian squad for three years, from 2013 when I got back for the tour of India, through to early 2016, when he headed to the UK to coach Surrey.

He never tried to overcomplicate things with me, and his quote, from an interview on the website cricket.com. au in April 2017, is a perfect summary of what we both believe batting is all about. It doesn't matter what you look like at the crease; making runs is what it is all about and as long as you can do that then there is nothing wrong with what you do when you have the bat in your hand.

I realise my technique is a point of interest for many, many people because I know I don't look like what you might call a classical player—someone like Greg Chappell, for example, who, when I look at footage of him appears upright, still, side-on and makes everything appear elegant and effortless. With me, I know I appear to be fidgeting as I set myself to take strike, and as the bowler hits his delivery stride I'm on the move across my crease.

But if you leave the fidgeting out of it then I actually think my technique is a pretty simple affair. Critics might think there are a lot of moving parts, that I get a long way across in front of my stumps and that the way my bat comes down from second or third slip might mark me down as something out of the ordinary. But if you analyse the positions I get into when I actually make contact with the ball, then I would argue I'm a pretty orthodox player. I have a solid base and my head is still and they are probably the key points for anyone trying to build a serviceable technique. I'm not one to overthink at the point of delivery, either. To a great extent it is a case of instinct taking over, and having fine-tuned my shots through countless hours at practice and having worked out what the bowler is trying to do—with the field he's set offering the best clue to that—it is almost a case of 'see ball, hit ball'.

As a youngster I never had any formal coaching but my dad was instrumental in helping to produce the basis for the technique you see today. At that stage of my cricketing life it was all about volume for me and I just wanted to feel bat on ball, and bat and bat and then bat some more. Dad didn't try to impose any particular style or approach upon me. All he did was try to get me to be as natural as possible. I've heard that Adam Gilchrist's father used to spend part of every net session telling his son just to have fun by trying to hit the ball as hard and as far as he could, and with Dad it was a case of much the same. We never studied coaching manuals and I think the only time I've read one was when I was studying for my Level 1 coaching qualification. Enjoyment was the name of the game when I was growing up and what I was doing when I faced Dad in my formative years is still the basis of my batting now. Much of what I do with my hands and feet has stayed the same.

Dad did challenge me in one major way, though. Every year from about the time I was ten, he would creep just a bit closer when he bowled so that by the time I was 15 he was bowling at me from maybe 16 or 17 yards away. It obviously shortened my reaction time and it certainly helped to speed up my reflexes and movements, and I think that approach has stood me in good stead ever since. It meant that when I graduated to senior cricket, the pace of the bowling and the speed of the game as a whole was much less of a culture shock for me.

Growing up, my first batting hero, the player I wanted to be like and the one I tried to model myself on, was Mark Waugh. I think that I can still see bits of what he did in my technique today—where my bat comes from in its down-swing and the way my hands can go at the ball—and one of my fondest memories of going to the SCG as a child was being there with my dad when Mark scored a hundred against South Africa in the New Year's Test of 1998. He brought up three figures with a glance to fine leg off Shaun Pollock, something I can still see in my mind's eye, and although you don't see it on YouTube if you look for that innings, I was the little boy who fielded the ball after it crossed the boundary, leaning over the fence to pick up the ball at the Paddington End before returning it to the fielder. Mark had the ability to make batting look effortless and he was a natural role model for me, especially as Mark's club Bankstown–Canterbury was only a few miles north of where I lived.

I do think that tennis and the fact I played it alongside cricket as a youngster has helped to shape my batting style and aspects of my cricket in a positive way. I can see it in footage of me clearing my front leg to play a big shot down the ground, almost as if I'm loading up for a big forehand, and there have been times when I know I've hit the cricket ball with top-spin. It actually prompted me to alter the grip of my bottom hand on the handle to try and stop that tendency and in doing so I believe I now hit the ball further as a result.

I've no doubt that playing tennis alongside cricket as I grew up has had a beneficial effect on my chosen career.

It has helped me understand different angles when I'm batting and fielding, and enhanced my hand–eye coordination. I also believe it's helped my footwork as it's led to me being fast on my feet, and when I'm at backward point or short mid-wicket in particular, the ability I have to push off one way or the other very quickly and powerfully has come from the need to do the same on the tennis court. I can also think back to Dad standing in front of the garage at the top of our small driveway at home, hitting catches to me using a tennis racquet and tennis ball while I fielded out in the street of the quiet cul-de-sac where we lived. Catching tennis balls like that taught me the value of soft hands, of cushioning the ball as you catch it, and my fielding has benefited as a result of that foundation.

I know there is a school of thought that says a child wanting to excel at a particular sport should start concentrating on it from an early age, but that's not my experience. I would always advise parents to encourage their children to play as many sports as possible for as long as possible before focusing on one, because the skills of one aren't necessarily exclusive, as I've found out.

I did play cricket for fun and enjoyment as a child but looking back now I realise that I was always someone who analysed his game—what worked for me and what didn't. I was never the biggest boy playing and I sometimes used to get out trying to hit over the in-field because at that stage of my life I lacked the power to play those sorts of shots effectively. There was an added complication at Casuarina Oval as the artificial pitch in the middle was set in a slight dip below the rest of the ground as it was filled in during the off-season to allow the winter sports to use the field. It meant that sometimes you could play a cracking shot only to see it stop dead near your feet, having hit the side of the lip from playing field to pitch. That was an encouragement to try and lift the ball but given I struggled to do that effectively, I had to adapt and find other ways to score. And Dad often told me that Don Bradman would say that if you don't hit the ball in the air then you can't get caught. It's funny, but that's been something that's stayed with me ever since.

As a teenager breaking into grade cricket with Sutherland District Cricket Club and the first-class scene at New South Wales, I think I can look back at the way I played and call myself fairly loose. I liked to feel bat on ball and play my shots, to get the scoreboard ticking over, but I was fortunate to have some terrific mentors at Sutherland who helped sand off the rough edges to my game. People like Phil Jaques, the former Australia opening batsman, and Trent Woodhill, who was one of the coaches at the club at that time.

Early in my first-grade career for Sutherland, when I was playing as an opening batsman, Phil gave me one piece of advice: 'Don't cover drive before lunch.' After that, he said, I could do what I liked. The pitch at the Glenn McGrath Oval does offer something to the bowlers in the first session but then it usually flattens out into what is one of the best batting surfaces in Sydney grade cricket. Playing those big cover drives early in my innings was undoubtedly a weakness at that stage of my cricketing career and when I first opened with Phil, against Blacktown, I was bowled for a duck. But after that, off the back of Phil's advice, I put the shot away, and went on to make 57 against North Sydney in my next match and it's advice I still try to live by today. I try to keep the big drive in the cupboard early on, only looking to play it if I get a very full-length ball that's right under my nose, and it is a method that works for me.

Trent, like Michael Di Venuto, has always been a coach I've listened to and respected and, also like Michael, he's one who looks to keep things simple. He recognises the value of seeing what a player does well and then trying to maximise that skill rather than seeking to force the player into doing what's regarded as the norm. When I was 16, he watched me trying to drive balls on middle stump back past the bowler and wondered why, with the technique I had, I was trying to do that. 'Why don't you hit those deliveries through mid-on and mid-wicket?' he said. 'Work on doing that well and you'll make a lot of runs.' He was spot-on.

The major change in my technique since I've come into professional cricket has been my preliminary movement, the movement I make with my feet as the bowler is in delivery stride, in order to get myself in a position to play the ball. When I started out I used to bat on middle stump, have no discernible preliminary movement across the crease, look to stay as still as possible for as long as possible and play predominantly off the front foot. But that all changed in Perth, out in the middle on day one of the Ashes Test against England in December 2013.

The England bowlers were bowling short at me and the WACA pitch was offering them a decent amount of bounce. I was finding that by batting on middle stump and pressing forward, I was something of a sitting target for their method of attack. I was stuck in no-man's land with nowhere to go. So I made a decision in mid-innings to alter my guard from middle stump to middle and leg, and adopted a preliminary movement that took me not only across my stumps but also back, something that gave me an extra fraction of time and also allowed me to be in a good position to either avoid the short ball or play the pull or hook shots.

It was one of those happy occasions where everything just clicked into place, it felt right and I went on to score a hundred that I can still look back on with a great deal of fondness. It was an example of me adapting to the situation, thinking on my feet and achieving a great result.

My movement across the crease means that as the bowler bowls I have my head in line with off-stump. And so whereas previously I wasn't always sure where my off-stump was—something that sometimes caused me to play at balls I could have left alone—now I am in a perfect position to be able to judge what to play and what to leave. And as I am able to leave effectively rather than get drawn into playing at wide balls, it can prompt bowlers to alter their line and attack my stumps, something I want them to do because working the ball off my pads is one of my strengths, which Trent recognised all those years ago.

The position of my feet can make an opposition bowler or captain believe that I'm a candidate for a lbw dismissal but my attitude is that I'll hit the vast majority of deliveries targeting my stumps. If I don't and the bowler gets me out lbw then I'll say 'Well bowled'. I actually like it when I realise opposition players are trying to get me out lbw because it means they will be bowling to what I regard as one of my strengths. I have total belief in my game and I think the figures back up the fact that any targeting of my pads is something I have coped with pretty well in my career. In my first 100 Test innings I was dismissed lbw 14 times. For another player in my era, Alastair Cook, his percentage is close to 19, while Sachin Tendulkar was sent on his way lbw just over 21 per cent of the times he fell.

That's not to say that my approach has been flawless. Over time my preliminary movement has got bigger and just occasionally it gets out of rhythm. In the Ashes series of 2015 in the UK, I found that I was moving a little bit too much and too late, with the result that I was actually still moving when the bowler delivered the ball. It was something I picked up watching videos of myself and I was able to correct it with Michael Di Venuto. Issues like that mean I will watch footage of myself every so often just to keep myself ticking over, ensuring I'm not moving too far and so losing my bearings and a knowledge of where my off-stump is. But I like to think I'm not one to over-analyse my game or spend hours going through footage of myself gathered by our assistant coach and video analyst Dene Hills. What I tend to do is to watch videos of myself on YouTube getting runs just for the feel-good factor. Viewing examples of me doing well is the best way to maintain confidence because it is a way of saying to myself: 'I've done it before and so I can do it again.'

Of course, the style I have developed as a batsman isn't going to work for everyone. My movement has allowed me to tighten up on what I play and what I don't play on or outside off-stump, and playing with greater discipline in that area was something I realised I needed to do after I was left out of the Test side in early 2011. But someone like David Warner, for example, would be crazy to replicate what I've done, as his great strength is through the off side and he likes to give himself room to play through that side of the ground. If he made that pronounced movement across the crease as the bowler bowled he would cramp himself for room and lose some of the scoring options he currently has through the off side thanks to his staying more leg side of the stumps than I do. Then again, I can't replicate what David does by going out and blazing away from ball one, hitting boundaries right from the start of my innings. My style is to be more patient and make the bowlers bowl where I have my best chance of success against them. Differences in style and approach like that are what make the game so good.

The key for any player is to identify where you score the majority of your runs and your main modes of dismissal so that you can maximise the former and minimise the latter. Even players like AB de Villiers, who I've heard described as a 360-degree batsman with strokes all around the wicket, will limit himself to certain shots in Test cricket. For example, he might look to cut if he's given some width or punch the ball back down the ground as his bread-and-butter shots, but he would probably put away the cover drive in much the same way that I do early in an innings.

Of course, it's one thing to have a routine to deal with each delivery I face, but I also have a routine that I stick to between deliveries too. If you bat for any length of time, then it's impossible to concentrate for every single second you are out in the middle. If you tried it then you'd be exhausted in no time at all, so you have to relax whenever you can. And it's also important to put the previous ball you've faced behind you and focus all your energies on the next one. After all, that's the only one that can get you out.

It's the art of switching off and then switching back on again, and different players have different ways of doing it. You can rest assured that every batsman has a method. If you watch David Warner, for example, you'll see that after each ball he unfastens the Velcro holding his batting gloves in place around his wrists and then, just before he settles back into his stance, he fastens them again.

What I look to do is move away from the crease and walk to short square leg, especially if a faster bowler is operating, one that has a run-up that allows me to take my time away from the business area of the pitch. And when it's then time to get back into my stance and re-gather my thoughts, I have a set routine. You might think my move-ments are just a series of nervous fidgets—and I accept I look very fidgety to the outsider—but they do serve an important purpose. I'll touch the top of my left pad, then the top of my right pad, my thigh pad and then finally my box, just a series of minute adjustments that get me back in the moment. Then, as I take my stance, I'll tap my bat down twice behind my right foot before looking up to track the bowler's approach to the wicket. And before I actually get into my preliminary movement, I'll make one more tap with the bat. It might seem strange but it's my way of ensuring I'm absolutely ready for that next ball, with nothing else in my mind. It's almost a case of being on autopilot.

I have reached the stage in my career, having played more than 50 Tests and close to 100 ODIs, where I am comfortable with my game but that doesn't mean I have stopped thinking about my approach and ways to improve or to minimise risk. My play of spin, for example, has evolved over time.

When I started out I spent a lot of time watching Michael Clarke and the way he went about combating slow bowling. He was light on his feet and looked to get down the pitch on a regular basis to keep the bowlers guessing about where they could bowl. Initially I looked to emulate that style, especially in the sub-continent. But after my dismissal against South Africa in Perth in late 2016 when I was given out lbw after I'd gone down the pitch, I reassessed that approach and subsequently looked to stay in my crease unless I was making a conscious attempt to disrupt a bowler's length.

Against spinners now, especially on the sub-continent, I will look to get a big stride forward with my bat out in front of the pad to combat the threat of lbw, and try and remove the possibility of an inside edge onto the pad, and I'll only look to drive if the ball is very full in length. If I'm playing off the back foot, then it's a case of getting right back as far as possible to give myself that extra split second, and, when I'm back there I'll look, wherever possible, to play with a straight bat to straight balls as the delivery that skids on is a threat. Showing the full face of the blade offers the best chance of combating it.

The point at which my game is at now means I use coaches more as another set of eyes rather than for advice or criticism. I know what I'm doing to the extent that I can avoid the need for much tinkering. When I go into a practice net I will usually ask a member of the coaching staff to watch my preliminary movement and where it is. Is it across to off-stump or middle and off? That helps me line things up in my own mind. I'm not bothered if a coach comes up and offers advice or an opinion because I'm at the stage in my career where I can take on board what I think is relevant and filter out what I regard as irrelevant. And ultimately I place a great deal of faith in my ability to problem-solve for myself. After all, no matter what a coach might say, I am the one with the bat in my hand who has to deal with any given situation out in the middle so I like to try and figure things out for myself wherever possible.

The best coaches I've worked with, people like Michael Di Venuto, for example, know not to crowd a player's head with lots of theories or ideas anyway. Sometimes it can be as simple as giving a player confidence through an affirmation that everything is okay. After all, they can often be the ones who know your game as well as you, if not better, thanks to countless hours throwing to you in the nets. The odd positive word here and there can be necessary, even for the best of players, because we are all human and we can all be prone to the odd moment of doubt, even when we have reached the top of our profession. I remember doubting myself during the Ashes series of 2013 in the UK. In the early part of the series I hadn't scored many runs. I hadn't nailed down my spot and having only been a late call-up for the tour I found myself looking over my shoulder at other players who might take my spot. 'I just can't get a big score,' I said to Michael at the end of one net session. 'You're not out of form,' he replied. 'Just out of runs—and they'll come.' He could see I was hitting the ball well enough and it was just one of those times when, as a batsman, you need a little bit of luck or a couple of balls in the middle of the bat at the start of an innings to get going. It was an invitation to stop thinking about all the possible reasons why I hadn't got a stack of runs and instead just back myself to execute the plans and the method I had in place. Sure enough it clicked for me in the next match at Old Trafford where I got 89 and then, in the final match of that series, at The Oval, where I made my maiden Test hundred. And for the most part since then I've not looked back.

CHAPTER 8
Phillip Hughes

Cricket is a game that creates wonderful highs but, in my career, it's also featured one dreadful, terrible low—the death of Phillip Hughes.

I can still remember the events of 25 November 2014 as if they were yesterday, as they are etched on my mind, and I'm sure the same is true of everyone who knew Phillip and certainly everyone connected with cricket on that awful day.

It was day one of a Sheffield Shield match at the SCG, with New South Wales playing South Australia. I wasn't playing in the game as I'd suffered a slight thigh strain during an ODI against South Africa, also at the SCG, two days earlier, and although the problem wasn't serious, I was left out of the match to rest, receive treatment and ensure I was ready for the first Test against India that was due to start just over a week later, on 4 December in Brisbane.

I'd been in to the SCG in the morning, during the first session, to see the Cricket New South Wales medical staff, and while I was there I was able to watch some of the action. South Australia was batting, Phillip was playing like a genius and it looked like a case of perfect timing from him. He had been the reserve batsman on the recent tour of the United Arab Emirates (UAE) where we played Pakistan in two Tests and, with Michael Clarke struggling with injury—something that had placed a question mark over his fitness to take part in that opening Test—Phillip appeared to be putting himself forward as the obvious candidate to fill that slot in the Test side if Michael wasn't able to get himself right.

I headed home after lunch with the instruction to keep icing my injury through the afternoon, and that was what I was doing, lying on my couch, when I received a text message from Richie Callander, the son of racing legend Ken Callander and a good friend of mine.

The message was that Phillip had been hit on the back of the head and that the players were coming off the field. That was unsettling but I'd seen and heard of plenty of players getting hit during my years of involvement in the sport and that knowledge meant my first thought was: 'I'm sure he'll be okay', rather than any major concern for his welfare.

But when Richie followed up by informing me that the matter was very serious and that I should get to the SCG as quickly as I could, I didn't need to be told a second time and I was up off the couch like a shot and on my way back to the ground.

I was living just under ten minutes' drive away but by the time I got there Phillip had already been taken away to hospital and the scene that greeted me in the New South Wales dressing room was one I never want to experience again. I looked around at the faces of the players and the colour had drained out of every single one of them. Everyone appeared to be in a state of shock and although I asked a few questions trying to get some more detail about what had happened, and whether there was any news of Phillip, no one was saying very much. Most of the players were just sitting around with blank looks on their faces and some were in tears. I stayed around in the room for a while but with no one really talking—there was an awful silence for most of the time—and with no one knowing what was going on, with the match or with Phillip, I headed back home trying to take in what had happened. What was clear from the reaction of the players and the fact Phillip was away from the ground and at hospital was that the situation was very serious. It was very hard to try and take it all in and I think my feeling was the same as everyone else's—I couldn't believe what had happened.

Phillip and I went back a long way and although he was playing for South Australia on the day the tragedy occurred, that switch had been a relatively recent event.

He was in his third season based in Adelaide, having originally switched states to try and revive his international career after missing out on a Cricket Australia contract in 2012. But he'd played all his junior and state cricket up to that point for New South Wales and that's how we met. Phillip was just over six months older than me and we first faced each other at junior level when I remember him scoring successive hundreds against my team. Even then it was obvious he was an exceptional talent as, although he was unorthodox, he seemed to pick up the length of the ball very quickly and was in position to play the shot he wanted almost before the fielders were ready. That ability to assess length rapidly is something the very best players have and Phillip certainly possessed it.

Our first time playing alongside each other was on a Cricket New South Wales under-17s tour of the UK the year before I went there to try and gain some experience as a club professional. We hit it off straight away. Our shared unorthodoxy as batsmen was something that drew us together, but we also shared a real passion for batting. Most youngsters like having the bat in their hands, but what drives players to the next level is that passion for the sport, almost bordering on an obsession, and that's what Phillip and I both had, I think. His desire to be the best he could be as a batsman drove his move to South Australia and also his stints in county cricket for Middlesex and Worcestershire.

Because Phillip's family lived a fair distance away from Sydney—Macksville is about 500 kilometres north and just as close to Brisbane—he would stay at my parents' house when we were both making our way on the fringes of the Cricket New South Wales squad as juniors, and we would then head to the SCG together for training. He was a great guy to be around, quietly spoken and not brash, and we always enjoyed each other's company.

When he died he was still taking his game forward. Right from the outset he was always strong through the off side and especially through the point region and the timing and placement of his cut shot was remarkable. He really was great to watch when in full flight and as a fielding captain you could have five fielders in the area square of the wicket and he would still be able to find the gap between them. The cricketing grapevine—together with video analysis of his game—meant sides eventually got wise to that strength and started to restrict him by tucking him up, not offering him any width. But as I saw first-hand in practice in the UAE during our series against Pakistan, and also during that morning session at the SCG, he had begun to develop a really good leg-side game. Now, when bowlers bowled straight to him, he was whipping them through the arc between square leg and wide mid-on.

I have to admit, though, the intricacies of Phillip's game was the last thing on my mind at a meeting of players at the SCG the day after the incident. We were briefed that day by both Doctor John Orchard, who'd attended to Phillip out on the ground, and Doctor Peter Bruckner, Cricket Australia's team doctor, and the fact John broke down in tears as he was explaining to us what had happened was a real hammer blow that told us all just how bad the situation really was.

What had happened was that Phillip had been struck on the left-hand side of the neck, just below his helmet, by a short ball and had gone down head first on the pitch. After John's intervention he was taken to St Vincent's hospital and had undergone surgery soon after arriving to relieve pressure on his brain caused by bleeding following the blow. But he remained critical, in an induced coma, and we were confronted with a very stark view of what would happen next. It was explained to us that it was believed Phillip was not expected to recover but, in the event that he did, he would be unlikely to be the person we had known because of the nature of the injury he'd experienced.

I still remember the moment I took in those words. I felt a mix of numbness and shock and it was a feeling that was shared by the entire group. It was like being punched in the stomach—the breath just went out of the whole room. None of us could believe what we'd been told.

I went to the hospital over the 24 hours or so that followed, along with not only all the players based in New South Wales, but also players and cricket officials from elsewhere, including national head coach Darren Lehmann, who'd flown in from Brisbane to be close to the situation and to offer what comfort he could. Darren had gone through a similar tragedy in 2004 when his mentor and mate David Hookes died from a blow to the back of the head inflicted during a night out in Melbourne, something, that like this situation, had come completely out of the blue. It meant that if anyone had experience of dealing with this sort of situation then it was him, but, in truth, I think he was just as stunned as the rest of us.

I think what really affected me—affected many of us players, perhaps—was the fact that this situation had arisen playing cricket. It wasn't as if Phillip had been involved in a road accident or been the victim of an attack while walking in the street. The ball hit him while he was doing something all of us had seen, done and been party to count-less times before. We'd all hooked short balls and hit them for four or six and the bowlers among us had all bowled plenty of short balls too. We were all aware of the dangers of such deliveries, but it wasn't something that ever really entered our heads when we played the game. Yet here was a situation where a player we all knew—and a very good player too, not a novice who couldn't handle himself at the crease—had been the victim of a freak accident that could have happened to any one of us. It was a confront-ing, sobering and frightening thought.

Despite being at the hospital for long periods over the time that followed Phillip's accident, I didn't actually go in to see him until it was time to say goodbye, after we had been told that his life-support machine was going to be turned off. Before then I just sat in the foyer, along with a host of others, including state teammates Daniel Smith, Stephen O'Keefe and Moisés Henriques, as a steady stream of people came through. It was difficult to know what to say or what to do; I just felt—and I think the same was true with others, too—that we should be there for our mate and his family, and also to offer each other whatever comfort we could in a shocking situation.

When I did eventually go in to see Phillip it was with Stephen O'Keefe. I would put it down as one of the toughest things I've ever done in my life. It made me feel sick, but I'm glad I did see him before he left us as it forced me to try and remember all the good times we'd had together beforehand.

The day after Phillip's life-support machine was turned off, on Friday 28 November, there was a meeting of players at the SCG. Something that was crystal clear from that get-together was that no one had any stomach to get back on the field and play, certainly until after Phillip's funeral. That meant a postponement of the first Test against India, but it wasn't debated for a moment, as it was clearly the right thing to do for Cricket Australia and the Board of Control for Cricket in India when they discussed how to go forward.

From a personal point of view—and as someone who was obsessed with practice—I didn't feel ready even for a net, or some throw-downs, and so the prospect of going out to play a Test match was the furthest thing from my mind. What those members of the Test squad—the likes of Shane Watson, David Warner, Nathan Lyon and Brad Haddin—who'd witnessed the incident first-hand must have been feeling as they took part in the first Test when it eventually got underway in Adelaide on 9 December I can't imagine, and the same was true of all those who were present at the SCG on 25 November. Certainly, I found the whole situation a very difficult one to come to terms with.

In the days after Phillip's passing and before the funeral I took comfort in joining with a few of the New South Wales crew, including players like Moisés Henriques, Stephen O'Keefe, Nic Maddinson and Ben Rohrer, spending time together at the Clovelly Hotel in Sydney, having a few drinks and telling stories, trying to celebrate Phillip's life. I think all of us wanted to be with other players at that time rather than be alone because the whole nature of the tragedy was that we knew it could so easily have been one of us instead.

All of us had either faced or bowled countless short balls during the course of our careers and even when any of us had been struck there'd never been any lasting damage; now, here we were, reflecting on another short ball that had actually ended a player's life. We had taken our sport for granted, forgotten about any dangers involved and just got on with things and now we had received a shocking jolt to let us know that it wasn't just a bit of fun but could also result in someone's death, even possibly our own.

But if I was feeling terrible about what had happened, I couldn't begin to come to terms with what was going through Sean Abbott's mind. Sean and Phillip had been friends—Phillip was still playing for New South Wales when Sean made his first-class debut for the Blues—and they'd been on tour together for Australia in the UAE just over a month earlier, so for him to have bowled the ball that ultimately led to the tragedy must have been like a 100-ton weight around his neck. Everyone at Cricket New South Wales and the cricket community in Australia was keen to rally around him, although it was difficult to know how best to do that. The message to him was that we all supported him and the fact he took 2–53 and 6–14 in his next match, against Queensland also at the SCG, spoke volumes for his strength of character.

I saw Phillip's parents, Greg and Virginia, at the hospital as Phillip's situation became clear, but I just wasn't sure what to say or how to approach them. I mean, if it was tough for us as players and friends of Phillip to deal with, for his parents to go through that just goes beyond any words. And the fact that Virginia and Megan, Phillip's sister, were actually at the SCG to watch him bat on the day itself makes it even harder for me to comprehend how the whole family must have been feeling and still feel to this day.

My memories of the funeral in Macksville on 3 December were of the immense sadness everyone was feeling, the intense heat of the day and also of the dignified way Michael Clarke carried himself. Michael, like me, had missed the match because of injury, but he showed his leadership qualities in the hours and days that followed by fronting up on behalf of the players to speak with media and delivering a heartfelt tribute to Phillip at the funeral itself. He was close to tears by the end of his eulogy and I know I was too.

The one thing that came through to me from that period between Phillip's injury and our resumption of cricket with the first Test was the feeling that nothing, and certainly not playing, felt as important as it had done before the incident. Before Phillip's death, when I was dismissed I would get upset with myself, but his passing was a watershed for me, and I'm sure for a lot of other players too, as it made me realise that, in the big scheme of things, losing my wicket was nothing in comparison to losing my life. I'm not saying it made me carefree or flippant in my attitude to cricket or to train with any less intensity after that time, but it certainly made me remember why I played the game in the first place—because I love it. It has its own pressures because I have responsibilities to myself, my teammates, my family and the cricketing community, but ultimately I'm thankful to be able to do something I have a passion for, and I've found that attitude has taken a weight off my shoulders in the years that followed.

I didn't feel able to pick up a bat again and practise until we arrived in Adelaide ahead of the rescheduled first Test and when I did so I started very gently, with just a few throw-downs from batting coach Michael Di Venuto. Some players, like David Warner, didn't feel able to bat at all— he just faced a few deliveries before he had to walk out of the nets and he ended up bowling instead—and the atmosphere around the group was one of apprehension. Our bowlers didn't want to bowl a short ball and, as a batsman, I certainly didn't feel like facing one. I remember the feeling that whenever a short ball was bowled it was much more of a big deal than it ever had been at practice beforehand. As time went by that feeling gradually settled down, but the memory of what happened has always stayed with us as players, to the extent that now, whenever anyone is struck in the head, then the first reaction is genuine concern. That was clear when Mitchell Johnson hit Virat Kohli in that

Adelaide Test and also, in the following year, when Mitchell Starc landed a bouncer on the helmet of Eoin Morgan in an ODI in Manchester. Before that summer of 2014–15, there may have been more of a feeling of 'Let's let him have some more short stuff', but now even though we are still determined to use the bouncer as an attacking weapon, we're also far more mindful of the effect being struck by a short ball can have.

In the aftermath of the incident at the SCG, and again after Phillip's passing, there were all sorts of views floated about on how to make the game safer. Any ban of short-pitched bowling was an obvious non-starter for me, because it's part of the fabric of the sport, and the game would suffer in its absence, as there are few more thrilling sights in cricket than a batsman hooking a fast bowler in full cry. Even if a ban had been considered, the issue of how to enforce it would have been another issue. Bowlers have to bowl different lengths depending on the type of pitch they play on in order to get a ball up to head height—a short ball in Dubai, for example, on a relatively docile surface would have to be much shorter in length than a short ball in Perth to get up to a batsman's head height.

The answer for me has always been in improving the quality of protective equipment and we've now seen that with the adoption of British Standard helmets across the game at the highest level. The main features of them are that the grille is now fixed and can't be adjusted manually as was the case in the past, and the gap between the grille and the helmet peak has been reduced and is now fixed to try and avoid the ball from sneaking through to strike the face. That fixed grille took a bit of getting used to for me because it meant the top bar was in a place where I'd previously been looking to try and locate the ball. It was a concern for me as having anything interfering with my vision made the helmet more, rather than less, dangerous in my view, but I got used to it and now playing with such a helmet has become second nature.

Neck guards were also introduced as clip-on additions to the helmet, aimed at reducing the consequences of a blow around the area where Phillip was struck, by dispersing the impact, but although I tried one for a while in the nets, I just couldn't get used to it. It just didn't feel right as I felt it restricted my movement as I turned my head, and so I opted not to use it. That might be seen as an unnecessary risk but my view is that while I need to be protected at the crease, I also need to feel comfortable, and for me a helmet without the neck guard works on those levels.

That first Test after Phillip's passing was tough for everyone in our side. It had only been a couple of months earlier that he'd been part of the squad in the UAE and now he was no longer with us. There was a great deal of emotion as we sang the national anthem ahead of the first day's play, but my main recollection of the period and the match itself was how flat the playing group was. Our changing room was like one where we'd just lost five games in a row. There was no energy, and none of the usual bubble you get within an Australian dressing room before and during a Test match.

It was tough but I think we all knew we had to get out and play the game because, however painful the situation was, we all had to try to come to terms with it as best we could. And I think we all did that with our performances in that Test match, and we continue to honour and respect Phillip to this day. When someone was a part of our lives as Phillip was for so many of us within the game, we will always remember him.

In the circumstances, I can count my double of 162 not out and 52 not out, and especially the unbeaten hundred in the first innings, as two of the more satisfying Test innings of my career. When I reached my hundred on the second day and looked up to the heavens as I stood on the number 408 that had been painted on the ground—a mark of respect for Phillip as he is the 408th player capped by Australia at Test level—there were tears in my eyes. I took off my helmet and Ian Gould, the umpire, very thoughtfully told me: 'Take your time, take all the time you need.'

It was actually an outstanding Test match, not least for the way we managed to win it on the final day when India seemed to be in a position to secure a remarkable win of its own. By that stage, Brad Haddin had taken over as captain with Michael Clarke out of action following a first innings hundred (128) of his own which was interrupted by a back injury and then a hamstring issue as he fielded, and Brad quickly showed himself to have something of a golden touch that day.

As Virat Kohli—who batted outstandingly well in that match and for much of that series—was easing India towards the winning line as it chased 364, we were looking a little flat and Brad said to me: 'You get out of bat-pad and out into the field to help me out with some energy.' I think that's the last time I've fielded bat-pad and I wasn't sorry to get out of there. Suddenly—not through any action by me, I might add—everything seemed to click for us, Nathan Lyon got on a roll by taking seven wickets in the innings and 12 in the match, and India went from 2–242 to 315 all out to give us a wonderful win by 48 runs.

We enjoyed the success and had a good get-together as a team in the dressing room after the match, remembering Phillip and delighted we could pay tribute to him by securing a win at a venue he called home. But at the same time we all knew that it was going to take more than just five days for us to get over the trauma we felt in the wake of Phillip's passing, and that was exactly how it proved, as playing again at the SCG in the final match of the series was just as testing for many of us, especially those who'd played in that fateful match and also those of us who'd played alongside Phillip at state and international level.

It was one of the toughest parts of my life so far and however long I play the game and am involved in it I hope I never have to experience anything like it again.

CHAPTER 9
Assuming the captaincy

I t was in the bar of the Sebel Playford hotel in Adelaide on the evening of 13 December 2014, after we'd wrapped up a thrilling and emotional Test win against India, that I first realised I had a chance of becoming Australia's 45th Test captain.

I was having a drink with Brad Haddin, and former captain and now Channel Nine commentator, Mark Taylor and my assumption was that, with Michael Clarke injuring his hamstring and back during the match, Brad would take over for the foreseeable future. He was the senior professional within the squad, the vice-captain, a mentor for me at state and international level—and someone who was always prepared to cut to the chase, as he showed again that night.

'You should give the captaincy to Smudge,' he said to Mark.

Now Mark wasn't just a prominent ex-player. He was also on Cricket Australia's Board of Directors and it was those Directors who were the kingmakers when it came to deciding who captained the Australian side. The selectors put forward recommendations, but the decision to say yes or no lay with Mark and his colleagues around the board table.

Brad's remark took Mark—and me—off-guard. 'Don't you want to do it, then?' he said to Brad with a smile, perhaps thinking he was joking.

'I'm not going to be playing for much longer and there's no point in putting in a caretaker like me who'll be gone soon. This'll be a good opportunity for you to look at a long-term candidate to fill the role. Smudge is your man,' said Brad.

'Are you serious?' said Mark, and then he turned to me and said: 'Are you ready?'

I had absolutely no doubts that I was and said so, and with that Mark said: 'I'll go and make some calls then.'

I'm pretty sure Brad had already had the conversation with head coach Darren Lehmann, himself a selector, because it only took until the following morning as I was relaxing with Dani in Adelaide doing some shopping, for my mobile phone to ring and it was National Chairman of the Selectors Rodney Marsh calling.

'We need to get this approved by the Board but subject to that approval, which I don't think will be a problem, we'd like you to captain the side for the rest of the series against India, and when Michael comes back we'd like to make you vice-captain,' he said. It all happened that quickly, and in less than 24 hours I went from a situation where the idea of captaining the side—at least at that point in time—hadn't entered my head to being all set to take on the role. It was pretty amazing.

I'd grown up with one aim in mind, to play for Australia, and although the thought of captaining the side was something I'd dreamed of, it had never been anything more than that—a dream—up to that point in time. Now the dream was about to become a reality.

It was only after Mark had left the bar on the previous evening that I allowed myself to start thinking for the first time what it would be like to lead my country and I thought to myself: 'This is actually happening.' I started to get a little excited and I know Dani felt the same way when I told her later that night too.

So when Rodney called me with the news, my answer was a simple one: 'Of course I'll do it, yes—and thanks.'

I never had any doubts in my mind about taking on the role, either. I'd done a fair amount of captaincy throughout my life, throughout the age-group levels as I grew up, a season in first grade for Sutherland, and with New South Wales and the Sydney Sixers. And so although I knew this was a serious step up, I wasn't daunted at the prospect in any way.

What was reassuring for me was that I knew Brad was in the team and that gave me a great deal of confidence. I was very close to him thanks to our time together, first at

New South Wales and then with Australia, and knowing I would be able to call upon his terrific cricketing brain and experience was a tremendous feeling. He was a fantastic sounding board, not just for me, but for Michael too and, just as importantly, he had respect throughout the group.

Not that, as I soon realised, any of the players had to be won over to the idea of me taking charge. I'd known several of the squad, players like newcomer Josh Hazlewood, as well as Mitchell Starc, Nathan Lyon and David Warner over a long period of time either through New South Wales cricket or our time together in the national side, while other senior players like Shane Watson—who captained the side when Michael Clarke was injured in India in 2013—Chris Rogers and Mitchell Johnson were very supportive. In fact, when the squad met up in Brisbane for the second Test of the series the whole group were very accepting of my appointment.

The speed of my rise from the ranks to the top job was best illustrated by the fact that in October in a tour game in Sharjah in the UAE ahead of our two-match series against Pakistan, when Michael and Brad were both off the field, it was Chris Rogers and not me who'd taken charge. And in early November in the ODIs against South Africa I wasn't even in the first-choice starting eleven in that format and only secured a slot in the side when Michael suffered an injury in game one of that series. Fast-forward less than two months and now I was in the Test match hot seat.

The call I'd taken from Rodney was on Sunday morning and by the following day we were in Brisbane, it was two days before the second Test and I was officially announced as the new captain.

I knew I wasn't going to be short of people offering their views on what I should do in my new role and how I should do it, but in the same way I had just a small group of people I trusted to chat with about my batting, the same was true when it came to discussing my promotion.

When I called my parents on that Sunday they were thrilled as it was justification for everything they'd done for me behind the scenes ever since I'd first had a cricket bat in my hands at the age of four. What came across to me when we chatted was the faith and confidence they had in me to do the job and do it well, which made me feel like a million dollars. They knew I was doing what I'd always wanted to do, that made them happy and that was enough for me. And Dad added: 'Just go out and have fun.'

Warren Craig, my manager since the age of 18 when I was breaking into the New South Wales squad, was used to looking after high-profile sportsmen and women, including former Australian fast bowler Glenn McGrath, and his advice was simple: 'Just do it your way and back yourself in everything you do.'

That first team meeting is now a bit of a blur. I remember someone—Darren Lehmann, I think it was—announcing that I was going to be captain and then it was my turn to speak and, as I recall, what I had to say was pretty short and sweet.

'I'm just taking over for three games and although I'll be doing it my way, I won't be changing too much,' I said.

That was because although I knew I was the vice-captain when Michael was fit to return, and so I had a pretty good chance of being the next permanent appointment, I also knew my role, at least for the time being, was that of care-taker captain.

By that stage Michael had sent me a text asking me to call him when I was free, and he was very generous in his congratulations when we spoke as he told me to enjoy the experience. 'Don't worry,' I said. 'I'll hold on to it for you.'

From there it was on to the media conference at The Gabba where everything was made official in a public sense and it was undoubtedly the largest media gathering I'd ever attended. Again, just a couple of months earlier, I couldn't help recalling I'd spoken to some journalists at the ICC Academy in Dubai as we prepared for the Test series against Pakistan and, by kindest count, there were maybe half a dozen reporters there plus a couple of cameras. My appear-ance then wasn't exactly a crowd-puller but now every television news network, plus national and international reporters as well as the massed ranks of the Indian media were in attendance.

Just for fun I looked back at the video of that confer-ence on ESPNCricinfo and I was pleasantly surprised at how relaxed I looked. I think that was a reflection of how I felt. This was where I wanted to be and I was pleased to be in that position.

The media gathering was just one aspect of my new job to get used to. Both Michael and Brad had told me that the on-field part of captaincy was the easy bit; it was all the off-field stuff, they said, that was the real drain on time and energy.

The role involved discussions with not only the media as the spokesman for the team but also with selectors and even board members. It was also a case of paying far more attention to the rest of the squad during net sessions, rather than just operating in my own bubble and preparing with just my own game in my mind. Ahead of team meetings it was no longer enough for me to know what my game plan was going to be against the Indian bowlers. Now it was a case of knowing what all my bowlers' plans were too and so it was a case of watching footage, analysing where the opposition batsmen scored their runs and what their weaknesses were.

At the same time I was quite clear about my main responsibility. I was in the side as captain, yes, but I also had to score runs. If I didn't do that then my place in the side was under threat because there are few, if any, teams that are good enough to carry a non-performing leader, no matter how tactically aware he might be. My desire, right from the outset, was to lead from the front, by example, and I knew the best way to do that was by producing big scores with the bat. If I did that then I felt that, with the quality of players at my disposal, everything else would fall into place.

An outsider looking on would only have noticed a few subtle changes to the way the side operated in that Gabba Test in comparison to what had gone on the previous week in Adelaide. It was only two weeks after the funeral of Phillip Hughes and so emotions were still raw within the dressing room, but having gone out and played as we did in Adelaide, we all now knew we could get on with the job at hand, however difficult that was.

What were those changes? Well, one of the first things I did was to make the group get-together out on the ground on match days a little bit later than had been the case under Michael. On the morning of matches players will go through their own preparations, whether that is having a bat in the nets, getting strapped up as a bowler or having a massage, but at a certain point in time the whole squad assembles on the outfield, the captain and coach say a few words about the plans for the day ahead and then the players and support staff break up into smaller groups and go through some stretches, loosening-up exercises and perhaps some fielding drills, while the bowlers might roll their arms over on a pitch adjacent to the one used in the match.

With Michael's well-documented back problems and the acute stiffness and soreness he experienced as a result of that, he would usually like to have that group meeting relatively early in the day because, understandably, he liked a decent amount of time to get loose. The downside of that was it meant if others wanted to go through their own preparations then they would have to be correspondingly earlier as would, therefore, every other part of their preparation, from getting up to having breakfast, and so Michael's timing for everyone to be 'on deck' was something that was not always universally popular. It was no criticism of Michael, but by shifting our get-together to a later time it meant the players could go through their individual routines at their own pace without one eye on the clock.

I took Michael's spot on the field, at second slip, moving from my previous place in the cordon at third slip, Shane Watson remained at first slip, and Shaun Marsh, back in the side in place of Michael, moved into the cordon in my former role. It meant that players used to looking for the captain in a certain position on the ground would still be looking in the same place. It also meant minimal changes to the cordon too, something I was keen on as continuity in that area was vital. Slip catching is a skill like any other in that the more you do it, the better you become, and having players in positions they are used to—Shane was a fixture in his spot and Shaun and I both knew what we were doing there too—gives confidence to the bowlers that when the edge is found then it is almost always going to be taken.

The other major issue of debate for me leading into the Test was where I would bat, as the order was something that was always determined by the captain. I'd slotted in at number five in the first Test in Adelaide and been success-ful there, one place behind Michael, and now Shaun, with experience of batting throughout the top order, was coming into the squad to replace him. In my first media conference as captain I was even asked about whether I was going to jump up to number three, the position Ricky Ponting held down as captain with such success over many years and one which was now occupied by Shane Watson. Shane was settled there and so I was happy to bat at number four with Shaun following me at five, something he had been doing with a degree of regularity for Western Australia. It wasn't a decision I arrived at on my own as I spoke with Darren

Lehmann and also Brad and Shane, as well as Shaun, and I decided that my moving up was one way I could follow through on my desire to lead from the front, by example. I obviously wanted those players ahead of me to cash in and make big runs, but at the same time I knew that the earlier I got in, the more chance I would have of affecting the innings and the match in a positive way. It wasn't a massive deal for me, but at the same time I wanted to be proactive and I thought that moving up the order was one way of doing that.

Mark Taylor presented me with my captain's blazer at the start of the first day and, like Warren Craig a few days earlier, his message was simple: 'Good luck, do things your way because you're the one who's remembered as the captain who wins or loses matches, and remember everyone is behind you.' That was appreciated, but it was a prelude to what turned out to be a real baptism of fire as, after I lost the toss on a very hot day, India took control with the bat and our bowling resources were stretched to the limits by injury and fatigue. Looking back, though, that was perhaps the best thing that could ever have happened to me at that stage of my captaincy career. If things had been an absolute cruise, with wickets falling at regular intervals and every bowling or fielding change I'd made turning to gold, then it would hardly have prepared me for any tougher times ahead in the future. As it was, at the end of the Test I thought that having coped with everything that was thrown my way in the early stages, I could cope with anything in the future.

I learnt a lot about myself and my style of captaincy during that Test match. Being calm was not something that came easily to me and if you look back at footage of that match, you'll see my frustration show itself from time to time, whether it was a shout, a wave of the hand or a look. I quickly realised that my body language was important as I was now the focal point for the rest of the team and everyone was looking to me for positivity. And I soon understood, too, that as captain, there was a camera on me at all times, either television or photography, and so I had to control my emotions to a far greater degree than I was used to doing previously. I quickly decided I had to come up with a coping technique to deal with any tension I was feeling at any point in time other than simply letting it out in full public view as I might have done in the past. My answer was to push my hands deep into my pockets and squeeze my thumbs hard. I found it offered a little relief for any pent-up feelings and it was something I continued to adopt from that time onwards.

The difficulties I experienced in the field after losing the toss on a decent surface began with Mitchell Marsh injuring his hamstring and he had to go off soon after lunch, unable to return to bowl for the rest of the match. Added to that was the fact that Mitchell Starc, back in the side in place of Peter Siddle, was really struggling for rhythm and Josh Hazlewood, on debut, was cramping badly. When all those factors were thrown together alongside India's decent progress, as Murali Vijay made an excellent 144, then I honestly thought that I was going to have to try and get through quite a few overs myself to give Mitchell Johnson a break. It was a bit frightening for a while and I had the feeling of havoc unfolding on my watch, right in front of me.

As it was I only bowled one over that day, just before the new ball was due, as did David Warner, as Shane Watson and Nathan Lyon stepped up, getting through more than 30 overs between them. And although we only took four wickets on day one, we managed to take India's last six wickets for the addition of less than 100 runs on day two to keep its score to 408—sizeable, but not match-winning.

It left us behind in the game and we were still in that position when Mitchell Johnson joined me at the crease on the third morning, one ball after drinks when Brad Haddin was dismissed with us still trailing by 161. From that point, however, we took the initiative thanks to some lovely clean striking by Mitchell while I went on my way at the other end. We added 148, of which he scored 88 of 93 balls, including 13 fours and a six, and although I was dismissed in the same over as him for 133, our tail then wagged so well through Mitchell Starc *(52)*, Nathan Lyon *(23)* and Josh Hazlewood *(32 not out)* that we added 107 for the last two wickets, runs that gave us a substantial lead of 97 and proved crucial in the final wash-up.

I would have to rate my innings, spanning just over five hours, as one of my best in Test cricket and certainly one of my most important. It was necessary to help us first achieve a position of parity with India after its decent first innings score, but also because it gave me huge confidence to know that I could still perform as a batsman despite the added pressures of leadership. I knew I had the support of the dressing room, but to actually go from thinking about leading from the front to then doing so, gave me a huge mental boost and I hope it also won over any doubters of my ability among the public who, because of my rapid rise to the captaincy, may have been wondering at the start of the match whether I was up to the task in front of me.

For us to go on and win the match from the positions we found ourselves in both on day one with the ball and day three with the bat was a fantastic effort, and I told the players so at the end of the match. I did some research that I mentioned when I spoke to them, that it was the first time in two years, since the Boxing Day Test against Sri Lanka at the MCG, that we'd lost the toss, bowled first and still gone on to win a Test. It was a tremendous achievement with a relatively inexperienced attack and I told everyone not only how proud I was of them but also how grateful I was for them to give me a winning start to my Test captaincy career.

We had been positive in chasing down the runs in the fourth innings, knocking off the 128 we required at close to a run a ball, albeit for the loss of six wickets. There was no pre-set plan to play in that way and I think it simply reflected the fact we were tense and wanted to get the job done. It was still a good surface and to win with a day to spare gave everyone a much-needed extra day of rest, something that was of vital importance, given that as the series timetable had been re-jigged there were only five days set aside in the schedule between the end of the action in Brisbane and a resumption of hostilities in Melbourne, with Christmas in between.

After Brisbane we drew the third and fourth Tests of the series, in Melbourne and Sydney, to seal a 2–0 series win and that, for the time being, marked the end of my time in the hot seat. We moved on to limited-overs cricket with a tri-series against India and England ahead of the ICC CWC and I slipped back into the ranks.

Throughout those three Tests in charge I only focused on the present and didn't allow myself to look down the road at what might happen in the future. It would have been easy to think about the possibility of captaining Australia in that World Cup with Michael still rehabilitating from his injuries, but my mind didn't work in that way. To start with, I'd never captained the ODI squad before and a World Cup was no place for a rookie captain, especially when there were experienced players like Brad Haddin, Shane Watson and George Bailey also in the line-up, with Shane and George two players who'd done the job previously. In any case, I was still trying to establish myself in the side again in that form of the game.

As it turned out, I did end up captaining the ODI side that summer, ironically at George's home ground in Hobart when he was suspended for a match against England after we had maintained a poor over rate in a match against India in Melbourne. And, just as I did when I first took charge of the Test side, I managed to score a hundred *(102 not out off 95 balls)*—this time batting at number three— as we chased down a target of more than 300.

If I had to assess my captaincy in those three Test matches then I would give myself a mark of maybe seven out of ten and admit that, especially in Melbourne and Sydney, I was too conservative. My delayed declaration on the final day in Melbourne snuffed out the chance of an Indian win, something that ensured we would regain the Border-Gavaskar Trophy, but at the same time it didn't give us enough time to bowl India out on what was still, even on the final day, a very flat pitch. And although we were more positive in Sydney, giving ourselves the whole of the final day to try and take ten wickets for victory, we again fell short, not helped by a surface that remained good for batting.

I would certainly do things differently in Melbourne if I had my time again, but at the same time I was conscious of the unique circumstances leading up to that point. Phillip Hughes's passing was still fresh in everyone's minds, all the players were emotionally tired after that terrible accident and the fact that the pitch in Melbourne offered so little to the bowlers meant we'd already spent 128.5 overs in the field getting India out a first time. There was also the matter of Shaun Marsh attempting to score a Test hundred and, although I knew it was a team game rather than one all about the achievements of the individual, it would have been needlessly cruel to deny him that chance. In the end he fell one run short when he was run out going for the landmark. The eventual closure was my attempt to take the pressure off the players as it came in the knowledge we could no longer lose the match and on that basis we could go out and relax, knowing the series was already won with us 2–0 up with just Sydney to come. If we won in Melbourne too then that was a bonus.

That final day declaration wasn't without its moment of controversy as the television cameras captured Darren Lehmann, rather than me, calling our last pair off. That vision was seen by some as confirmation that it was the coach and not me who was pulling the strings, but that couldn't have been further from the truth. I was also signalling for Nathan Lyon and Josh Hazlewood to come off the ground, but as the team's viewing area was hidden away underneath a tiered stand on the members' side of the ground, I wasn't easily visible from the centre. On that basis, quite a few people were signalling, but it was Darren who was seen. The criticism that followed did sting me as I knew the truth of the matter but perception was a tough thing to fight against. It was just an indicator to me that although things had started well for me, they wouldn't always be perfect.

The irony was that I found working with Darren very easy and we clicked very quickly as captain and coach. I knew he was a big supporter of mine, something that dated back to him seeing me score that 90 I mentioned earlier, for New South Wales in a Sheffield Shield match against the Queensland side he was coaching in late 2012, runs that were scored in a low-scoring match in Canberra. The start of his time as coach of Australia coincided first of all with me becoming a late inclusion in the Ashes touring party of 2013 after we had worked together on the Australia A tour earlier that year and I quickly went on to establish myself in the side. We both had a similar outlook on the game and it proved to be a terrific partnership that was resumed after Michael retired following the losing Ashes series of 2015.

CHAPTER 10
Mentors

Throughout my career I've been fortunate to have some tremendous people in my corner, assisting me to develop from a youngster with potential into an Australian captain.

Several of those connections are well publicised, the likes of Michael Di Venuto and Darren Lehmann within the national set-up, for example, and they have been pivotal in helping me kick on from being a player on the fringes of the national set-up to achieving the batting and captaincy success I have enjoyed.

But aside from that duo, there have been plenty of others

who have been equally significant in my growth as a player and a person, and chief among them have been my parents and especially my dad, Peter.

Earlier in the book Dad outlined the regime we adopted when I was a junior, and reminding myself of the details of it now, well over a decade later, has been a fascinating experience.

It's worth confirming something that Dad said in his chapter, that he in no way forced me to go through the hours we spent together and it was actually quite the opposite; I loved the game so much from an early age that it was me dragging him to the park night after night and not the other way around. I just wanted to play all the time and I was so fortunate that Dad had a job that allowed him to spend so much time with me.

Looking back now I can see that the net sessions we had at Casuarina Oval really did give me a head start against everyone else in my age group as I grew up. I can't believe that anyone worked as hard as we did in those sessions but the key to be able to put in so much time was that, from my perspective, it didn't feel like work at all but just fun. I enjoyed it and that enjoyment of playing the game is something I've managed to take with me throughout my career, no matter who I've been playing for or the context of the match in question.

Dad's contribution to my development as a cricketer went far beyond just bowling to me in the nets, though. Like most parents of cricket-crazy children, he was my taxi driver too and thanks to my progress as a junior, that was an onerous task in itself.

There were plenty of occasions when I would play a club game in Sydney on Saturday and then have a representative game elsewhere on Sunday, sometimes as far afield as Canberra, Hawkesbury or Newcastle. If that was the case, then we'd jump in the car straight after the match on Saturday, he'd drive to the next venue, then we'd stay overnight, I'd play on Sunday and then we'd drive back that night with him needing to be ready for work on Monday after having anything but a relaxing weekend. That became the pattern of his life during summers as I was growing up but I don't ever recall him complaining about having to put his life on hold in order to help me. I know some might argue that it's what being a parent is all about, but I also think it's fair to say that what I needed from my dad asked an awful lot of him.

Some of those trips also doubled as driving instruction for me after I reached the age of 16, as Dad would often let me take the wheel. And I reckon I lost count of the number of times he sat beside me as I drove to and from the SCG for New South Wales' age-group practice twice a week, with matches on a Sunday.

As time has gone by, Dad's developed a fascination for the little details of the game. He mentioned in Chapter 2 that his first love as a child was rugby league and he came to cricket after that league bug had bitten, but since then, not only because of my rise within the game but also through his own curiosity, he's allowed himself to become immersed in it, just like me. That curiosity and his scientific background led him to conduct an experiment into the relative qualities of traditional and new-style bats. He took what you might call an old-school blade, full of linseed oil and without the thickness of modern bats, and then a recently made one, including that thicker blade, and placed them, one after the other, in a workshop vice. He then dropped a cricket ball onto the bats from the same height in order to see what the new design meant for the hitting power and sweet spot—the ideal position to make contact with the ball—of each.

What he found was that the sweet spot of the older bat was just as good as the newer one but that there was a better response from the new bat when the ball made contact away from what might be regarded as the middle. It's just one illustration of Dad's attention to detail and I think it is one characteristic I've inherited from him.

Dad was never a loud or pushy parent or someone who was determined to live out his fantasy of being an excellent cricketer through me. All he did as he bowled to me was occasionally point out alternative ways of dealing with a particular type of delivery. Being a fairly headstrong young bloke and a typical teenager, I would regularly try to rebel against his advice and I often thought: 'Let me get on with it myself. Let me go!'

Our net sessions were enjoyable but also ultra-competitive, and they became even more so when we ended on the scenario of me needing to score 20 to win from 12 balls. I think that's helped me in later life and is evident in my desire to always, wherever possible, try to win a game. And the hours we put in during our sessions together certainly gave me a fierce cricketing work ethic which I've retained, even though Dad is no longer steaming in off his long run at me every evening.

When Jeff Thomson was inducted into the Australian Cricket Hall of Fame during the Allan Border Medal awards night in 2016 he made a speech that had everyone in stitches as he cursed about this, that and the other, but at the heart of what he said was something serious, that the main reason for the success of players like him—and me—at international level is people like our parents who, although they are rarely recognised in any formal way, make huge sacrifices to help us achieve our dreams. My parents, and especially Dad, are a perfect illustration of what Jeff was talking about. I owe them everything.

As I developed as a cricketer and moved up towards first grade at Sutherland District Cricket Club, Australian opener Phil Jaques and coach Trent Woodhill played pivotal roles in helping me progress. Sutherland was Phil's club in Sydney grade cricket while Trent was a coach there and they helped me bridge the gap between junior and senior cricket.

Trent tells the story of when he first saw me, when I would have been around 16 years old. It was a game of touch football with shirts against skins and I ended up on the side of the skins team, in other words, playing with my shirt off.

At that age I was a chubby and slightly awkward lad but Trent said that as soon as I got into the game that I tore shreds off the opposition and the competitive player he saw in that moment, was someone who immediately captured his attention.

We hit it off, I think, because I was someone who, as a cricketer, was always a bit different, in the way I picked up the bat, the technique I had, and where I looked to hit the ball. The fact I was different appealed to Trent, who is drawn to players who do things in ways that are not what you might call the accepted way. He's also worked with David Warner and Nic Maddinson, which is a further illustration of the idea that he enjoys working with players who row their own boats, and with flair, too. There is a view that cricket is fixated on what I might call the eye test, that someone who looks good technically will always get the nod in a side ahead of someone whose technique is a bit more homespun. Trent has railed against that with his support of players like me, and I think that thanks to the success I've had, that attitude, if it ever existed, is starting to change.

Trent picked up on the fact that in order to get the best out of me as a junior I had to be challenged and put in competitive situations as much as possible. If I wasn't put in a situation like that then I was open to accusations of being lazy and not working hard enough. And while, to an extent, that may have been true, when I was eventually dropped from the Test side and had come to terms with that, getting back to that place was the sort of challenge I needed and it brought out the best in me.

Trent's mantra to me was that rather than looking to change what I did to suit what might be called the orthodox way of playing, hitting balls on off- or middle-stump down the ground, I should instead focus on the fact I was already hitting those balls pretty well through mid-wicket and look to hone that skill to an even greater degree.

Up to the ages of 22 or 23, much of the work I did with Trent was a matter of 'grooving' my game. Having played a bit for Australia, but not having found a way that worked consistently for me, it was a case of trying to achieve that silver bullet for success. And although I've now worked out a method that has brought me that success—Trent now says that the best coach for Steve Smith is Steve Smith—I stay in touch with him and it's a two-way conversation. I'll have the odd net with him if I ever feel that something isn't clicking, while he'll very occasionally get in touch via a WhatsApp message or text if he spots something that I'm doing at the crease that he feels isn't quite right.

As an example, before I scored my maiden Test hundred at The Oval in 2013, Trent wanted to make sure I was playing with my hands in front of my back pad, in other words not getting them too far ahead of my body. His view was that by having my hands back there, I was storing my power, which I could then unleash in my shots. It also meant I was playing the ball later, which is one of the secrets to successful batting. Pushing hands out and searching for the ball is a sure way to be dismissed, especially if the ball either swings or seams. Trent's pointer certainly helped me succeed in that Test match.

One of the virtues of the advice Trent has given me over the years is that he'll not look to fill my head with theories and all of his advice is practical advice that I can put into practice, even under pressure, because it is simple and clear.

These days I actually regard him as much a psychological coach as a technical one, as one point he always drills home when I ask him for advice is to stick to my strengths. It can be easy to overcomplicate batting and think about what the bowler is doing or what the pitch is doing. But he always tells me to play the ball that's being bowled, as that's the one thing I can control, know where my scoring areas are and stick to them.

It's not unusual for players at the top level to have a mentor they go back to time and again, especially if it's someone who's worked with them since their junior days. That's not a criticism of coaching within any of the teams I've played for. People like Michael Di Venuto have been invaluable for me, but he and most other coaches I work with as members of team support staffs have finite amounts of time to deal with each individual in those teams and are also unlikely to have seen me over many, many years. In Trent's case he has seen me for a long, long time, has seen my technique evolve and he probably knows my game better than anyone else apart from myself. And I'm not alone in having someone like Trent to call upon if I ever feel I need some technical guidance. Michael Clarke had Neil D'Costa while Kevin Pietersen had former Sri Lankan coach Graham Ford. There are many other examples of top players with mentors outside formal team coaching structures.

I've already written about Phil Jaques' advice to me before we opened together in first grade for the first time, about not driving before lunch, but he also gave me another piece of wisdom that has stuck with me. Phil said I should always try to line my head up with the bowler's hand and if I did that then making a quick assessment of the line of the ball was always far more straightforward. That tip, coupled with the development of my back-and-across technique in late 2013, made it far easier for me to know what to play and what to leave alone outside the off-stump.

Having a player and person of Phil's stature around as a sounding board as I developed at grade level was another vital part of my growth—he was someone who commanded instant respect because of what he'd done at state, county and international level. It certainly helped me when I graduated to the New South Wales side that within the dressing room there was a person I already knew well, who gave me an extra degree of reassurance. I knew that he was in my corner and felt that I belonged at that level, which was a huge confidence booster for a young bloke making his way.

Phil was a great advocate of me at state level and he told a friend of mine that once he'd seen me he was pretty sure I had what it took to go on and play for Australia. What he liked, he said, was the way I was able to use my hands to manipulate the ball into gaps and also my fearlessness at the crease. There was one occasion in a grade game when, facing a free hit, I practised hitting it left-handed. The boys on the sidelines urged me to do it for real so when the ball was bowled I did face up left-handed and hit it for six. It was that ability to do something out of the ordinary which gave Phil the belief that I could progress with my game.

Phil, like Trent, was someone who saw me as a slightly chubby teenager, but he never nagged me about the way

I was in those early days. Instead he led by example and of all the players I worked with in the early stages of my career, he was one whose work ethic rubbed off on me. Phil, for his part, always believed that once I got inside the state system and saw what others like him were doing to maintain their spots, then I would be carried along and eventually become one of the most fervent trainers, and that's exactly how it's worked out.

Phil left New South Wales to coach Queensland—although in June 2017 it was announced he was heading back to Sydney to work as the state's batting coach—but we kept in touch, partly through having a mutual friend in Luke Dudman, a former teammate of ours at Sutherland, and even as recently as December 2016 I worked with him in the nets at The Gabba in the build-up to the Test series against Pakistan. I used him to throw to me because, being left-handed, his angle of release replicated the left-handers in the Pakistan bowling line-up. As with Trent, having someone working with me who has known my game for a long period of time was invaluable and I was delighted to follow up the work we did with a hundred *(130)* in the first innings of that Test, an achievement that helped set up the match for us.

Brad Haddin was another player I gravitated to once I made it through the New South Wales dressing-room door. Over the past few years he has been a terrific supporter of mine as well as a fantastic sounding board, just like Phil.

My first meeting with Brad was an odd one as it came when I dismissed him in a grade game when Sutherland played against his side, Eastern Suburbs, in March 2006.

It was a bizarre dismissal, too, as although it went down in the scorebook as 'caught and bowled Smith' it involved Brad—who'd already taken quite a liking to my bowling and had scored 65-odd by that stage—trying to clobber me through the in-field. I had a man in short on the off side and before the fielder had a chance to get out of the way, Brad had clubbed it straight into his foot. While the fielder reeled away hopping about in pain, the ball looped gently to me, and as soon as I caught it, off went Brad without a backward glance.

When I came into the New South Wales system, Brad was the next cab off the rank as Australia's first choice wicket-keeper. Adam Gilchrist's stellar career was winding down, and what I saw in Brad straight away was his excellent work ethic. He understands the game inside out and front to back. He is a tough taskmaster and that means he has the potential to rub people up the wrong way, but he had no agendas and all he wanted was to be the best he could be, and for the team he was playing for and the players around him, to be the best they could be. His work ethic resonated deeply with me.

Brad was certainly a hard player and his combative approach to playing New Zealand in the 2015 ICC CWC final wasn't to everyone's liking. Brad did pick the odd verbal battle on the field that day but what he was trying to do was to avoid playing the Black Caps at their own game, as they had become a very quiet side to play against. Brad, quite rightly, believed that we played our best when there was a bit of an edge in the middle and he helped create that combative atmosphere that day without ever letting it get out of hand.

The more I played and the closer I got to the Australian side, the closer Brad and I became. We both liked talking about the game and I liked to be a sponge for his knowledge, although he's joked that my means of extracting that knowledge was both unorthodox and costly to him. He reckoned my mode of operation was always the same: I'd go to his room for a chat, order room service and a movie while I was there, talk cricket and then head off, leaving him with the bill. He reckons his advice to me cost him AU$500 per week when we were out of Sydney!

The thing that made Brad willing to keep footing those bills was, I think, that he saw me as a cricketing investment, for New South Wales and Australia. My presence in his room was proof to him that I wanted to learn about the game, and he was willing to give me his time because he saw when we practised or played together that I was a player who could not only listen, but also put into practice what I'd heard very quickly. He liked that.

We certainly spent a lot of time in each other's company on the 2013 A tour of the UK, Ireland and Scotland and he was constantly in my ear to make sure I did everything I could to impress the powers that be, as he had an inkling, even then, that there was a chance for me to be elevated to the senior squad for the Ashes series. Brad urged me to get as fit as I could and when someone of his stature tells you to jump, your natural reaction is always to comply. I'm glad I listened in that instance.

Brad, like Trent Woodhill and Phil Jaques, was never hung up on my unorthodox methods with the bat and he believed I would always be a pure batsman rather than a leg-spinner. Brad felt I was pigeon-holed as a bowler because of the media and public's desire to find the next Shane Warne, but that I always had the talent to make it in a batting role, and although lots of people have picked up on my habits and movement across the crease, as Brad said to me, I was still when the bowler let go of the ball and I played it under my eyes. They are the fundamentals of batting and I'm glad I've been able to back Brad's judgement in my ability.

I'm also glad that it was Brad who was at the other end when I made my maiden Test hundred at The Oval in 2013 as he was responsible for giving me the confidence to reach the milestone with a six. Jonathan Trott was bowling his gentle medium pace and in between overs I said to Brad that if he pitched the ball up then I was confident in my ability to put him back over his head for a maximum. 'If you think you can do it then go for it,' was his message. 'Just clear your head.' That idea of clearing the mind of everything else apart from the next ball was one that both Trent Woodhill and Brad pushed me to do and it's a method that has served me well. And when Trott gave me just the ball I wanted then the result was a great way to reach a landmark in my career, one that I'll never forget.

Of course, I owe Brad a whole lot more than I can ever repay, no matter how many room service bills I cover, as he stepped aside and advocated I get the Australian captain's job when it became vacant in late 2014, when he could just as easily have laid claim to it as the incumbent vice-captain. It would have been a worthy honour at the end of an outstanding career. Brad could see the bigger picture for Australian cricket and for that I am forever in his debt as it gave me a terrific grounding in the job so that when Michael Clarke stepped down after the 2015 Ashes series I was already primed and ready to go.

Having Brad alongside me when I took up the captaincy during that India series was priceless as he has one of the best cricketing brains I know. I took Michael's spot at second slip in the three Tests I led the side in and so was right next to Brad for much of the time and the chance to pick his brains was invaluable. It's something I like to do with all the wicketkeepers I work with and I do the same now with Matthew Wade. They're in the best spot to see what's happening with the ball, the movement of the batsmen's feet, and the fact they both read the game so well is a bonus.

And although Brad's now no longer a part of the international scene, I still pick those brains of his whenever I get the chance. We will chat over a coffee or message each other pretty regularly and, although he's happy to praise me, he'll also often look to challenge me, asking why I did something, whether it's a bowling change or a field setting. That sort of approach, ensuring I'm continuing to try and take my captaincy forward, will stand me in good stead, I hope.

It was Brad who suggested I approach Mark Taylor to try and use him as another sounding board and someone I could chat with. Brad's theory was a sound one: here was a person who'd captained Australia, so he was well placed to understand the challenges and the pressures I was under and could offer a sensible perspective when I needed one.

Mark had originally heard of me from former New South Wales player and selector Marshall Rosen, who gave a good report of me, saying that I was a talented batsman who played the ball late. Mark is now honest enough to admit he couldn't quite see at the start of my career just how good things could become for me, but he's been someone who I've looked to take into my confidence especially since I've become permanent captain. Indeed, he was the man who handed me my captain's blazer when I was first made captain in 2014 and I still remember his advice on that day. He said that listening to other people was good but that I had to be my own man as the wins, losses and draws would go against my name as captain, as they did against his name when he led the side.

We met ahead of the home summer of 2016–17 and caught up either side of that on a semi-regular basis for a coffee, although we also meet at matches given his role as a Channel Nine commentator. There is a view, I guess, that me being friends with someone who has the potential to be a critic of mine and my team, and also someone who's a Cricket Australia Director, is a bit too cosy, but I don't think of it in those terms. My perspective is that here is someone who's done the job I'm now doing, has been in my shoes, and so why wouldn't I want to get his perspective on the game and how we're doing as a side with me in charge?

We don't always agree on everything. I read his comments in the media after our home season in 2016–17 that he thought I'd had a good summer as a player and a leader but that his only question mark against me was man-management, as he felt the issue of Glenn Maxwell's comments that he should be batting ahead of Matthew Wade at state level should have been dealt with more quickly. I thought we actually handled that pretty well, that he was fined by the leadership group and we moved on, but Mark and I can agree to disagree on that one because as he well knows, there are very few cut and dried answers when you hold the role he once held.

I'm happy to chat with other past captains for their perspective too, but given that Mark and I both live in Sydney and he is present at all our home international matches, he is a good fit with me and I'm delighted he's agreed to listen to me and, more importantly, give me his views on my captaincy and ways I can improve on it.

There have been plenty of other people who've played roles in my career and will continue to do so and I'm grateful to them all. Having those ears to bend, usually in confidence, is a vital part of what I do.

CHAPTER 11
Routine, habit and superstition

The keys to my success as a cricketer are repetition and routine. Repetition is the process that has allowed me to develop my skills so that I end up doing things automatically. Hitting hundreds of balls pitched in a certain place in a certain way and in a certain direction during numerous training sessions over a long period of time means that when I face that same delivery out in the middle, I don't have to think about what I'm doing. My body simply goes into autopilot and the shot I've been rehearsing over and over again is the result. That is the side of the game that spectators don't see.

Alongside that process, routine, for me, is just as important. By having a standard order of doing things it allows
my mind to focus on the actual act of playing or practising
cricket. I heard a story about Barack Obama that during
his two terms as President of the United States of America
he only used to wear grey or dark blue suits. His thinking
was that he had enough decisions to make during each and
every day without needing to make another one about what
he should wear, so he boiled things down to the basics,
allowing him to focus on more important things. The same
is true with me having a routine.

When it comes to training or playing, I'm always up
early in the morning. I still have that excitement about
getting to a cricket ground, that anticipation and enjoyment
of what I do and hopefully I'll retain that for as long as I'm
involved. Breakfast is a must and then I'll always look to
go to the venue ahead of the rest of the playing group. I like
to get there early, have a chat with the coaching staff, have
a look at the pitch, get my gear in order and also have a bit
of 'me' time where I can think about what I'm aiming to
achieve during the day. If it's a training session it may be
that I want to practise a particular shot or do some work
on my fielding skills. What I don't ever do is just practise
with no purpose; if I attend a session then my aim is to
get something from that session. Practice for the sake of
practice is a waste of time.

I think my desire to be early to the ground comes from
Dad. He has always had a similar mindset and he's passed
on the desire to be early to me. I hate being late and I love

Early days: with my grandfather—Mum's dad—Walter soon after I was born. I think I may have inherited my reflexes and ball skills from him. (Family collection)

First Christmas: with sister Kristie in Sydney; Melbourne would be my preferred destination during the festive season in years to come. (Family collection)

Away days: a family portrait during our time in New Zealand, our location because of Dad's work, although we were back in Australia by the time I started school at Alford's Point Public School. (Family collection)

Back in Australia and happy about it: at Redland Bay in Queensland, where we stayed with Mum's parents before relocating back to Sydney. (Family collection)

Anyone for golf? Trying out one of my granddad's clubs for size in Queensland. He only began playing after he retired but was a natural. I play occasionally, not seriously but always competitively. (Family collection)

Soccer star? Not quite. Here I am, on the right, playing for the Menai Hawks. What position did I play? The same as most children at that age: just running around after the ball! (Family collection)

All white now: dressed in what I reckon is my first set of whites and back in Sydney. I was probably five years old at this point and already the cricket bug had bitten me. (Family collection)

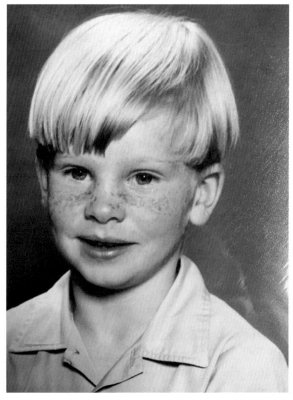

Old school: a portrait from Alford's Point Public School, just around the corner from the family home. (Family collection)

Goal machine: soccer players get to keep the match ball when they score three goals; I'm not sure how many I got on this occasion but I just loved sport as a child. (Family collection)

Look at the camera! I'm not sure what distracted me during this photo but my time with Ilawong juniors was my first exposure to the team environment. (Family collection)

Cricket Christmas: by 1996 Santa was fully aware of my obsession and that year's sack of gifts included a set of stumps, some batting gloves (below the baseball mitt), a video game and a book. I couldn't get enough of the game, even then. (Family collection)

Model cricketer: a portrait as an under-10 player; even then I didn't bend my front leg very much when playing forward! (Family collection)

Fostering a passion: preparing to represent the Sutherland Shire Junior Cricket Association in under-10 Foster Shield action. I obviously worked hard shaping the peak of my cap! (Family collection)

The start of something special: here I am, front right, with the 10A age-group at Ilawong Cricket Club, when my parents started to think I might have some potential in the game. All I was thinking about was how much fun I was having. (Family collection)

Milo moment: bowling at the Sydney Cricket Ground during the lunch break in the Australia–South Africa Test of 2002. Who knew I'd be back there as Australian captain 12 years later? Not me, that's for sure. (Family collection)

Making a racket: tennis was my other real sporting passion as a child. I was never as good at it as I was at cricket but it was fun and kept me entertained and fit during the winter. (Family collection)

Dressed for success: at home in Alford's Point with my favourite Australia One-Day International shirt, from the late 1990s. I loved that shirt and wore it all the time, as you can see by the state of it! (Family collection)

Shire enjoyment: here I am, front left, in a Sutherland Shire Junior Cricket Association team photo with my dad, a pivotal influence on my life and my cricket, just behind me. (Family collection)

It's catching: I never stopped playing for a moment as a child, whether it was nagging my dad to bowl to me or here, getting Judy Shackle, my parents' friend, to join me in a game of catch in the back garden at home. (Family collection)

It's catching—again: I loved fielding, even as a child, and here I am for Ilawong demonstrating my catching skills. (Family collection)

Where it all began: going out to bat with opening partner Matt Hughston on my first-grade debut for Sutherland, against Gordon at Killara Oval, in November 2006. I scored 2 and 69 over two weekends and was on my way. (Family collection)

Baggy white: when my cricket gear got delayed in transit en route to the UK in 2007 I ended up wearing borrowed kit—including a jumper far too big for me—during my time at Sevenoaks Vine Cricket Club. (© Peckasprints)

Living the dream: having fun with Tom Ward, the son of Tony and Julie Ward. They helped turn my trip to the UK in 2007 from a potential disaster to a fantastic life and cricketing experience. (Family collection)

Family times: with Dad, Mum and sister Kristie at Christmas 2011, during my time out of the Test side. (Family collection)

'Don't cover drive before lunch!' Opening for the first time for Sutherland with Phil Jaques, with his advice still ringing in my ears! (Family collection)

A big bang in the Big Bash: one of my dad's photos, of me playing for the Blues in the 2009/10 domestic Twenty20 tournament, something that catapulted me into contention for a place in the Australian side. It's funny to see Phil Jaques over my shoulder on the advertising board, even there! (Peter Smith)

Ready for action: warming up with ball and bat for my One-Day International debut, against the West Indies at the Melbourne Cricket Ground in February 2010. Note Michael Clarke stretching his back in the first photo, something he had to do just to get onto the field. (Peter Smith)

Happy days: celebrating after I had Kieron Pollard of South Australia caught by Phillip Hughes during the 2010 Big Bash League. I finished as New South Wales' most successful bowler in the tournament with seven wickets, form that helped take me to the ICC World Twenty20 with Australia. (© Getty Images)

Baggy green dreams: another of Dad's photos, capturing me at the nursery ground at Lord's moments after I received my baggy green cap from Ricky Ponting ahead of my Test debut against Pakistan in 2010. (© Peter Smith)

It's good to be back: Phillip Hughes and I share a laugh during a media conference in Perth after my recall to the Test side to face England in December 2010. I wasn't laughing when my comments about 'having fun' made me a figure of fun for the opposition. (© Getty Images)

Is it a bird or a plane? Me demonstrating my aerial skills in the IPL, saving a boundary for the Pune Warriors against the Kolkata Knight Riders at a packed Eden Gardens in 2012. My time with Pune Warriors wasn't full of joy but I love the whole IPL experience and never stop learning when playing in it. (© Getty Images)

being first, even in simple things like getting to the airport well ahead of a flight time. When it comes to cricket I just love that extra 15 or 20 minutes to potter about, relax and ensure that I'm not rushing as I complete my preparations for a training session or match.

In the practice nets there's obviously a pecking order, with the frontline batsmen always getting the chance to take first strike and that's something I've always sought. When Michael Clarke was captain, I still made sure I had my pads on and was ready to go in second after him. I'm not a great one for sitting around and doing nothing. I want to be on the go.

Michael was one of the players I shadowed in my early days, both with New South Wales and Australia, along with Ricky Ponting and Michael Hussey when I made it into the national side. I've mentioned previously that I based a lot of my early thinking on how to play spin bowling from watching Michael Clarke. When it came to each of those players, I tried to be like a sponge, soaking up what they were doing and trying to take the best of it and adapt it for my purposes. Ricky was incredible in that everything he did in training seemed to be at a million miles an hour, and when it came to fielding drills he was always at 100 per cent on the basis that his intensity at practice had to be identical to a match situation or else it was pointless. I learnt from that trio, and Ricky in particular, that the act of practising at high tempo meant actual competition was less of a step up.

I'm definitely a creature of habit, but there's one aspect of my preparation that's changed in a major way since the

Test tour of the Caribbean in 2015, and that's the number of balls I hit in the nets, either on a training or match day. Up until that point, I always hit countless deliveries and throw-downs, as I just liked to feel bat on ball. When I was younger, still developing my game, that was no bad thing for the reason I've already mentioned—improving my skills. But over time I realised there was a point where I was in danger of actually batting myself out of form, especially if I didn't hit the ball as well as I wanted during any particular session. Doubts had the potential to creep in and there was a danger of it becoming batting for the sake of it.

I recognised the issue but actually breaking the habit proved tough as it formed such a pivotal part of my routine. After all, I'd broken back into the Test squad and become a regular on the back of following that approach. But thankfully the decision to change was actually made for me by the state of the practice pitches at Sabina Park in Jamaica during that 2015 tour. The pitches simply weren't up to scratch and so I was forced to resort to throw-downs on the outfield instead. When I then went on to score 199 it showed me that I could still perform well without facing a high volume of balls, either in the lead-up to or on the day of matches, and so that's been my method since that time.

As an example, for the tour of India in 2017 I batted for long periods in the nets in Dubai during our preparatory camp and also once we arrived in Mumbai, but once the series started I reduced the numbers of lengthy batting sessions I had. Instead it was a case of hitting a few balls, making sure everything was in working order, and then stopping, ensuring instead that I was in the right physical and mental state to perform. And as was the case in the Caribbean, match days saw me try to limit myself to a few throw-downs on the outfield. This actually became even more important as the series wore on, as having spent so much time on the field it was vital that I saved as much energy as possible for the match situation. I knew I was hitting the ball well, I had my plans against the Indian bowlers and it was just a case of trusting those plans and going out and executing them to the best of my ability.

Of course, I'd never rule out going back to a routine that would see me hitting a large volume of balls in the nets. If there was ever a time when I was out of form and felt there were aspects of my game I needed to work on to an intense degree, then that would be an approach to be considered. The advantage I would have if I opted to go down that route would be that, having tried both options with success—high and low volumes of balls faced—I could switch between the two without feeling too stressed about the change.

The most important part of any batsman's kit is the bats he uses and I'm no exception. I usually carry between seven and ten with me at any one time as it's nice to have options and I like to have plenty of spares with me in case any break. I can use one that's straight out of the factory but I prefer to knock them in during training wherever possible, and that means I always have a handful that I'm comfortable with at any one time.

When it comes to bats then I'm quite pedantic, as you might expect, in the same way that a top golfer is about his clubs or a snooker player is about his cue. The weight I use is always the same, somewhere between two pounds, nine ounces to two pounds, nine-and-a-half ounces or 1.162 kilograms, and I don't change bats depending on the format I'm playing. I know some players prefer heavier bats for the shorter formats, but while they might feel it gives them the ability to hit the ball harder and further, if I use a bat that's any heavier than my preferred weight then I notice it in the pick-up and I struggle to swing it in the way I want.

I've used the same weight bat ever since I was 18 years old and even though I'm now much fitter and stronger than I was then, it's something I'm completely comfortable with, a bit like an old pair of running shoes or an old t-shirt that fits perfectly. And I'm fortunate that my bat manufacturer, New Balance, will tailor the bats I'm sent to fit in with my personal preferences. I like the back of the bat to be quite full rather than have a large taper on either side of a point running down the middle, and I also like the toe of the bat to be cut in a straight line rather than tapered upwards at either edge. Both of those preferences give me confidence when the bowler is running in as, when I look down at the bat in my stance, they make me feel it is as wide as it can be.

I only use one rubber grip on my bat, although there was a period in late 2013 and early 2014 when I switched to two. That was forced upon me because during the Boxing Day Test match at the MCG, England batsman Michael Carberry swept a ball hard into my right hand while I was fielding at short leg, bruising it quite badly. I was struggling to grip the bat so I added another grip on one of my bats ahead of the next Test in Sydney as that meant my hand didn't have to close over the handle to quite the same degree. I used that bat at the SCG for that match and scored 115. It meant I stuck with the bat—and the two grips—through the tour of South Africa that followed, including the hundred I made at Centurion in the first Test, the innings I rate as my most important and significant in that form of the game. By the time we got to Cape Town for the final match of that series, the handle was starting to flex on its way to breaking and although I don't like changing bats during an innings, it just didn't feel right so I was forced to do so. It was back to one rubber but with my hand fully healed by that stage I kept hitting the ball well scoring 84 and 36 not out and I've stuck with one grip again ever since.

The number of pairs of batting gloves I have is something of a standing joke within the dressing room, as is the way I keep them in order, as I number each pair. As you will have gathered, I'm very particular when it comes to my gear and I don't like to use gloves that haven't been manufactured and sent to me as a pair, hence the idea of numbering them by making a small mark in pen on each one. I probably carry between 12 and 15 pairs with me at any one time because I'm a big sweater out in the middle and I like to change them frequently, maybe every 20 to 30 minutes, or even more often than that if it's especially hot, as I don't want to bat with wet gloves or get them so wet that they won't dry reasonably quickly once I've swapped them. As a junior I did use fingerless inner gloves to absorb the sweat from my hands but after starting to play professionally, I found I got a better feel for the bat handle by not using them. In a year I probably get through between 30 and 40 pairs of gloves depending on how much I bat.

Perhaps the habits I have that provoke most eye-rolling and amusement among my teammates are my use of football socks when I bat and my insistence on taping my shoelaces to them before I put my pads on.

I started wearing football socks—plain white for Test matches and blue, red and white Sydney Roosters socks from my favourite rugby league side for one-day internationals and Twenty20s—that run up my calves and finish just below my knees for batting in around 2012 and have stuck with the habit ever since because I like the way they offer an extra layer, in addition to my trousers, between the pad straps and my legs. But the taping of the laces to those socks only started during the Indian Premier League (IPL) of 2016.

When I batted I always hated to look down and see my shoelaces. Don't ask me why, but I always found them a distraction, especially if they weren't tied neatly. It might seem like a strange thing to notice but I did notice it and I didn't want to. To cover them up I used to ensure the bottom of each pad was over the tongue of my shoe and I also folded the laces under my batting trousers to ensure they didn't pop out unexpectedly.

That was fine on national duty as Cricket Australia—issue batting trousers always had enough fabric to ensure I could get a decent fold in them but that wasn't the case when I went to play for the Rising Pune Supergiants—the trousers had much less fabric in the front—so I had to find another solution.

The answer was to tape the laces to my socks before I put my pads on, winding the tape around my ankles twice to keep them in place, and the first time I did it, against the Gujarat Lions in Pune, I scored my first hundred in the shortest form of the game, 101 from 54 balls. As a creature of habit and finding something that worked for me, I stuck with it to the extent that even when I was back on international duty I still kept doing it. The only issue I found at first was ensuring the correct tightness of tape—if it was too tight it would restrict my running and if it was too loose there was always a chance of the laces working free. But in the 18 months after I started the habit I never had an issue with it in a match.

Using one of Adam Zampa's hairbands was something else that became a habit. It started during the home summer of 2016–17, as I decided I was going to grow my hair but in doing so I found it was distracting me by coming down onto my forehead inside my helmet. Adam had been using a band for a while and during the ODI series against Pakistan I asked if I could use one for an innings in Perth. As was the case with the shoelace taping, it proved a hit straight away as I scored a hundred *(108 not out off 104 balls)* the first time I tried it and so, again, I decided to stick with it.

Headgear has always been a bit of an issue for me because I have a very small head in comparison to most other people, certainly most players in the Australian squad. When I first came into the limited-overs side I just couldn't get a cap that fitted me and so I had to resort to either gathering the fabric of the cap up at the back and taping it into a fold so that the cap fitted securely on my head or, more often, just not wearing a hat at all. As I became more of a regular in the side I felt more confident to let Cricket Australia know about my issue and, to its credit, the staff ensured the manufacturers made hats of my size, even coming along to measure me for the purpose. Usman Khawaja had the same issue and now actually asks for the 'Steve Smith size' when he puts in requests for caps and sunhats.

Are all these things stupid habits or crutches that take away from what I'm trying to do, which is to play cricket to the best of my ability? I don't think so. In fact, I find they help me because they actually take my mind off the pressures of the game. Everyone's different and every player has routines and habits that make them who they are. Steve Waugh had his red rag, Shane Warne had his ham and pineapple pizzas and I have the tape that holds my laces in place. It's just me, it's who I am, and I reckon my performances over the past few years haven't suffered because of anything I do. On the contrary, my figures seem to indicate that whatever I've been doing, it's worked.

Although I love the game, I still regard myself as a terrible watcher. I can watch and enjoy a match if I'm not involved, but if I've been dismissed and have to sit on the sidelines then I find that a very frustrating experience as all I can think about is the runs that I'm missing out on scoring. I've had to become better at sitting and watching because as captain I know I need to set an example, but at the same time I also use the thought of that frustration as one of my motivations for doing well.

If it's raining and no one's out on the ground, then that's a different matter, and my habit of choice in that situation is to work on a crossword puzzle. I first got interested in them when I used to help my grandmother as a child, although at that stage all I was really doing was reading out the clues rather than filling in the answers. Nowadays I'll carry around a book of them or pick up the newspaper and have a go over breakfast or a coffee, or sit around with teammates in the dressing room. When I got back into the Australia side in 2013 Chris Rogers was usually someone who you could expect to be working on a crossword puzzle during a rain delay. Adam Voges was also someone who enjoyed the challenge and now I can turn to players like Moisés Henriques, Patrick Cummins and Nathan Coulter-Nile for assistance. The attraction of crosswords is that they make me think about something other than cricket and in any downtime that I have I find them a very useful outlet.

Since becoming a regular at international level, one aspect of my life that has improved almost beyond measure is awareness that I am what I eat and drink. When I was starting out in the game, I think it's fair to say I was a bit of a party boy and I liked a drink, and when I left home and moved into my own apartment I didn't pay much attention to what represented proper nutrition. My home was close to a number of restaurants and cafes and so cooking was a very rare occurrence, eating out was commonplace and even if I had a night in watching a movie with my housemates then it wouldn't be unusual for my evening meal to be a packet of peanut M&Ms.

As I grew older I realised—and was educated at state and international level—about the value of eating and drinking in relation to the quality of my own performances and so I started to make better choices. I began to eat more energy foods like pasta when I felt I needed a boost or if I was spending a lot of time playing or training, but if I wasn't doing as much then I'd limit my intake of carbohydrates in an attempt to maintain and control my body weight. A large part of my diet now is lean meat and vegetables and I've cut out chips and junk food. It's not rocket science, it's about giving myself the best chance of being successful, and my results have shown me I've been on the right path.

Having said that, I do allow myself a glass of wine with a meal every now and then, or a drink when I'm with my teammates if we do well or win a match. I'm a believer that you have to let your hair down every so often and unwinding is absolutely vital after the five days of intensity that comes with Test match cricket.

I did follow the habit of many cricketers down the years of not eating duck, but that changed when I was on the Ashes tour of 2015. Our hotel in London had an excellent Chinese restaurant on the top floor and I took my parents and Dani there for a meal the night before the Lord's Test. They served delicious duck pancakes and I tucked in, only to realise afterwards what I'd done. I'd never done well at Lord's before, but I needn't have worried as I made 215, my maiden Test double hundred, and I've not avoided duck since.

I love chocolate too, but I do try to limit myself, using it strictly as a reward if I do well. It was an idea I got when speaking with Adam Goodes, the Sydney Swans Australian Rules Football player, as he told me that whenever the Swans won and he did well he used to treat himself to a block. I decided to take up that idea so now, whenever I get a hundred, I buy myself a block of chocolate.

My primary focus has always been cricket to the extent that everything else has always come a distant second, including getting my full driving licence. I had my provisional 'P' plates soon after my sixteenth birthday but with cricket then taking centre-stage, it took years for me to get around to doing my driving test. It meant that when I got the call to captain the Australian team in 2014 I was still on those P plates, something that might seem ironic given I was being handed the keys to the national side. I know Ricky Ponting was another player who learnt to drive relatively late, but minor sacrifices like that just haven't seemed important in comparison to doing what I love.

CHAPTER 12

Centurion 2014—Autopsy of a Test innings

Every player in even the briefest of careers is likely to be able to look back at a passage of play, an innings or a spell of bowling and regard it as significant in the context of that career.

For me the innings that fits that bill, in Test match terms at least, is my fourth Test hundred, the 100 I made against South Africa at Centurion on 12 and 13 February 2014.

That may come as a surprise to some people given several other innings I've played that could be regarded as important. There was my maiden Test hundred, of course, 138 not out against England at The Oval in 2013; the 111

I made against the same opponent at the WACA in Perth later that year after I revamped my technique in mid-innings; the 199 I scored against the West Indies at Sabina Park in 2015 that showed me that my desire for endless practice wasn't necessary after all; my 215 at Lord's just over a month later, a maiden double-hundred, that helped us level the Ashes series; and the 109 I scored on a deteriorating pitch in Pune against India in 2017 to help secure the lead in a series in which we were given little chance of avoiding a whitewash by those outside our group.

Each Test hundred I've scored obviously means a great deal to me but at the same time I know that when I raised my bat skywards on the second morning of that opening Test against Graeme Smith's side having reached three figures, it was the moment when I knew I really had made it at the highest level. Everything clicked, I played as well as I could and I did so to produce an innings that was important not only for me personally but also for the team.

The build-up to that Test and the series was an interesting one. We were off the back of our 5–0 whitewash of England that saw us regain the Ashes, and for me things had gone pretty well. After failures in the first two matches in Brisbane and Adelaide I scored that hundred in Perth and followed it up with 115 in Sydney. Both innings helped rescue us from tricky situations and my effort at the SCG meant I'd scored three hundreds in six Tests.

That was enough to ensure I went into the South Africa series full of confidence, but at the same time I knew the task in front of me personally and the team as a whole was hardly straightforward. We were up against a side that had lost just one of its previous 19 Tests and hadn't been beaten in a series, home or away, for five years. And although we hadn't lost a Test series in South Africa since the country's readmission to international cricket in 1991, a statistic like that is pretty meaningless as history doesn't win matches—playing well in them does that for you.

Our preparations for the opening match were disrupted by bad weather. Our training base was Potchefstroom, a quiet university town a couple of hours' drive from Johannesburg and a place Australian sides had used to prepare for series in South Africa ever since doing so successfully in 2003 ahead of that year's ICC CWC. The facilities and the stadium there were excellent but unfortunately heavy rain meant our warm-up match was washed out and we had to make do with hastily arranged practice among ourselves back in Johannesburg, at The Wanderers, to get ready for the series ahead.

That did not concern me too much. Conditions in South Africa were not that far removed from Australia—the pitches were hard and faster bowling was the order of the day—so there were no issues from that point of view. Although I'd not played a Test at Centurion, I had played there previously—a rain-affected ODI in October 2011 when I hadn't batted and a Champions League Twenty20 match for the Sydney Sixers against the Northern Titans in October 2012 when I was run out for three and we won off the final ball chasing 164. The surface for that match had plenty of pace in it and in fact it wasn't dissimilar to the WACA, so I was sure it would be pretty similar for the Test, given pace was one of South Africa's strong suits.

I knew that my ability to combat Dale Steyn, Vernon Philander and Morné Morkel would determine whether or not I made a success of the tour and so my thoughts going into the opening match were all about figuring out how they would try to bowl at me, and what I would do to try and counter that. I was helped by the fact that although I'd not played Test cricket against South Africa at that point, I'd faced all those bowlers at some stage of my career—albeit my exposure to Vernon was just one Champions League Twenty20 match for the Sixers against the Cape Cobras in Chennai in September 2011. So that made working out a strategy to face them that little bit easier. None of them were unknown quantities.

My planning to face that trio, as well as Ryan McLaren, another seam bowler and someone in the side to try and plug the huge hole left by the retirement of Jacques Kallis, involved some studying of videos of the bowlers in action, as well as discussion with batting coach Michael Di Venuto and net sessions to put the plans into action. At that stage of my career I was very much all about a high volume of balls faced when it came to my preparations as a batsman. And although the rain had ruined our chances of outdoor action in Potchefstroom, it didn't stop me testing out Michael's throwing arm in the indoor nets. Those practice surfaces had some pace in them, which was handy, and the same was true of the net pitches at Centurion too in the lead-up to the Test.

Morné Morkel's main asset was his height, which allowed him to generate steep bounce. But although that made him awkward to play, I also felt it reduced his means of getting me out. It meant most of the balls he delivered would bounce over the stumps, making a bowled or leg before wicket dismissal unlikely—especially on what was expected to be a hard and bouncy surface—unless the ball was very full indeed. As such, my plan was to leave as much as I could and wait on him to get either too short, in which case I could cut or pull, or too full, in which case I could drive.

Dale Steyn had pace, was skiddier than Morné and I thought he would attack the stumps more, but he also had the ability to shape the new ball away and the old ball back in getting reverse swing. My desire with him was to ensure I waited for a ball that was right under my nose before I attempted a drive, as his main method of getting me out was likely to be to encourage me to play away from my body and edge behind the wicket. And I knew both Vernon Philander and Ryan McLaren were bowlers who tended to operate on a line just outside off-stump and they, too, would be likely to try and play on my patience, hanging the ball out there, trying to encourage me to play a rash shot.

It all meant that much of my time in the nets with Michael and also up against our bowlers—Jackson Bird, Ryan Harris, Mitchell Johnson, Peter Siddle and James Pattinson—at Centurion in the two days before the Test was spent trying to leave the ball as much as I could and being sure where my off-stump was.

Different players have different habits when it comes to the pitch on which a match will be played. Matthew Hayden, for example, liked to go out to the middle the day before play and visualise facing the opposition's bowlers, thinking how they would bowl and where he would hit them. He even went to the extreme of sitting at one end of that pitch, just off the cut strip, with his shoes off, perfectly still and in his own world, trying to picture the action that would take place when he batted. I know others opt not to look at the surface until the morning of the match on the basis that it could still change and so they don't want to have any preconceptions about it before the time comes to bat or bowl. I don't fall into either of those two camps, and ahead of the Test I was relaxed about walking out to the middle to take a look at what we would be playing on, something I do ahead of every game. I don't go through any visualisation routines but instead just try to figure out what the pitch will do based on grass cover and how dry it is, and also have a look at the distance to the boundaries on either side of the pitch. I like to understand whether or not one side is shorter than the other and which way the wind is blowing, as that can affect my choice of shot, especially if it's a matter of whether or not to loft the ball. Hitting in the air into the wind can be something that's fraught with danger. One thing I did realise in the days leading up to the match, as we went through our fielding drills, was that the outfield was very fast and that if I hit the gaps with any shot I played I would get full value for it.

Wanting to face a high volume of balls meant I still felt underdone despite half-hour sessions in the nets—situated just to the right of the playing area, behind the hospitality chalets, as you look out from the main grandstand—against our bowlers two days before the Test, and then some local bowlers the day before, so I resorted to more throw-downs with Michael just to top myself up. They took place in the indoor nets located in the bowels of that grandstand and, as in Potchefstroom, those surfaces had decent pace in them. My purpose was two-fold: to feel bat on ball and to rehearse leaving as well as playing the ball, something I found was made easier by my new trigger movement that saw my back foot go back and across to off-stump just before the bowler delivered. It meant that as I received the delivery my head was in line with off-stump and so I was in an ideal position to know what I could play and what I could leave. One of Michael's tasks during our sessions was just to keep an eye on my foot movement and to let me know if I was ever going either too far across or not far enough. He was happy and so was I with the work we did.

Because there's a responsibility on players to get their own preparations right, team meetings before matches such as this don't tend to drag on too long, with around 30 minutes being about the maximum. A typical meeting sees our video analyst offering up shots of batsmen and bowlers and what they are looking to do. In the case of the opposition's batsmen, there'll be some clips of how they have been dismissed and graphics of where they score their runs. But those things are not dwelt upon mainly because it is expected that players do their own research using that footage and information. Before that main meeting of the whole touring party, batsmen will get together to discuss tactics and bowlers will do likewise so that when everyone gets together, that gathering is simply all about the conclusions reached in those batting and bowling discussions. The group discussion is usually led by the head coach and the captain and they may ask others to weigh in, but this meeting was straightforward with just two main messages: that the first Test was important in setting the tone for what lay ahead and that we should look to give the ball to Mitchell Johnson whenever we could! He was fresh from terrorising England's batsmen by taking 37 wickets at 13.97 in the Ashes series. He had done much the same to South Africa during our tour there in 2009, and having faced him in the nets in the lead-up to the match I could confirm how frighteningly fast he was. We all felt his presence was a huge psychological boost for us.

Once a team meeting breaks up then players will go their own way and there's no set way of spending the night before a match. Some players just lounge around in the team room getting massages—the fast bowlers usually fall into this category—while the medical staff will also tend to use that room as a place where treatment is administered. Others will get together to have a meal and as, on this occasion, we were staying next to what was probably the biggest collection of restaurants in the country, all part of the Sandton shopping and entertainment complex, there was no shortage of options. For my part I chose to have room service with Dani and just try to switch off as best I could before the action got underway.

My evening before the Test was more than a little unsettled as I found out I was set to drop down the order to number six, something I wasn't overly happy about. Unlike the Ashes series where we kept the same top six—and indeed the same starting 11—for all five matches, there was a great deal of uncertainty surrounding our order before Centurion. George Bailey had been dropped for the tour, with Tasmania's Alex Doolan, who'd been added to the squad as injury cover for the final Test against England in Sydney, and Shaun Marsh selected for the trip. Shaun then picked up a calf injury during the limited-overs series against England and withdrew from the tour squad, replaced by Phillip Hughes. However, Shaun made a quicker-than-expected recovery from his injury, proving his match fitness by playing in the Perth Scorchers' Big Bash League final victory *(Marsh scored 63 not out off 43 balls)* and so was drafted back into the squad when Shane Watson, who'd batted at number three during the Ashes, sustained a calf injury of his own after we'd arrived in South Africa.

It meant there would be at least two changes in the batting line-up from the one that played against England and the selectors settled on Alex Doolan, who had been on the fringes of selection since the previous summer, and Shaun Marsh coming in for George Bailey and Shane Watson, with Phillip Hughes and all-rounder Moisés Henriques missing out. But having settled on who would play, there was then a decision to be made by the captain Michael Clarke on who would bat in which positions.

Alex, making his debut, moved into the number three spot vacated by Shane Watson and that left the question of where Shaun would bat. He had batted at three in all but one of his previous eleven Test innings (when he came in at number ten because of a back injury in the Cape Town Test of 2011 when we were bowled out for 47) but with that spot taken he would have to slot in elsewhere. The opening partnership of Chris Rogers and David Warner was a settled pairing—so that left numbers four, five and my spot during the Ashes series—up for grabs.

I was happy at five. My desire was always to bat as early as I could so I could try and influence the match as soon as possible, and I thought I'd made the position my own by scoring all three of my hundreds from there, but the decision was made by Michael to put Shaun in at four while the captain (who'd occupied that position during the Ashes series) moved down to five and so I had to drop to six. A creature of habit, I was disappointed with the decision but I decided to let it go and opted not to argue about it with either the coach or captain. It was just a case of making the best of my situation.

That simply added to thoughts racing through my mind on the eve of the match and I slept poorly, although that wasn't unusual for me at that stage of my career. I found it hard to switch off from thinking about what was to come and all the possible scenarios that could confront me and I was restless ahead of the action getting underway. I did, though, have a decent breakfast the following morning. As a child I used to avoid it, although I'm not sure why, whether it was superstition or nerves, but as I grew I realised the importance of getting some energy inside my body, something emphasised to me by the team's support staff, and I had some Weet-Bix.

Centurion is located just outside South Africa's capital city, Pretoria, but teams and officials always opt to stay in Johannesburg as the hotel used by Cricket South Africa is superior to anything closer to the stadium. Doing that means a 45-minute journey north by road, although it is freeway virtually the whole way so it is not the toughest assignment. A trip of that length will see players listening to their own music using headphones, some will sit and read while others will chat quietly. The buzz that morning was actually all about the IPL as the start of the Test coincided with the auction ahead of the 2014 IPL season and I found that a very helpful distraction. Rather than thinking about what was to come, players spent the journey chatting about who had been picked up by which franchise—and who had been passed over. I was chosen by Shane Watson's side, the Rajasthan Royals, which also included fellow Australians James Faulkner, Brad Hodge, Ben Cutting and Kane Richardson. I was actually the franchise's most expensive purchase on auction day, for US$666,000, although that was dwarfed by quite a few of the picks by other teams, including India's Yuvraj Singh, who fetched a price of more than US$2 million to go to the Royal Challengers Bangalore; Kevin Pietersen of England, who cost Delhi Daredevils US$1.5 million dollars; Mitchell Johnson who went to Kings XI Punjab for just over US$1 million; David

Warner who was picked up by the Sunrisers Hyderabad for US$916,000; and Michael Hussey who was chosen by the Mumbai Indians for US$833,000.

I had an iPod with my own playlist that also helped to pass the time and at that stage of my career my routine extended right down to the last song I had to listen to before I arrived at a venue and that was '23' by Jimmy Eat World. It was a song I really enjoyed and what I wanted was to ensure it was going through my head as I stepped off the transport and into the dressing room as I found it relaxed me.

I had a net session ahead of the day's play, although not a very long one as there was obviously only a certain amount of time between arriving at the ground and then going through our group warm-ups and some light fielding drills. The weather was fine and it felt like a good day to bat and so no one was more surprised than me when Graeme Smith opted to field first when he won the toss. It looked like a good pitch to me, rock-hard, but even on day one there were cracks to be seen. Those cracks made the pitch become more and more uneven in bounce as the match went on and played into our hands with South Africa batting last, but if we hadn't made a decent first innings score then that would have been far less of a factor in our favour.

With us batting first it was a case of me having some time to relax, although that time wasn't all that long as it turned out, as both David Warner and Chris Rogers were dismissed within the first nine overs. My own preference as a batsman waiting to go in was to watch the action live in our viewing area at the front of the dressing room rather than on the television inside the dressing room, despite the fact I disliked our vantage point. The dressing rooms at Centurion are at the extreme end of the massive grand-stand that covers one side of the oval, and so when the bowler has that grandstand at his back and he's bowling to a left-hander, then we were situated above deep extra-cover and therefore almost side-on to the play. I find that sitting square of the wicket can be quite disconcerting because it can give the impression the bowling is quicker than it actually is. It's all about perceptions, of course, but it's much harder to track the flight of the ball from side-on and when all you see is a bowler's delivery followed by the ball thwacking into the wicketkeeper's gloves 20 to 25 metres back then that can be unsettling to even the best of players.

My own preparations to bat began when Chris Rogers was the second man out. I changed out of my training gear and put on my whites and football socks, as well as my thigh pad and abdominal protector and laid out my pads, gloves, bat and helmet alongside me when I returned to my seat at the front of the dressing room. My pads went on at the fall of the third wicket, Alex Doolan, four overs before lunch. The batsmen dismissed, after they'd got changed out of their whites and lost their initial frustration, shared information on what was happening out in the middle. As was clear from what I could see—I watched every ball— and from what they said, there was a bit of bounce in the surface, as we'd expected, as well as some movement in the air and off the seam, to judge by not only our dismissals but also the times when the batsmen were playing and missing and the movement of their feet. As the first session continued and the ball lost its initial hardness it looked as though batting became slightly easier but it was still a challenge, that was plain.

Lunch brought the question of what to eat, which was tricky given I was next in. Eating too little had the potential to leave me short of energy out in the middle but eating too much could leave me feeling sluggish and lethargic, not ideal with Morné Morkel and Dale Steyn set to be in operation. I settled for some grilled chicken and vegetables—not a big meal but enough to tide me over. The food was served in the dressing room in big metallic trays that allowed players and staff to help themselves, with fish and pasta also available.

During an interval the not-out batsmen will often share their impressions of the pitch with those still to bat, not in a formal way, but usually just by the odd comment here and there. Generally, though, they are left to relax as much as they can, and the non-playing reserves will be buzzing around at a distance ready to assist them in anything they need, whether it's drying their gloves or pads—usually done by putting them out in the sun—or getting them some food while they relax.

It was the seventh over after the interval when I was finally into the action, although I wasn't on strike straight away thanks to Michael Clarke's dismissal, a top-edged hook to fine leg off Dale Steyn, caught by Vernon Philander. The batsmen crossed and so Shaun Marsh took strike for the final ball of the over.

I hadn't batted with Shaun in a Test before Centurion as the start of his career, in Sri Lanka in 2011, coincided with my two years out of the side, but straight away I found him a very easy player to bat with. He called well, ran well between the wickets, and he came across as a very relaxed person in the middle, despite the fact we were 4–98 when I came to the crease.

My arrival prompted a change in the attack with Vernon Philander being replaced by Ryan McLaren, something that surprised me given I was new to the crease. Philander had bowled eight overs before lunch and another three straight after the interval but I thought with a new batsman at the crease, Graeme Smith would have persisted with his two best bowlers in tandem for a little longer. Not that I was complaining as Ryan McLaren gave me a juicy half-volley that got me off the mark as I crunched it square on the off side for four.

It was nice to get underway immediately but I'm not a player who tends to fret if I'm still to score, or someone who is especially concerned about feeling bat on ball at the start of an innings. As I wrote earlier, that was something that did concern me earlier in my career but experience had removed the desire to get on with things. There are some who I've known who are like that—Michael Clarke and Adam Voges were always desperate to get that first run on the board—but I can block out those sorts of feelings. That might seem odd given my sleeplessness before the match but much of that was worrying about what might or might not happen. Once I was out in the middle then I was in control of my own destiny and that made me far more relaxed. And I've always had the attitude that a half-volley is a half-volley if you are on zero or 100 and it should be put away.

I was content to wait for a very full-length ball or something angling into my pads in order to score and I actually left three of the next four balls I faced, allowing them to pass harmlessly through to AB de Villiers behind the stumps. Patience had been my watchword in the build-up and now was the time to put it into action. And although I respected Ryan McLaren, I also felt he would give me something loose now and again. It was just a case of waiting for it and not doing anything rash in the meantime, especially given our situation.

It was Dale Steyn, who bowled a five-over spell after the interval, who gave me my next run as I worked a ball backward of square on the onside for a single. The ball was into its 37th over now and so had lost that initial hardness but Ryan McLaren reminded me there was still plenty of reason to be on my guard as he nipped one back at me quite sharply, although the resulting leg-before-wicket appeal was stifled as the ball would clearly have gone over the top of the stumps.

After my first-ball boundary I scored just that single off Dale Steyn from the next 14 balls I faced, but although I am someone who looks at the scoreboard at regular intervals during an innings, I didn't feel under any pressure to lift the tempo at that early stage of my time at the crease. I knew that at that point it was all about consolidation and earning the right to bat later in the innings when the bowlers were tired. It was a warm day and I felt the best time to bat would be in the final session, especially given the speed of the outfield. Shaun was thinking the same way and when we came together between overs all we tended to say to each other was 'Keep going' or 'Don't give it away'. He wasn't a big talker and that suited me as I felt I knew what I had to do, and so it was just a case of getting on and doing it.

Morné Morkel replaced Dale Steyn after the latter's post-lunch burst and straight away he presented that different challenge that I'd been preparing for. I was relaxed enough, after the tea break, to actually upper-cut him over the slips for four, using the extra bounce he generated. Before I played the shot, the thought did cross my mind that if he bowled it in a certain area then I would simply help the ball on its way over the slip cordon, especially as there was no third man in place that meant the shot carried with it no real risk of being caught, but it wasn't a shot I practised before the match and I hadn't played it in a Test previously. It was pure instinct.

Morné Morkel gave me another interesting moment later in my innings when I punched him back down the ground for four, through mid-on, when he pitched the ball up. He's not one to say a great deal out in the middle but as I admired my handiwork and just jogged down the pitch he turned to me and said: 'That's a good shot!' I was lost for words in response and as I settled back into my stance I thought: 'That's odd, he's complimented me!' I'm absolutely certain there was no sarcasm involved—it *was* a very good shot anyway—and he was 100 per cent genuine. It just goes to show that not every word said out in the middle is an out-and-out sledge.

Robin Peterson, the left-arm spinner, came on for the 41st over, replacing Ryan McLaren, and by that stage I was seven off 22 balls. Robin wasn't a big spinner of the ball and

I wasn't expecting the surface to offer a great deal of turn as well—and sure enough it didn't—and so I never felt my outside edge was likely to be threatened by his stock delivery. So on that basis I straight away set out to try and mess up the length that he wanted to bowl. I knew his role in the side was primarily to try and keep things tight while the quicker frontline bowlers rested and so my plan was to try and ensure he wasn't able to settle into a rhythm of bowling lots of dot balls and slowing our scoring rate too much while the likes of Dale Steyn and Vernon Philander were out of the attack. I skipped down the pitch to his second ball and although I only defended it into the leg side, my idea was to make the bowler think, and to let him know that if he kept trying to bowl the same length then I was willing to use my feet and hit him over the top. It was a game of cat and mouse and when he dropped the ball a little shorter on the final ball of the over, maybe suspecting I would use my feet again, that gave me the chance to work the ball into the leg side for a single.

It was during this part of my innings, with Morné Morkel bowling with good pace and control, that I became becalmed, going 18 balls for just two singles at one stage. There was just one occasion when I lost my patience and was drawn into a loose stroke outside the off-stump by him, flapping at a ball that beat the outside edge, but other-wise I felt relaxed and focused only on the next ball I was going to face. That really is the key to batting as, whatever has gone before, the next ball you face is the only one that can get you out. It's always a case of focusing concentration and energy on that delivery.

I broke those shackles by doing what I'd been threatening to for some time, using my feet to Robin Peterson and hitting over his head for four and then, two balls later, I used my feet again and worked him into the on-side for two more. I was perfectly happy to see him in the attack and I felt there was a strong case for Graeme Smith rotating his faster bowlers instead but I also knew it was a balancing act for him, too, as if he did bring them back and they didn't break through then that might affect their ability to come back again later in the day when the second new ball was due. Robin was in the side to bowl and Graeme had to show some faith in him to do just that.

The South Africans, Morné Morkel's compliment apart, were very quiet on the field, even when I came to the crease, which surprised me a little at that point given they were in the driving seat. There was very little chat on the ground aside from the usual encouragement for the bowlers and in fact the only time I can remember being involved in anything vaguely fiery during the series was in the second Test in Port Elizabeth when I was playing pretty well in a difficult situation as we struggled to avoid the threat of the follow-on. I edged Dale Steyn through the slips cordon for four and then, later in the over, clipped one through mid-on, an authentic shot to the boundary. He gave me the most almighty spray, no doubt frustrated given the luck I'd had with my first four of the over, but then, having done that, he apologised to me. Just like when Morné Morkel gave me a compliment at Centurion, it took me completely by surprise.

Dale Steyn and Vernon Philander had both got through 11 overs each before the drinks interval in the afternoon session, and out in the middle it seemed South Africa went into a bit of a holding pattern against us at that stage, playing a waiting game before those two could return to the attack and also trying to test our patience with the bat. Whether that was the right approach given we were four wickets down and Graeme Smith had put us in to bat was debatable but confirmation of that strategy seemed to come from the line that Ryan McLaren bowled at me at stages during the run-up to tea. I got the impression he was deliberately bowling a metre or so outside the off-stump, waiting for a mistake—what professional cricketers sometimes call 'hiding the ball'—but it wasn't a game I was prepared to play and I was happy to let the ball go rather than chase it. Robin Peterson had no bat-pad fielders close-in catching for me in front of the wicket, another indication of that holding pattern idea, but instead opted for two fielders on the drive in the covers, again looking to take advantage if I went for the big shot through the off side. And again, I wasn't playing ball.

The benefit of my approach came when Vernon Philander came back into the attack just before tea and straight away, having seen me leave the ball from Ryan McLaren, he was tempted to go too straight to me and I was able to clip him through square leg for four to get the scoreboard moving again for me. To the outsider, strokes like that from me look like they contain an element of risk but they also represent my strength and I would back myself to clip the ball away through the on-side, even through square leg, 99 times out of 100, and the ball that's either too full or too straight is always the one I'm on the hunt for. By that stage the ball was in its 49th over too and there was precious little swing for the bowlers, either orthodox or reverse.

That boundary off Vernon Philander brought up the 50 partnership, the cause for a handshake and a simple 'Keep going', and it followed another handshake when Shaun Marsh brought up his 50 with a pull for four off Ryan McLaren. There was a time, so Ricky Ponting once told me, when the Australian way was a proper manly handshake and glove-punches between batsmen were ridiculed. It's not something that crops up any more as changing room chat, and with so many of us having now played in tournaments all around the world and with and against players from a host of different cultures, it's a case of whatever feels natural at the time.

Dale Steyn came back into the attack for a couple of overs before tea and straight away started with a deep point, which did surprise me a little bit. It wasn't as if I'd looked to dominate very much up to that stage, although the irony was that my first scoring shot off him in that spell was a push out to that spot for a single, which would have been four had the fielder not been there. In the handful of overs left before the interval there was a case for Graeme Smith attacking a bit more, as Shaun and I were obviously keen to ensure we didn't expose a new batsman just ahead of the break but at the same time, and especially since I've become captain, I don't mind a sweeper in that spot. It stops the scoreboard getting out of control for the fielding side, gives the bowler confidence to pitch up outside the off-stump knowing he's got that protection, and bear in mind too that with the fast outfield at Centurion, Graeme knew that anything timed even reasonably well that beat the in-field was usually four.

Morné Morkel bowled one over before the break at the other end from Dale and the two raced in trying to get the breakthrough, but in Morné's case he got a bit carried away when he banged one in way too short, it hit a crack, cleared AB de Villiers and went for five wides. Far from intimidating me or making me fearful of the bounce Morné was generating, I was quite positive about that happening as I felt those cracks were only going to get wider as the match went on, something that did actually happen.

At tea I'd worked my way to 29 from 67 balls with three fours; Shaun and I had added 78 and the two of us were very happy as we walked off the ground. It's a long walk up steps from the field into the dressing rooms, something that's great if you're taking applause from the crowd, and backslapping and congratulations from your teammates, but not so much fun if you fail. In this instance the words were all positive from players and coaching staff but although we knew we'd done well, we also knew we needed another good session to consolidate and reinforce our position. South Africa, when Graeme Smith put us in to bat, would probably have been looking to get us out for less than 250, and so at 4–176 we still had plenty of work to do to reach that mark and beyond.

What we did know was that we were in for a long final session of the day, likely to be two and a half hours, as South Africa had only bowled 54 overs up to tea. I knew that if Shaun and I could bat for the first hour or so after the break then we would be in a position to try and cash in as tiredness inevitably started to affect the bowlers and fielders.

Twenty minutes isn't a long time when you're a not-out batsman. By the time you get to the dressing room and sit down, there are five minutes gone already and with the need to get ready to go out again at the end of the break you probably only have ten minutes of quality rest time where you can try and switch off, unwind, process what's happened on the field and try and take in some refreshment. The reserve players brought me a banana and a protein bar and I had some water too but my regime during this innings was just to sit quietly and do nothing, not even taking my pads off. Some players might like a dry shirt or a dry pair of trousers, but I didn't feel the need for either. I was comfortable in the gear I had on.

I did think about my innings—what I'd done to that point and what I needed to do after tea—but by and large it was just a case of switching off after the period of intense concentration. The coach, Darren Lehmann, came up to me and said 'Well played' as did a few of the players. I'm not someone who minds people coming up to me and saying something, as I'm not that intense in that situation. The only thing I can't abide in those circumstances is someone coming up and fiddling with my bat, not that anyone did on this occasion. The bat I was using was the one with the two rubber grips that I'd started using after the hand injury I'd suffered during the Melbourne Test against England, and having scored a hundred with it in Sydney, it was something that felt good so I wanted to keep it going for as long as I could.

Starting again after an interval can be an issue at times. The bowlers have had a break and it is a case of switching on again, but it's not something that I find too much of a problem and, sure enough, I felt great as soon as I reached the middle. My first two boundaries after tea were the upper-cut and on-drive off Morné Morkel I mentioned earlier and I really did feel very comfortable at the crease. There wasn't much movement now for the faster bowlers, either off the seam or in the air, but I knew this was a crucial stage of the match because if Shaun and I could continue our partnership then it would go a long way to putting us in the box seat.

Dale Steyn opened up after the break along with Morné Morkel and in the absence of much assistance for him he opted to put the ball outside my off-stump and invite me into a loose shot. In his second over after tea there were five balls I didn't play at, four which were wide and one short delivery. It again emphasised my discipline in the innings, a determination to make the bowlers bowl to my strengths rather than looking for scoring opportunities that invited risk.

The cracks were still playing the odd trick and in the fifth over after the break I almost chopped on a ball from Morné Morkel that cut back sharply, although the ball eventually ran backward of square for a single. Apart from that, though, I felt pretty much in control of what I was doing.

Morkel came off following a four-over spell after tea, to be replaced by the off-spin of Jean-Paul Duminy. It was a victory of sorts to have forced South Africa into introducing a sixth bowler, but at the same time I knew it was no time to switch off. That was a possibility, however slight, especially when facing a bowler who, on that surface, wasn't going to turn the ball very much at all. There was also the danger of thinking it was time to cash in against a part-timer in the absence of the big guns, but for both Shaun and myself it was just a case of trying to continue to bat rather than think about any need to play big shots. A five-day Test match is a long time, especially on a surface that would clearly get harder to bat on, so runs made in the first innings would always make things easier later in the match.

Duminy's approach was an interesting one, as he operated around the wicket to me. Off-spinners normally do this if the ball is turning sharply as it brings the lbw dismissal into play if a bowler can pitch the ball in line with the stumps and then spin it back, but there was no spin to speak of from this surface. His plan, instead, was to use the angle across me to try and get me edging behind the wicket or to run past one as I looked for a big shot down the ground. I was happy, though, to once again bide my time and wait for the right ball to hit and after playing out a maiden I stood at 38 from 98 balls faced.

There was actually a double-change as Graeme Smith had withdrawn Dale Steyn, and replaced him with Ryan McLaren for the preceding over. I faced him in the second over of his spell and greeted him with a cover-driven four, one of my best shots of the innings as it beat the deep point on the boundary, so well did I time it. It was another three overs from McLaren before I got something else that I regarded as hittable as he continued the policy he adopted before tea of operating to that fifth stump line against me. And when I got the ball in the areas that I wanted I took advantage, first dropping the ball into a gap on the on-side and scampering two before then crashing a full ball through extra-cover for four to reach my fifty from 118 balls including seven fours.

That two was just about the riskiest thing I'd attempted, as the throw to the bowler's end could have left Shaun short of his ground if it had been a direct hit, and to an extent it was a slight misjudgement. McLaren's line outside the off-stump meant he was operating to a packed off-side field and that, in turn, meant there were gaps on the onside with just a mid-on and a fine leg in position. We took the fielders on and won, but having done it I knew there was no need to be quite so cavalier in future.

The quickly taken two and the aggressive drive for four had nothing to do with any nerves as I approached my fifty. By that stage of my career I had moved past the idea of getting nervous close to landmarks. Being near my first Test hundred at The Oval made my heart beat a bit faster as it was only two Tests earlier that I'd been dismissed for 89 at Old Trafford but now I was calm and I just saw this half-century as a stepping stone to a bigger score.

Shaun Marsh reached his hundred with a nudge backward of square on the on-side off Duminy and I was delighted for him. He batted patiently, hadn't really looked in any trouble and was the perfect partner for me in this innings. Watching him bat the way he did, it was incredible to think it was only his second Test hundred and his first since reaching three figures against Sri Lanka on debut more than two years earlier. He has the ability to make batting look very easy indeed and did so in that innings.

Shaun benefited from South Africa's holding pattern of using Duminy and McLaren in tandem and I'm sure he would have been delighted to be moving towards his hundred with those two in operation as opposed to any other members of the home side's attack. But at the same time Graeme Smith was also mindful that the new ball was due just a handful of overs later and he wanted the likes of Steyn, Philander and Morkel to be as fresh as possible to use it. It was a tough balancing act for the fielding captain.

Philander came back in place of McLaren for the 72nd over and I was able to pull him through straight midwicket for four when he dropped short. With Philander bowling that sort of length then I knew I was winning the battle because his stock length is full and tries to induce a false stroke from a drive. But it illustrated how nothing much was happening for South Africa at that stage and that Shaun and I were nullifying them, making them bowl in ways and in areas they weren't comfortable with. Having said that, I almost fell to the next delivery when Philander dropped short again and I miscued to mid-wicket, short of any fielder, with my bottom hand coming off the bat, just about the ugliest shot I played in the innings. To an extent it was clever bowling from Philander as the last thing I expected from him, especially after my previous shot, was another short ball, and perhaps it was one of the few times—maybe the only time apart from my dismissal—when I let a desire to be aggressive take unnecessary hold of me. I just lost a little concentration in the over, as I then looked to drive only to miscue when not quite to the pitch of the ball, and it was just a case of re-gathering my thoughts and realising there was plenty of work still to do.

I chopped Duminy, still operating round the wicket, away to deep point for two to bring up the 150 stand and my share of it—66, from 133 balls, with eight fours—was another illustration of my patience and the fact Shaun had dominated the partnership. It was that patience and discipline that was a key to my success in the innings. It might not have been champagne batting but it was a case of playing the situation—the need for a partnership, the need for crease occupation and the belief that the pitch wasn't going to get any easier for batting as the match progressed—and that was what gave me so much satisfaction at the time and still does. And as the new ball approached, with Graeme Smith turning to Robin Peterson alongside Duminy, I felt we had South Africa on the defensive for the first time in the match.

Oddly enough, Smith didn't take the new ball immediately. He actually waited until the 83rd over before doing so when he threw the ball back to Philander. Part of that may have been down to a desire to give his faster bowlers just a little bit more of a break and part of it may have been down to the fact we weren't scoring very quickly, as both Shaun and I knew the importance of not taking risks so as to ensure we were at the crease when the quicks came back for another burst. Philander's first delivery with the new ball—taken at 4–263 with Shaun on 110 and me on 73—was something of a loosener (it was the second ball of his spell) and was floated up wide outside the off-stump. My aggressive tendencies took over and I just threw my hands at the ball with no real movement of my feet. It wasn't the best of shots, especially in the circumstances, but I was seeing the ball well and instinct took over again. I got away with what was still an error of judgement as the ball sliced off the outer half of the bat away on the off side for four, but it just emphasised the need to maintain the discipline that had served me so well in the innings up to that point.

I wasn't tired, either mentally or physically, at that stage and the shot against Philander actually illustrated how good I was feeling. The second new ball with the close of play looming had the potential to be a difficult time for us but I felt very positive. The bowlers were tired, it certainly hadn't been South Africa's plan to be in that situation when we were asked to bat first, and often the new ball can be a good time to bat as, given it's harder, it can come on a little quicker and make timing easier. I produced two far more convincing cover drives for four from Philander and Dale Steyn and they took me into the eighties.

The false stroke against Philander acted as an alarm for me in that I realised I had moved away from the discipline outside the off-stump that had served me so well throughout the innings. So when Steyn offered me six deliveries in a row that I didn't need to play, I ensured I didn't. That was poor bowling with the second new ball by the side's premier fast bowler, but it also helped me get back into the groove of playing balls only when they were in the areas I was looking to score from.

Those leaves also showed how calm I was. At that point there were five overs left in the day and I was close to three figures, but there was no feeling in my mind about that landmark. It didn't enter my head to try and get there before the end of the day's play and so avoid the potential for a sleepless night. I knew sleep would be difficult anyway with the innings set to go through my head and it was now just a case of trying to repeat the processes that had served me so well during the day. I wanted to be positive against the new ball, but there was no point in throwing away all the hard work that had got me to that position in the first place. I still had to play each ball on its merits.

Steyn did tempt me to play at the odd ball wide of the off-stump, but the balls I chose to try and hit were ones I felt confident I could score from, and in his last-but-one over of the day I cut a ball hard into the ground, over point, and away for four. I was happy to cut from that wide line but not to drive and so it was Steyn's length that encouraged me to believe I could play the shot and have success with it.

There was just one more alarm for me ahead of the close, and it came when Morné Morkel replaced Philander for just one over. He raced in and gave me a rearing ball that I just managed to play down from in front of my face, away from any close catchers. It wasn't the sort of ball I would ask for after close to four hours at the crease but, on the other side of the coin, batting for that length of time meant I was better able to deal with it. It also served as an encouragement to me—and to the rest of the team sitting on the sidelines too, I'm sure—that there was still plenty in the surface that allowed the faster bowlers to inconvenience batsmen, and as we had Mitchell Johnson in our side it was something South Africa would have been aware of too.

I walked off 91 not out, out of a total of 4–297, with Shaun Marsh on 122, and it represented a terrific first day of the series for us. That was reflected by the mood in the dressing room too. It wasn't euphoric but it was very positive, as you might expect given we had been 4–98 just after lunch, and there are few better feelings that walking off to the shouts of your teammates and pats on the back, as Shaun and I got then. The two teams' dressing rooms at Centurion are next to each other and South Africa would have heard how good we felt about the day's play. We had a short debrief in the dressing room and Shaun and I chipped in about the surface and how we thought South Africa had bowled, with lessons to learn for us. With the cracks on the pitch it was impor-tant for the faster bowlers to run in and really hit that pitch as hard as they could to try and exploit any uneven bounce rather than just put the ball in the right area.

For me the regime after play was simple: to rehydrate and replenish my energy levels. I usually like to take water after an innings although if it's especially hot and I'm cramping—it wasn't and I wasn't in this innings—then I'll take an isotonic shot to boost my system. I'm not a big fan of an ice bath but I had to have one here to help reduce the lactic acid build-up and so reduce stiffness from muscle fatigue. And once I got back to the hotel it was room service and a massage in the team room, another way of looking after my muscles after a long day.

I'm not a good sleeper when in the middle of an innings and this night was no exception even though I was tired. I found myself replaying the innings in my head and sleep only came with difficulty. I will admit I felt a little fatigued on day two when we arrived at the ground, more mentally than anything after all the concentration of day one, but at the same time physically I felt good. After all, if you can't feel good when you're due to bat in a Test match and already have 91 against your name, then when can you feel good?

The outdoor practice nets, after our sessions on them ahead of the Test, were a little worn and so I opted to go indoors again with Michael Di Venuto ahead of play. It was just a case of feeling bat on ball as much as anything and by my standards at the time it was a relatively short session— about 15 minutes—before the squad assembled for a brief chat about the day to come with the emphasis on more of the sort of intelligent cricket we'd produced on the first day.

I wasn't nervous as I went out with Shaun but I did get a terrific wake-up call first ball as Vernon Philander nipped the ball back off the seam and had a big appeal for lbw against me turned down. What saved me was the extra bounce in the surface as the ball struck me above the flap of the pad.

I was certainly made to work for every one of the nine runs I needed for my hundred that morning. Philander nagged away around off-stump getting just a hint of movement away in the air, although I was again pleased to show plenty of patience against him, while Steyn had better control than on the previous evening and made me play a lot more. The ball continued to misbehave every so often too, with one delivery from Steyn that I left flying off a crack and rising from just short of a length to armpit height, although thankfully it was too wide to cause me any issues, while another squatted lower than expected and I squirted that to square leg for a single. Steyn also produced a nasty ball from back of a length that went past my outside edge and a ferocious short ball that cleared everyone, including wicketkeeper AB de Villiers, for five wides.

Steyn bowled with some serious pace on that second morning, getting one ball to cut back and hit me in the thigh pad before it looped to slip, but when he offered me width and something that was a little bit short, I was good enough and quick enough to pounce, cutting him through point for my first boundary of the day, which took me to 95. Another single squirted through square leg in the following over, from Philander, took me to 96, and although once I got within a boundary of three figures it was tempting just to let the adrenaline get the better of me by looking for the big, pressure-relieving shot, I had worked too hard for too long to think about giving it away and so was determined to continue to try and be as patient as I could be.

Finally I got some respite when, after five overs apiece,

Steyn and Philander gave way to Robin Peterson and Ryan McLaren. Peterson came on for the 101st over. I was surprised with the choice of Peterson when the ball was eighteen overs old and Morné Morkel was available, but I wasn't complaining, skipping down the pitch to clip Peterson through square leg for a single before twice clipping McLaren through the on-side for singles to move to 99. Graeme Smith had obviously left that gap there to try and get me to play across the ball but, as ever, I was completely confident in my ability to hit straight balls in that area.

The second of those singles got me on strike against Peterson. It's a funny aspect of cricket that suddenly, when a player is close to a landmark, all fielders seem to be on their toes far more than is the case at other times and that can be a cause for anxiety and wondering where the all-important run will come from. But I was actually quite relaxed about things. I knew it would come from somewhere and sure enough, to the third ball of the over, a ball that skidded on with no spin, I squirted it behind square leg for a single to bring up my milestone.

I might not have shown it but I felt quite emotional and very elated to get to my hundred. I'd helped dig the team out of a decent-sized hole and to do it alongside Shaun Marsh, a player coming back into the side, and so with something to prove, made the moment doubly pleasing. More than anything, though, the innings gave me confidence and belief that I really had arrived as a Test batsman. To score those runs against a top Test attack, against a team that had an exceptional home record and in conditions that were tricky, made me realise I had the ability to really make something of myself at the highest level. Whatever job you do, imagine doing it to the very best of your ability in the most testing of circumstances, coming out with flying colours. That's how I felt when I raised my bat that morning.

After all that, however, the end came for me suddenly, in the next over, and it was a bit of an anti-climax. I pushed hard at a ball from Ryan McLaren and edged to Robin Peterson, who took a comfortable catch at second slip. It was a decent ball, it nipped away off the seam and drew me into the shot but it was a ball I'd been leaving countless times during the innings and it was, without doubt, a lapse in concentration on my part. The relief of reaching my hundred undoubtedly played a part and that was disappointing.

It meant I walked off with a mix of emotions—elation, yes, at scoring a Test hundred, an important innings for me and the team, but also frustration at getting out in the way that I had. I was satisfied with what I'd done, but at the same time that frustration was there, as once reaching three figures it is often the best time to bat. The job isn't done, but having achieved something it can be a time to play with a bit more freedom, score more quickly and really turn the screw on the opposition.

As a child I tended to get pretty upset when I was dismissed and would shout and carry on when I got back to the dressing room. I've settled down from that over time and although I do get angry when I make a mistake, if I get a good ball then I can be fairly relaxed about getting out. I was calm by the time I got back to the dressing room this time, helped by the fact it was a long walk from the middle and boosted by the applause I got from the crowd. It's hard to be too angry when you raise your bat as you walk off. Since the death of Phillip Hughes I've certainly been calmer after being dismissed, whatever my score, as that really brought home to me that there's no point, when you've got out, in getting too worked up. It's only a game, after all. My career yes, but still only a game.

Michael Di Venuto and Darren Lehmann both came up to me and said 'Well played' and I knew they were right. It had been hard work, especially on that second morning when my last nine runs took 14 overs, but my hundred was my reward for the thought I'd put into the innings before-hand and the execution of my plans once I got out in the middle. It was a template for me for the time ahead and I really do feel that it marked the point where I actually believed that international cricket was where I belonged. Before that innings it was something I'd wanted to believe. After I walked off at Centurion I knew it was.

CHAPTER 13
Away from the game

I was 20 years old when, sitting down one day to lunch with my manager Warren Craig at Homebush Bay in Sydney, he made what I thought at the time was a very interesting remark.

'You need to develop some interests outside the game,' he said. 'It's all very well to have cricket as your main focus when the going is good, but when things aren't going so well you need to be able to take enjoyment out of other things as well.'

Warren knew what he was talking about. He'd managed Glenn McGrath through his successful career, helping him make the transition from player to former player and,

Prior warning: celebrating the wicket of England wicketkeeper Matt Prior with Phillip Hughes during the Lord's Test of 2013, one of the few happy moments we had as a side during that match as we were thrashed by 347 runs with a day to spare. I took four wickets but made only 2 and 1 and wondered if my return to the Test side had stalled again. (© Getty Images)

Shield success: celebrating after captaining New South Wales to success in the Sheffield Shield in 2014. I made 75 and 103 not out against Western Australia in the final in Canberra to help us seal the title, part of a dream summer for me that included two hundreds in an Ashes whitewash. (© Cricket NSW)

'I've made it!' That was my feeling as I raised my bat to acknowledge the applause for my hundred against South Africa at Centurion in February 2014. I really did feel I'd finally arrived as a Test cricketer and still rate the innings as my best and most important in that format. (© Getty Images)

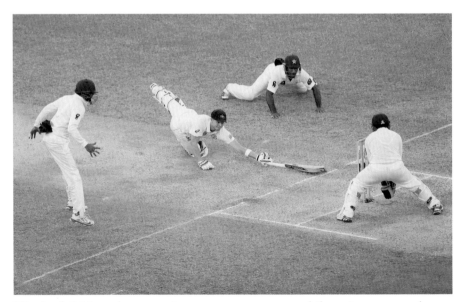

'Get back!' I just about survive a run-out attempt while trying to save the Dubai Test against Pakistan in October 2014. I batted for long periods in the two-match series but we were thoroughly outplayed in alien conditions. (© Getty Images)

Never forgotten: acknowledging my great mate Phillip Hughes after reaching my hundred in the Adelaide Test against India in December 2014, our first match after his tragic death. (© Getty Images)

'Good luck, mate!' Receiving my captain's blazer from Mark Taylor, a great mentor of mine, ahead of my first match in charge, at the Gabba in December 2014. Nathan Lyon (left) and Shaun Marsh look on approvingly. (© Getty Images)

Here goes: tossing the coin at the start of my first Test as captain, alongside match referee Jeff Crowe (in the cream hat), India captain Mahendra Singh Dhoni and Channel Nine's Mark Nicholas. Our security manager Frank Dimasi (with phone and sunglasses) records the moment, next to media manager Kate Hutchison. (© Getty Images)

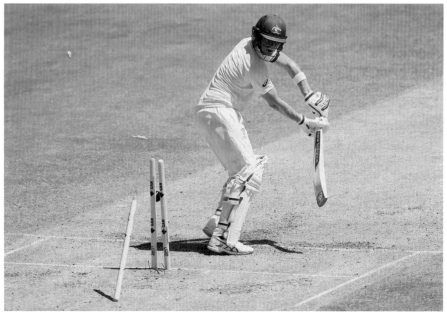

The end of the beginning: India's Ishant Sharma bowls me off the inside edge to end my innings of 133 in my first Test as Australian captain in Brisbane in December 2014, an effort that proved to me I could lead and score runs. (© Getty Images)

'Good catch, Smudge!' Being congratulated by one of my mentors, Brad Haddin, after catching Mohammed Shami during the Melbourne Test against India in December 2014. Brad's decision not to seek the captaincy in Michael Clarke's absence gave me the chance to lead the side. (© Getty Images)

Leg-side love affair: if a bowler strays onto my pads then I back myself to score runs more often than not and here's another example. (© Getty Images)

Satisfaction: posing with the Allan Border Medal, awarded to Australia's top male cricketer, in 2015. I also collected the Test and One-Day International Cricketer of the Year 2015 Awards and the Sir Garfield Sobers Trophy for ICC Cricketer of the Year 2015, all part of an unforgettable few months for me and the team. (© Getty Images)

Practice makes perfect: all those years of catching drills with Dad pay off as I snare an edge from Henry Nicholls of New Zealand during our victory in Christchurch in February 2016. Our 2–0 series win took us—briefly—back to the top of the Test rankings. (© Getty Images)

'Yes!' Joy unconfined from me and Shane Watson after I hit the winning runs in the ICC Cricket World Cup final against New Zealand at the Melbourne Cricket Ground in March 2015. (© Getty Images)

Mob rule: I'm engulfed by teammates after the winning moment in Melbourne. My face says everything about how I'm feeling. (© Getty Images)

Champions: celebrating with teammates and showered by tickertape as we lift the biggest prize in international cricket following our victory against the Black Caps. (© Getty Images)

Winners are grinners: lapping up the atmosphere during our lap of honour after Cricket World Cup final success. It was the climax of a remarkable season that saw us ride a rollercoaster of emotions with huge highs like this, and also the terrible low of Phillip Hughes' death. (© Getty Images)

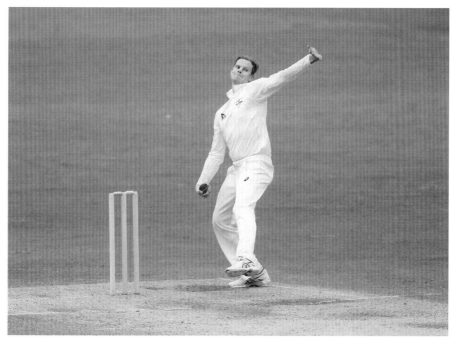

Turning it on again: at the bowling crease during the tour match against Kent at the start of the 2015 Ashes tour. I picked up three expensive wickets that day but ended up bowling just 11.4 overs on the trip, a reflection of my desire to concentrate on my batting. (© Getty Images)

Let's get on the field: waiting with David Warner to take the field during the opening Ashes Test of 2015, at Cardiff. A great thinker on the game, David is a joy to play alongside and I think we make a terrific team as captain and vice-captain. (© Getty Images)

Lording it at Lord's: I'm ecstatic after reaching my double hundred at The Home of Cricket during the Ashes series of 2015. It helped us to a series-leveling win but then successive crushing losses at Edgbaston and Trent Bridge ended our dreams of retaining the urn. (© Getty Images)

What a feeling: taking the applause from a full house at Lord's and a standing ovation from the members in 2015 as I walk off after scoring my maiden Test double-hundred. To achieve that and for the side to go on and win the match really was a dream come true. (© Getty Images)

Worth the wait: my only wicket of the 2015 Ashes series and no wonder I look pleased, dismissing England captain Alastair Cook as we closed in on a consolation victory at The Oval. (© Getty Images)

Pause for thought: the faces of coach Darren Lehmann and myself say it all as we join in the applause to remember Phillip Hughes exactly a year after he died, during the inaugural day–night Test against New Zealand in Adelaide. It was a time to reflect on the fact that our great mate was no longer with us. (© Getty Images)

'I'm embarrassed to be sitting here.' Facing the media after our capitulation against South Africa in Hobart in November 2016, our fifth successive Test loss. (© Getty Images)

The gathering storm: heading out for the toss at the Sydney Cricket Ground ahead of the West Indies Test in January 2016. The grey skies were a prelude to three days of the match being washed out, condemning it to be a draw. (© Getty Images)

Winners are grinners again: celebrating with my teammates after our clean sweep of the Test series against Pakistan in the summer of 2016/17. The way we turned our form around with four successive wins was a tribute to the new players introduced and a tremendous effort after our terrible run of defeats. (© Getty Images)

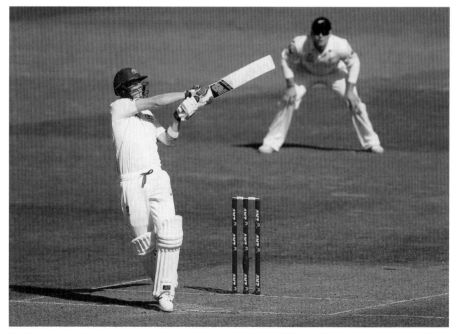

Pulling out the stops: more runs as part of my 71 on the opening day of the two-match series against New Zealand, in Wellington in February 2016. (© Getty Images)

Heading for victory: celebrating my hundred in Pune in February 2017, an innings that helped set up our first Test win in India for 13 years. It was one of three centuries I scored in the series, all of them complete with my lucky headband! (© AP Photo/Rajanish Kakade)

Bright spot: acknowledging the applause for reaching fifty against England at Edgbaston in June's ICC Champions Trophy. I was out soon afterwards and the match was ended early by rain. Poor weather and our on-field struggles made it a tournament to forget. (© Mike Edgerton/PA Wire)

Christmas: with partner—and now fiancée—Danielle Willis in Melbourne ahead of my first Boxing Day Test as captain, in December 2014. (© Getty Images)

having looked after me for two years at that stage, he'd seen how much I obsessed about the game as I sought to make a success of my chosen career.

It's true that, up to that point in my life, cricket had been front and centre for me, with everything else running a distant second. When I was in the UK playing club cricket for Sevenoaks Vine in 2007, Tony Ward, who I was staying with at the time, joked to a club official that I loved the game so much I even slept with my bat.

I didn't quite go to those lengths, but Warren's observations, along with those of a few other people I respected, made me reflect upon where I was in my life and now, while cricket is still my number one priority, I've gradually moved to a position where I take an interest in lots of other things away from the game that give me pleasure. And those things have, in turn, helped to take my mind off thinking about the game 24/7.

I was quite resistant to the idea of having anything other than cricket to think about when I first got into the Cricket New South Wales structure as a rookie, even though the state had a welfare program pushing players into diversifying in that way. The idea was—and still is—to give players other strings to their bows and ensure that if things don't work out on the field then there is a plan B and something to fall back on career-wise, or some other skill learnt that could make you attractive to potential employers.

I did get as far as considering doing a business course online but at that stage of my life my mind always came back to the same thought: when I wasn't playing or training then I wanted to be in a position to enjoy my relaxation time and not have to think about something that needed to be done. So, on that basis, I always shied away from that sort of commitment.

Of course, as I became more and more high profile through becoming a member of the Australian side, the potential for me to become associated with businesses to help them market themselves and their products grew and, whether I liked it or not, I came to realise that came with the territory.

But the good thing from my perspective was that Warren was quite selective in helping me choose likely partners, and we had a series of criteria that we used to help in that decision-making process if companies approached him expressing an interest in wanting to work with me. Those criteria were that the brand had to fit in with cricket, it had to fit in with what I was all about—a young, fit and healthy athlete—and resonate with me so I would feel comfortable promoting it. We also both agreed there had to be an upper limit of companies that I could be involved with, as too many would have the potential to impact negatively on my ability to manage my time.

One thing I've become acutely aware of is my appeal to young fans of the game, and on that basis it's made me even more conscious of doing the right thing in terms of what I endorse. As an example, in 2016 Warren was approached by a leading multinational snack food brand with a proposal for me to endorse a well-known product. There's no need for me to name the brand here but I decided it didn't fit in with the image that I wanted to portray, so I knocked it back. The bottom line for me is that any money I might earn from such endorsements is less important to me than the image I put forward to the next generation of players and supporters, and that is something I will always seek to live by wherever possible. The companies I do work with—Sanitarium and its Weet-Bix brand, Fox Sports, Commonwealth Bank and New Balance—all share my values of getting young people fit and active.

If that seems like a relatively small list of companies for a person whose profile is as high as mine as captain of the national team, then it is because it fits in with Warren's and my aim of not overcommitting me. Having too many brands to endorse doesn't work on a number of levels, not least because it would then be a question of trying to find the time to look after them. If companies are prepared to support me then I have to be prepared to do the same in return and with our playing schedule involving pretty much through-the-year action, the opportunities to lock time away in my diary to attend events is strictly limited. On top of that, there are commitments that Cricket Australia agrees with its commercial partners and, along with all the other contracted players, I am locked in to attending a set number of those during any given year too. And with those factors to consider, Warren is always conscious that when I do get downtime then he doesn't want to be filling it all up with endless promotional activities, as that would be a recipe for ensuring I never get that switch-off time that's always been so important to me.

A greater awareness of business through these endorsements has given me the confidence to look around off my own bat and over the past two years I've developed an interest in investing in start-up companies, both at home and abroad.

Before you get the idea I'm too focused on business and not focused enough on cricket, I'd point out that investing in this way is something I've been involved with since 2015 and the period since then has coincided with me playing the best cricket of my career, so it certainly hasn't affected me in that sense. And the investments I've made involve only a relatively small percentage of my income. What I've found is that the whole process has been thoroughly enjoyable, a good diversion from a diet of cricket, cricket and more cricket, and one that has whetted my appetite for greater involvement in the business world once my playing career winds down.

I think of my investments as a hobby, and one that has the potential to make a lot of people, not just me, very happy. Another hobby I have that has that same potential, although in a different way, is my interest in racehorses.

My attraction to the sport developed in a fairly standard way. Once I turned 18, just like many young Australians, the idea of a beer at the pub while having a bet on the horses was a very appealing one, but although I enjoyed it, it wasn't much more than a passing interest at that stage.

That changed when my friend Richie Callander introduced me to the idea of ownership, and as a result I now own small shares of two geldings, Hogmanay and Cauthens Power, both trained by Chris Waller, one of New South Wales' leading trainers. Hogmanay is a four-year-old and Moisés Henriques is also part of the syndicate of owners, while Cauthens Power is a five-year-old originally out of New Zealand.

I've never had the chance to make it to the track to watch them race—and win—on a Saturday, but I have managed to attend a few midweek race meetings when my schedule's allowed, although I've never made it to the winner's enclosure in person yet.

I'm not one who has a copy of the form guide under his arm at all times and I'm not so obsessed that I'll go and watch either of my horses train. But what I will do is watch my horses race online if I know they're running and I've got access to the coverage. It's something that gives me a lot of enjoyment although I know it's not something that will ever make me rich.

Most cricketers will follow most sports because sport is what we love. I think we all enjoy watching people compete, especially if the standard of that competition is high and, for me, the two sports I'm most passionate about outside of my own are rugby league and tennis.

My rugby league side is the Sydney Roosters, which would surprise people familiar with the city's geography as, coming from Sutherland, a long way from the Eastern Suburbs, the club isn't one that you would think I would be barracking for.

My attraction to the Roosters came from following Brad Fittler. He was my favourite player when he was at Penrith and I began taking an interest in the game, and when he moved to the Roosters my affiliation moved with him.

Brad's obviously long since retired but I'm still following the team, and although I've not been able to get to a game in person for the last couple of years, I do watch them online whenever I get the chance. And as the side trains in the SCG sports complex it's often the case that I'll cross paths with members of the squad.

I can't say I'm best mates with any of the current line-up, but I'm on nodding terms with the likes of captain Boyd Cordner, Jake Friend and Mitchell Pearce and they all come across as good guys.

Tennis was my winter activity growing up and although I don't get the chance to play much these days, I'm still in love with the sport and watch it as much as I can. For me, the Australian Open tennis in Melbourne in January is as much a part of the summer sports scene as any cricket match and there's nothing I like better during those two weeks than tuning in to a night session after I get back from a day's playing or training. Perhaps the biggest thrill of my sporting life outside of cricket was meeting and getting the chance to chat with Roger Federer in Sydney a couple of years ago.

Roger is someone I've idolised as a sportsman for his longevity and the way he conducts himself on and off the court. I got my introduction to him when he was playing in a Fast4 Tennis event in Sydney—the format of the sport billed as tennis' equivalent of Twenty20. Warren teed the meeting up through Lleyton Hewitt, who was playing Roger, and originally he was going to keep it a secret from me and give me a big surprise.

But when Warren told Dani about the planned meeting she thought I should be told beforehand as she figured—probably quite rightly—that I'd be so in awe of him that I might end up tongue-tied. By giving me a bit of notice I could at least get used to the idea of a catch-up with the great man.

I was like a child at Christmas when Warren let the cat out of the bag and all I could keep saying was 'The Fed!' And when the time came to actually meet him he was every bit as impressive as I thought he would be, and we chatted for about 20 minutes. He was honest enough to admit he didn't know very much about cricket, but he did say that wherever he goes in the world he tends to watch whatever sport there is on television so he had actually heard of it and seen some cricket as well. That night was also the first chance I had to meet Lleyton and he was just as impressive. I've got enormous admiration for both men as they have managed to remain at the top of their chosen profession for well over a decade, which, in sporting terms is a lifetime. Lleyton really has carried the Australian flag superbly throughout his time at the top.

For some players, any time away from the game and commercial appearances involves family time at home, but I'm still at the stage in my life where those considerations aren't things I have to worry about. On that basis, my primary way of relaxing away from cricket is to travel.

It may seem odd to some readers that someone who spends much of his life living out of a suitcase in hotel rooms as I do, is happy to do the same thing when I'm not playing, but it works for me. In 2016, after we won the ODI tri-series in the Caribbean against the West Indies and South Africa, Dani and I went on to the USA for a trip that combined a stop in Boston to visit the New Balance head office along with a holiday in New York, and we headed to the USA again after the Champions Trophy in 2017.

New York is something of a favourite destination of mine as it is such a fantastic place to explore, and Dani and I can spend four or five hours walking the streets there without anyone batting an eyelid at us given cricket's low profile in the country. The fact we can walk from one end of the city to the other means there is plenty of scope for exploring the place, as well as assisting in maintaining my fitness levels between cricket commitments, and with so much to see and do there, I'd happily live in New York tomorrow if the chance presented itself. There's obviously no chance of that at the moment, but once I finish playing, who knows where I might end up.

Dani has been a breath of fresh air in my life since we got together in the early part of 2012, and I reckon I was the happiest man alive when she accepted my proposal on top of the Empire State Building in New York in June 2017. We met at a time when I was out of the Australian Test team, but still enjoying life, perhaps in hindsight a bit too much. It was during the inaugural season of the Big Bash League, the summer I was part of the victorious Sydney Sixers line-up—I actually hit the winning runs in the final against the Perth Scorchers at the WACA—and I was on a night out at Scubar, a backpackers' bar in Sydney.

I'd seen Dani across the bar and was trying to pluck up enough courage to go over and chat to her and to work out what I might say if I did, when a male friend of hers who was part of a group with her that night, recognised me, came over, and started to make conversation. It turned out to be the perfect opportunity for me to introduce myself to Dani and I was delighted that we hit it off straight away.

I pretty quickly realised I enjoyed being with her and within a couple of weeks I took her to meet my parents, the first time I'd ever done that with a girlfriend. Soon after that I took her to Hawaii for a holiday, the sort of long-distance trip that can either make or break a relationship in its early stages, and thankfully for me it was the former rather than the latter.

I think meeting Dani was life's way of helping me to grow up. By the time we got together I'd already moved out of home and had my own place, but it was something of a lad's pad with housemates, including my New South Wales teammate Stephen O'Keefe. There was one occasion when I went out and bought a table tennis table on the spur of the moment only to find that when it was opened out it took up most of the living space in the lounge. It meant we had some great games of table tennis but it wasn't necessarily the most practical thing to do. Dani's arrival on the scene quickly made me realise what my priorities were, my housemates moved out and she moved in.

Dani didn't know a great deal about cricket when we met but as I quickly discovered she is very smart and now understands the game pretty well. I've even had her feeding me balls into the bowling machine at the SCG nets when I've gone down there for a hit on my own. She doesn't comment on my technique, and that suits me fine, because there are times when all I want to do is to feel bat on ball without a coach's input and she's able to help me with that whenever I need it.

Dani tends to travel with me pretty much everywhere I go when I'm playing and I find it great to have her around. Anyone reading this book will have realised there are times when I find it hard to switch off from thinking about the game, and that's even more so since I became captain, and so having someone around who's not involved with the team and the game, is very helpful for me. Regardless of the day I've had I can get on with the rest of my evening with her and she'll be the same person with me whether I've scored a duck or a hundred.

There is a view, of course, that having wives, partners or children around the team can lead to a dilution of team spirit but, although I guess I'm biased thanks to Dani, that's not my experience and I think you'll get the same answer from Darren Lehmann and David Warner, among others, too. As a team, we're on the road together so much and we see so much of each other every day anyway that I think it's actually good to get out of that bubble when we can and I, for one, am all in favour of families being with us whenever possible. We're fortunate now that we earn enough money to have that luxury, and Cricket Australia has also been supportive with dedicated family windows during summers and tours when they actively assist wives, partners and children travelling with players. Warren believes I play better when Dani is around and I think there's some value in that argument for the reasons I've already mentioned.

Dani and I have plenty of interests in common, whether it's going to movies and watching DVD box sets, walking or even going to the gym, as she'll head for the treadmill while I go for the weights. Our time together has certainly coincided with an improvement in my training regime, something that has led to a definite change in my body shape. I'm now at the stage where I actually enjoy going to the gym, whereas for the first few years of my career I regarded it as more of a chore that had to be done.

I'm conscious of the fact that Dani's put her life on hold to a great extent in order to be with me, as she's highly intelligent and has graduated in commerce and law and would be a great success in life in her own right if she chose to focus on her career. She's yet to decide what she'll do with that qualification but in the meantime we're working together on one of my other new interests, property development and management.

I own a portfolio of properties in Sydney and Brisbane that I rent out, but I've also now taken an interest in buying and doing up property too, and our plan is for Dani to take a hands-on role with that as she has a flair for interior design.

I'm fortunate to have had Dani come into my life and, with an increasingly fulfilling existence away from cricket, I know I have a lot to be grateful for.

CHAPTER 14

Cricket World Cup 2015—Some things are just meant to be

When I was a small boy playing with my dad at Casuarina Oval, the thought of any involvement in the winning moment of an ICC CWC final, and doing it on home soil, simply never entered my head. After all, why would it?

Being part of a moment like that is something that has been granted to only a very small group of players from around the world—although our coach Darren Lehmann has done it twice, first hitting the winning runs in 1999 then taking the winning catch four years later—but I joined that group on 29 March 2015 when I hit New Zealand fast bowler Matt Henry into the on-side for four to secure the title.

I can still see the moment in my mind's eye. Defeat was impossible by that stage, with two runs to get and seven wickets and 17 overs in hand, and although I felt utterly relaxed at the crease I also felt an incredible buzz at the prospect of all our efforts reaching fruition.

The atmosphere within the MCG was incredible too. As I settled myself at the crease, Jimmy Barnes's 'Working Class Man' was blaring out over the public address system and although, as a batsman, you usually switch off from all external sound, it was impossible to ignore the energy from the crowd.

On that basis I reckon that, whatever Henry had sent down, I would probably have looked to hit it away for the winning runs. So when he delivered a slower ball, just short of a length, it gave me the perfect opportunity to seal the deal. What I produced wasn't exactly a thing of beauty; it was no classical cover drive or a shot like Mahendra Singh Dhoni produced four years earlier when he on-drove the ball into the crowd at the Wankhede Stadium in Mumbai to secure victory for India, but prettiness came a distant second to effectiveness in the circumstances for me—as it often does.

I produced a slightly ugly stroke that was half-whip and half-pull but as soon as I hit it and got it past the fielder at mid-wicket then I knew that was it and that we'd won. Shane Watson and I ran the first run simply out of habit, both of us with our arms raised, before the boundary was signalled, at which point I took off my helmet and dropped it, along with my bat, at the non-striker's end and then leapt into Shane's arms as we met in mid-pitch. By that stage our teammates were all racing out from the boundary's edge to join in with the celebrations and it really was a moment that will live with me as long as I draw breath.

There were a lot of emotions coursing through my mind at that stage. There was joy and pride, obviously, as well as relief, that we'd done what we'd set out to do at not only the start of the tournament but also the start of the season, and the relief also came from the fact that the season, which had actually begun with a tri-series in Zimbabwe that also involved South Africa in the middle of 2014, was now finally over. And it was impossible not to think of Phillip Hughes too, as his passing was a tragedy that dominated the landscape of the season.

And from a purely personal perspective, the win really was the icing on the cake as it was the culmination of an incredible season for me. Even in November 2014, I wasn't a first pick in the line-up and now here I was in the thick of things in sealing the win that made us all national heroes. We all knew it was our one shot at winning a CWC in our own country—it had been 23 years since the previous one was held in Australia and we knew we'd all be long-retired by the time it returned again—and to be able to achieve that ambition was something that could never be taken away from us.

The speed of my rise up the ranks in the one-day side came thanks to Michael Clarke's injury problems and without those problems I might never have had the chance to press my case. I got an opportunity in Zimbabwe when he suffered a hamstring injury and then had another in the UAE against Pakistan when the same issue dogged him. I got 101 in Sharjah, batting at number three in the opening match of a three-game series, on a tough, slow surface and that gave me an enormous amount of belief in my ability to be a first-choice member of the side.

Even then, however, nothing was guaranteed and when we returned to Australia for a five-match series against South Africa to start the international season at home, I was again on the sidelines as Michael returned, only coming back for match two when he was again laid low by injury.

This time I batted at number four, behind David Warner, Aaron Finch and Shane Watson, but by producing scores of 10, 73 not out, 104 and 67, I actually managed to establish myself in the one-day line-up for the first time so that when Michael eventually came back it was going to be someone else rather than me who missed out.

That hundred against South Africa I regard as one of my best innings in international cricket, not least because it was against some outstanding opposition bowlers including Dale Steyn, and also because it played a vital role in helping us recover from being 5–98 to chase down 268 for victory. Without it I may still have found myself starting the CWC down the pecking order, but it showed everyone watching I had what it took to succeed in the top order in that format. It was the ultimate confidence-builder as far as I was concerned.

What pleased me most about the innings was that I remained calm and composed throughout—except for the final ball I faced, when I missed an attempted big hit trying to win the match with the scores tied—something that was absolutely vital in the circumstances we found ourselves in. The asking rate was well above a run a ball from a long way out and because we'd lost the rest of our top-order players very early in the piece it was up to me to drive the chase, something I did in partnership, first with Matthew Wade, and then James Faulkner. What we did really well was to bring the run-rate down bit by bit rather than going mad, and it meant that although we were in a tricky position, I never felt it was out of our control.

It was the innings that made me one of the starting eleven for the side in one-day cricket come what may, but the fact I had to produce something like that in order to force my way in was a pretty good indicator of where we were as a side at that time. To have scored a hundred in difficult circumstances in Sharjah and still not be certain of a spot just illustrated the strength at our disposal.

My effort in Melbourne against South Africa really was the start of what I regard as the best and most consistent period of my career up to the middle of 2017. From the beginning of the home summer in 2014 until the end of the CWC I felt absolutely in control of my batting and my life. I felt completely at ease every time I went to the crease and it felt like only a mistake by me, or an absolutely unplayable ball, was going to get me out. I revelled in the extra responsibility that came with the Test captaincy and then being pushed up to number three in the one-day line-up during the tournament, and although I've played well and very consistently since then, that four-month run of form really does stand out in my mind as the best I have ever played. If I could have bottled the feeling I had during that period then I would have done.

As we headed into the World Cup I think everyone in and around the squad knew we had a great chance of success. We knew we were a good side, we had a terrific blend of youth and experience, some tremendous power hitters and dangerous players right through our list and our fast bowlers were intimidating, especially in our own conditions. Tournaments are never won on paper but our line-up looked formidable and that was exactly how it turned out. I was certainly full of belief that we could win the tournament, something that was only reinforced in my mind by a strong showing against England and India in a tri-series beforehand.

From a personal point of view, the pivotal game for me was when we played Afghanistan at the WACA ground in Perth, as that was the match in which I was pushed up to number three in the list. James Faulkner was recalled to the side after recovering from a side strain picked up during the tri-series and in order for him to come back, someone had to miss out, and that someone was Shane Watson. Shane had been the man occupying the number three position, but with him out of the line-up and Michael Clarke only just back in the team after his back and hamstring issues, and him comfortable at four, it created a vacancy immediately behind the openers David Warner and Aaron Finch.

I'd started the tournament at four against England, then dropped down to five for the match against New Zealand in Auckland that saw Michael come back into the side, and although my scores up to that point had been five and four, I was relaxed about moving up the list. You could argue that after my two failures I should have been nervous about having George Bailey, our reserve batsman, breathing down my neck, but I was more excited than anything else at the prospect of batting at first wicket down. If you ask most batsmen in international cricket where they'd like to bat, especially in one-day cricket, then virtually everyone would reply it has to be somewhere in the top four. Doing that means you'll get the chance to face plenty of balls and can therefore influence the course of the match to a far greater degree than by batting down the list. I knew my game inside-out by that stage and I certainly didn't have any fears about facing the new or newish ball, and so it just felt right for me to be in at number three.

If there was extra pressure or expectation on me to prove myself in that position, given we were playing against a lesser-ranked team, then I didn't feel it. It was just a case of me doing what I'd done throughout the previous three months, which was scoring runs by playing my way. It certainly helped me that David Warner played so well at the other end as we added 260 in 35 overs and he made 178 before being dismissed with 12 overs still to go. For my part I threw away the chance of a hundred, out for 95 from 98 balls, but the dismissals of David and myself were an indication of the way we wanted to play as a team. There was no thought of personal milestones and it was a case of going as hard as we could in the knowledge that we had batting power left in the dressing room. Darren Lehmann's constant message to us was that if we had wickets in hand going into the closing overs then he wanted us to reach for the sky. He would rather we lost wickets trying to put the game well and truly out of the opposition's reach than settle for a mediocre score by pushing the ball around. His approach had an element of risk about it, but the confidence that existed within our group meant we were happy to embrace that positive option, and the success we had proved it was the right way to go about things.

I've mentioned already how relaxed I was feeling and I think the same was true throughout the whole squad, something that really stood us in good stead. Plenty was written beforehand, and even during the tournament, about the added pressure of being a host country and how only very rarely did a side staging a CWC actually go on and win it. Australia had failed to get past the round-robin stage in 1992 and we had some of the players from that group, Ian Healy and Stephen Waugh, plus our bowling coach Craig McDermott, speak to us about that. They all admitted they thought they would cruise through and when they lost a couple of games early on and also suffered an injury or two, then the pressure grew to an intolerable level. It showed us that while peaking at the right time in a tournament was important, it also emphasised that we had to start well too in order to get to the business end of the tournament in the first place, and that's exactly what we did when we thumped England by 111 runs after scoring 9–342 in the opening match. What we did throughout that

CWC was actually revel in the fact we were at home rather than feel burdened by it. Familiar faces, familiar places and venues, and familiar conditions surrounded us, and that helped a great deal. It even allowed us to have a couple of days at home after that England game, something none of the other teams, with the exception of New Zealand, were able to do.

Our only real blip in the tournament came against our co-hosts in Auckland and it was probably, in retrospect, the best thing that could have happened to us. We got our approach wrong that day and it showed us that although we had plenty of power in our batting line-up, we still needed to play with our heads too.

The build-up to the match was dominated by discussion of the short straight boundaries at Eden Park and predictions in the media of scores in excess of 400. When Michael Clarke spoke with journalists after the match, he certainly thought we had been a bit too focused on the idea of hitting sixes down the ground rather than playing in our usual way, and maybe he had a point. We certainly paid the price for going too hard and to be bowled out for just 151 with almost 18 overs unused, even though the ball was swinging for Trent Boult, was pretty much unforgiveable. If we'd just taken any thought of those short straight boundaries out of our minds and batted normally then the opportunities to play big shots down the ground would almost certainly have come. We got fixated on the dimensions and it cost us.

The fact we almost pulled off a remarkable win was down almost entirely to some superb fast bowling by

Mitchell Starc, who tore through the New Zealand middle and lower order with a series of fast, full-pitched late in-swingers, but it wasn't to be. The positive, however, was that it was a match that I felt really kicked us into gear, because after that we really moved up to another level and never looked like being touched.

The margins of our victories after that point illustrate that view very well—275 runs, 64 runs, seven wickets *(with 34.4 overs in hand)*, six wickets *(with 16.1 overs unused)*, 95 runs and then seven wickets in the final against New Zealand. There were times in most of those matches when we were put under pressure and in each instance we came through with flying colours. At the same time, my own contributions after shifting to number three were 95, 72, 65, 105 in the semi-final against India at the SCG and an unbeaten 56 in the final. Getting runs at the back-end of the tournament really did give me a huge amount of satisfaction.

The innings of 72 against Sri Lanka makes me laugh when I think about it. It was scored in 88 balls but when I got out, looking for a big shot down the ground, there were still 17.3 overs left and I wondered aloud to Darren Lehmann when I got back to the dressing room whether I'd started to look for a big shot and a major increase in the tempo of the innings too early. In fact, what I did by getting out was to bring together Shane Watson and Glenn Maxwell who then proceeded to blitz the bowling to all parts of the ground in incredible fashion. They added 160 in just 14 overs and when their stand was complete I eased up to Darren with a smile on my face and said: 'Maybe

I went hard at just the right time after all.' My getting out was the catalyst to a remarkable partnership that was one of my highlights of the entire tournament.

Playing in a CWC, doing well personally and being part of a successful team means I have a wonderful collection of memories to draw on. Wahab Riaz's duel with Shane Watson in the quarter-final at the Adelaide Oval was certainly something I'll never forget. It really was a ferocious spell of quick bowling from Wahab and I spent most of it in the best place of all—the non-striker's end. I seemed to always be able to work a single off my hip and expose Shane to the majority of the onslaught and although he had some good fortune, being dropped at fine leg from a top-edged hook shot, it was some of the most compelling cricket of the tournament. There wasn't much we could say when Shane and I met in mid-pitch between overs as we both knew we had to get through the spell. All I said was 'Watch the ball closely' and the fact he was still there at the end was testimony to his character. It was a curious passage of play, too, as Wahab kept stopping at the end of his follow-through to clap, trying to rouse his teammates, and that was something I've not seen before or since. But from my point of view it was great to get runs in tough circumstances. There was a little bit in the pitch for the faster bowlers with some grass left on by the curator and in addition to some seam movement on offer there was also some swing too. Having said that, the ball came on to the bat beautifully and I felt in control from the very first ball I faced. As soon as I was underway with a boundary through square leg off Sohail Khan, I never looked back. I felt my cover-driving in that innings was the stand-out and I know that when I'm cover-driving well, with my nose right over the ball, then my game is in excellent working order. That's certainly how it felt that night.

In terms of feeling relaxed, it was a case of more of the same in the semi-final against India when I scored 105 from 93 balls in what was my best innings of the tournament. It was one of those occasions when, to use the sports psychologist's expression, I was in the zone. Absolutely everything felt as though it hit the middle of my bat, I felt no nerves at all, was just in the moment and found I was almost on autopilot. I'm at my best when I don't overthink or overcomplicate things out in the middle, and this was a case in point, although, as I mentioned earlier, I felt like that for large parts of that home summer. It was an excellent pitch, and although it looked dry and appeared likely to offer plenty of spin later on, it actually held together throughout the course of the match and was great to bat on.

As was the case at the same venue against Sri Lanka when I got out with loads of overs in hand—I was dismissed in the semi-final with almost 16 overs left—that was in keeping with our philosophy of going hard when we had wickets in hand in the knowledge we had plenty of power still to come. With India's batting line-up, we knew we'd need a substantial total. When we finished with 7–328, I felt that was just about par with a shorter than usual boundary on one side of the ground.

When India got away to a flying start it appeared likely we'd need every one of the runs we had on the board, but the pressure of having to score more than a run a ball through-out the innings, and in a semi-final too, became too much for its batsmen eventually, and once we got the first two wickets—Shikhar Dhawan caught at deep point and then Virat Kohli, bounced out by Mitchell Johnson—I always felt we were in control.

As I've said, I'm not a great sleeper ahead of big matches and that habit has only intensified since I've become captain, but although I didn't get that much rest before the final against New Zealand, the main reason for that was excitement rather than nerves. To play in a CWC final is like having all your Christmases come at once and that's certainly how I felt immediately beforehand. It certainly felt different from anything I'd experienced before as a player. When I walked out onto the ground ahead of our warm-ups that day, the crowd had come in very early on and helped to create an amazing atmosphere.

I think it was actually a blessing in disguise that we lost the toss, as we would have batted first had we won it. The problem with batting first against a side including the likes of Martin Guptill and Brendon McCullum at the top of the order, is that you can look to go too hard too soon, thinking you need a big score to try and put the match beyond them, but chasing removed any of those issues and given I'd marshalled a chase against South Africa on the same ground just a handful of months earlier, I knew it was something we could cope with.

As it turned out, by fielding first it allowed us to get over any nerves we might have had very quickly as a group and as soon as Mitchell Starc set the tone by bowling McCullum in the very first over, then I don't think any of us were ever in any doubt that it was going to be our day. The noise around the MCG when that wicket fell is still something that I remember even now, more than two years later, and just the thought of it sends a shiver down my spine. The roar seemed to bounce around off the stands.

There was a suggestion we were more aggressive as a team than we had been in the round-robin match against New Zealand, more in-your-face, but I'm not sure that was the case. I think any aggression we showed was more in the execution of our skills than any over-the-top body language or chat. There was a confidence in our squad that we were the better side and that if we let our skills take over then the rest would look after itself, and I think that's what happened on the day.

It was just about the perfect game of cricket from our perspective with early wickets and then a rousing perform-ance to wrap up the New Zealand innings after Ross Taylor and Grant Elliott had effected a recovery of sorts. We would have taken having to chase 184 on that pitch every day of the year, and the fact we did it with such ease was an illustration of that point.

I never felt nervous during my innings, although I did have that shiver down my spine again as I walked out to bat because of the noise that seemed to echo around the venue. For me it really was a case of 'see ball, hit ball' without over-thinking things. There was no need to be concerned with run-rates chasing such a relatively small target so I knew that if I remained in the middle then the odd bad ball would come along and we would get the runs without a drama.

David Warner and Michael Clarke both got after Tim Southee's bowling but part of the reason for that was the attacking fields set by Brendon McCullum. At one stage he had three slips and a gully, I remember, based, I'm sure, on the fact that he knew he had to bowl us out to win. What that did was offer up gaps in the field that we were able to exploit and it seemed we were scoring pretty much a boundary per over for a lot of the time.

Very little was said by the batsmen out in the middle as we all knew our jobs, and although I was relaxed, I didn't allow myself to see the finishing line until we'd got to the position where we needed about 20 to win. At that stage, with eight wickets in hand, I knew we couldn't lose so it was possible at that point to try and savour what was unfolding, knowing it was the culmination of a lot of hard work by me and my teammates over a long period of time.

I did the team's lap of honour draped in an Australian flag given to me by someone in the crowd and it couldn't have been a more perfect evening. Dad was there, as he had been for the semi-final, and he came down to the dressing room afterwards to share a drink and enjoy the moment. Mum was absent, but she followed the action from home. She's never really enjoyed watching matches and gets bored very quickly.

The celebrations lasted right through the night, as we went back to the Langham Hotel and partied on the roof until the sun came up before a few hours of rest, a gathering at Federation Square to allow the public to share in the triumph and then another get-together with family and friends at a Melbourne restaurant. It really was an amazing 48 hours at the end of an amazing tournament and an amazing season.

Something that the victory did for me was to make me realise how much I wanted a time like that again in my career. Yes, to be part of a CWC–winning side was an absolute highlight and only our Ashes triumph of 2013–14 comes close to rivalling it from my perspective. But I don't want that success in Melbourne to be my only one in a global tournament and it's what I now use to motivate myself to achieve something similar in the future. Winning big games and enjoying the success with teammates is one of the main reasons I play the game, and rather than being satisfied with having joined a select group of people who have winners' medals, I want more of those moments before I finally bring down the curtain on my career.

As for that win in Melbourne, I knew it was my time when, on 16, I chopped a ball onto my stumps from Henry only for the bails to stay on. That summed things up for me during that CWC—some things were just meant to be.

CHAPTER 15

Two tours to forget—Sri Lanka and South Africa 2016

There is no point in sugar-coating the tour of Sri Lanka in mid-2016, or the ODI series in South Africa that followed it. Both were disasters.

It's true we won the two limited-overs series in Sri Lanka that followed the Tests—although I missed the majority of those matches, resting at home—but they followed a 3–0 defeat in the long-form games. And by the time we had been pummelled into submission in South Africa, losing the ODIs there 5–0, it felt like we had forgotten how to win cricket matches.

At the start of the trip, in mid-July, everything seemed

to be set fair. We arrived in Sri Lanka full of optimism and with good reason. We had a decent record there over the years—we'd only lost one Test in five tours—were up against an inexperienced home side short of confidence after a difficult tour of the UK and without retired stalwarts like Mahela Jayawardene and Kumar Sangakkara, while our most recent action—albeit in a different format—had seen us secure a ODI tri-series against the West Indies and South Africa in the Caribbean.

An indication of how fragile the home side was feeling came immediately before the first Test in Pallekele. We were due to receive the ICC Test championship mace, awarded to the top side in the rankings in the game's longest format, after moving to number one following our victory in New Zealand earlier in the year, but the Sri Lankans refused to allow me to be presented with it in front of the media. The implication was that such a presentation might affect the home side's already shaky nerves. Psychologically it was a shot in the arm for us, but that was about the last one we received for the best part of a month.

It's easy to look back and be wise after the event but perhaps we should have seen the trouble to come right from the outset. Our one warm-up match ahead of the Pallekele Test was against a side cobbled together in the absence of not only Sri Lanka's leading players, but also their second string, too, as Sri Lanka A was in action at the same time in the UK. It meant we had a very easy win in just over two days and the reality was it represented very poor preparation for what lay ahead. There was no high-quality spin in the opposition ranks and the pitch assisted the faster bowlers as much as the slow men. It turned out to bear little resemblance to the surfaces we would come across during the Test series.

Did the build-up lead to overconfidence on our part, or any degree of complacency? No, I'd like to think not, but after the first day of the opening Test it was impossible not to be delighted with our position and confident we would cruise to victory given we bowled Sri Lanka out for 117 just after lunch and had replied relatively strongly up to an early close that came at tea time because of rain.

I still wonder whether things might have been different had we played that final session. Usman Khawaja and I were dealing with the Sri Lankan spinners with relative ease, knocking the ball about into the gaps and not looking in a great deal of trouble, and had we gone through to the scheduled close of play that night in the same mode then we would already have been in the lead by some distance and all set to dominate the game. But instead we produced an ordinary batting display when play resumed on day two and I have to shoulder my share of the blame for that.

I have always set out to be positive wherever possible and to dominate the opposition bowlers because I believe if you can put them under pressure by looking to score runs, then they are more likely to err in line or length. But I made a massive misjudgement by attempting to put that philosophy into play from the first ball I received that morning from spinner Rangana Herath.

I looked to go down the pitch and hit him over the top of the in-field but he saw me coming, beat me in the flight and I ended up missing the ball, the second ball of the second over of the day and was stumped by a comfortable margin. And when he dismissed Usman in his next over we were always going to struggle to secure a massive, match-winning lead.

If I had my time again, of course I wouldn't run down the pitch in the way I did. But my dismissal was symptomatic of the way we approached the tour from a batting perspective—we let ego take hold rather than playing the conditions.

Instead of seeking to dominate the spinners, as we would look to do in Australia on pitches where the ball doesn't turn a great deal, we should have been far more inclined to sit in, work the ball around and wait for the bad ball—as we had done on that first afternoon before the rain intervened. And we should have been content to tick along at two or three runs per over instead of looking to score more quickly as we would do at home.

Also, we should have been far more inclined to allow ourselves, as right-handers, to get beaten on the outside edge. When you play against the turning ball and a delivery spins past the bat, the natural reaction in your head as a batsman is to think 'I didn't look good there, so I should cover the line of that turning ball'. Too many of us thought like that for too long, even though a ball that turned in that way was the exception rather than the rule. What it meant was that when the ball didn't turn and just skidded straight on, all too often we were playing for the magic ball instead. We lost countless wickets that way during the series with batsmen either bowled or lbw, beaten past the inside edge of the bat, and that was criminal. I was just as guilty as anyone else, too, and my dismissal in the final innings of the series, bowled by Herath trying to cut a ball that skidded through rather than turned, was a perfect illustration of how we kept making the same mistakes over and over again.

It wasn't as if we didn't talk about the issue either. We had countless discussions and team meetings, all of them excellent, about how we would put our egos away, play the line of the ball, get our bats out in front of our pads and if we got beaten past the outside edge by that magic ball then, so what? We had to be willing to look silly but the reality was that when it came to putting those plans into action in the middle we failed dismally.

Our tormentor-in-chief was Herath, who took 28 wickets at 12.75 in the series and more than half of those—15—came from batsmen falling either bowled or lbw. I was fortunate, along with Nathan Lyon, to get the chance to pick his brains after the series when the two teams got together in the Sri Lanka dressing room once our defeat in the third Test was sealed, and listening to him explain how and why he did what he did was fascinating.

Herath said that, in essence, he just looked to land the ball on roughly the same spot ball after ball and, to that plan, he added his own variations and the vagaries of the pitch to help him achieve results. He would not only vary his pace, but also his position on the bowling crease and even the height of his bowling arm at the point of delivery. All the changes were subtle but they helped to create doubts and questions in the batsmen's minds. The additional problem for a batsman was that there was also natural variation to deal with—the fact that some balls spun while others didn't. A lack of spin might be prompted by the leather of the ball coming into contact with the pitch rather than the seam, but whatever the reason it was an added complication for a batsman to deal with. Herath admitted to me that even if he tried to spin six balls hard, some might not turn at all and he had no idea which would bite and which would simply slide straight on. And if the bowler had no idea then you can imagine the problem in dealing with the situation with a bat in your hand 20 metres away. It was another illustration of why we should have been playing the line of the ball rather than for turn but it was something we could not get our heads around out in the middle.

The batting let us down in Sri Lanka, there is no doubt about that, but it would be wrong to lay the blame for our Test losses solely at that department of our game and the defeats were a collective failing rather than down to one aspect of what we did or didn't do. The fact of the matter was that time and again we got ourselves into excellent positions with the ball, but we never managed to nail down the home side's coffin lid. It was a trend that started in the second innings of the first Test and kept repeating itself, just like our batting woes.

In Pallekele we took four Sri Lankan second innings wickets before the opposition took the lead and even allowing for the brilliance of 21-year-old Kusal Mendis, whose 176 was one of only two scores over 50 in the match (an illustration of how tricky conditions were for batting), we should have managed to restrict the home side to a lead well below the 267 it eventually achieved.

The pattern was repeated in the second match in Galle where we took a wicket with the first ball of the match and had Sri Lanka 2–9 only to see it recover to 281. And then in the second innings we reduced it to 5–98 and 6–121 only to see its batsmen reach 237. But worst of all was the final match in Colombo where Sri Lanka posted 355 after being 5–26 inside the first 90 minutes, and then it followed that with 8–347 declared having been 4–98.

The honourable exception to our bowling failings was Mitchell Starc, who took 24 wickets at 15.16 and was brilliant throughout the series. He swung the new ball in and then got reverse swing with the older ball and his pace throughout many long, hot days was always nudging up close to 150 kilometres per hour. He delivered more overs than any other seam bowler in the series and his 11 wickets *(5–44 and 6–50)* on a slow, spinning pitch in Galle was surely one of the great displays of fast bowling there can ever have been in the sub-continent. It was just a shame we could not back him up.

Nathan Lyon, by contrast, had a tough time. When the Sri Lankan batsmen defended against him he looked menacing, but they broke his spell and frustrated him by looking to play the sweep shot at regular intervals. The way for Nathan to combat that would have been to fire the odd ball in much quicker as variation, but he struggled to mix things up in that way and so although he got 16 wickets at 31.93—only Herath and Starc took more—he was played with relative comfort by the home side's batsmen. By the time we arrived in India for our tour in early 2017, he had learnt those lessons and looked much more effective, but I just wished he had been able to adapt a little quicker in Sri Lanka.

Of course, a Test series like the one we endured in Sri Lanka is full of what ifs, and another one came in the shape of a hamstring injury to Stephen O'Keefe. Just before he suffered a problem in the first Test, as Sri Lanka was trying to build some sort of lead in its second innings, I thought he looked as though he could take a wicket with every delivery he bowled. He was operating in a similar manner to Herath and had he played for not only the rest of that Test but also the matches that followed then perhaps, just perhaps, the results might have been different and Sri Lanka wouldn't have wriggled off the hook each time we thought we had them. His departure meant a call-up for Jon Holland but with the best will in the world it was asking a great deal for an uncapped player, even one with the depth of first-class experience Jon had, to fly in and adapt to the demands of the situation without missing a beat.

Problems like the injury to Stephen contributed to an atmosphere of feeling the world was against us and, as captain, I probably didn't do enough to stamp down on that mood, which became more and more prevalent within the camp as the series went on. We weren't happy with the pitches prepared for the series, especially in Pallekele and Galle, feeling they were far too weighted in favour of the home side, and we also felt the practice facilities served up for us were far from satisfactory too as the net pitches very rarely replicated the conditions we encountered out in the middle. It was frustrating, but the truth of the matter was we should have dealt with things far more positively than we did. By the time we got to Colombo for the final Test, a real siege mentality had set in. The fact I lost all three tosses in the series didn't help either as that condemned us to bat last each time in conditions suited perfectly for Sri Lanka's spinners, but that was something beyond my control.

As a captain, defeat, especially in the manner it arrived, was a real shock to the system, particularly as it was so unexpected. I had been in charge for 11 Tests before the tour and had never lost, winning seven and drawing the other four, so it was a new experience for me and not a very pleasant one, as it asked questions of me both from a personal and a tactical standpoint.

First of all there was my own behaviour around the touring group. I tried not to alter my behaviour and I always sought to make sure I was visible to the players and available to speak with them if they wanted. I'm not a shouter and there would have been little point in me becoming like that in any case, as I believe flying into a rage every time things go wrong is just the type of approach guaranteed to get you off-side with most of your teammates, who look to you, as captain, for calmness and leadership rather than senseless anger. I tried to remain upbeat in my body language, but things did occasionally get the better of me on the field from time to time with the odd shout or gesture of frustration here and there when things went wrong. I just couldn't help myself.

I can say now, looking back, that I learnt a lot about

the art of captaincy on the sub-continent from that tour, painful though the lessons were at the time. The Sri Lankan batsmen liked to hit boundaries and, at times, I needed to be a bit more defensive in my thinking by working with the bowlers to dry up those opportunities. In Australia the first thought is always to attack but I realised that restricting scoring can be just as effective in Asian conditions. If you can go at two runs per over then that can, and will play, on the patience of batsmen in those conditions, batsmen used to scoring freely, and that can be just as effective as posting a whole host of attacking fielders that, at the same time, leaves gaps for rapid run-gathering.

It was still a case of fine margins, of course, and although we were ultimately well beaten in each Test, we got into positions to rule over each match only to fail to do so. We held first innings leads in two of the matches so obviously we did things right some of the time—just not for long enough.

There was the odd bright moment for me personally as I managed to score a Test hundred *(119)* in Colombo, although even there it was a bittersweet achievement as, rather than being the bedrock of a consolation victory, it turned into a footnote instead. We reached 1–267 at one point with myself and Shaun Marsh *(130)* both reaching three figures and putting on 246 for the second wicket, only to collapse again, so it was not an innings I will remember with a great deal of joy. I played well, as did Shaun, who was terrific in his first match of the series, but it is hard to take any pleasure in individual success when the team is losing, especially when you are captain.

Criticism, from the media and the public back home, arrived in the wake of our defeats and unfortunately I have to admit that most of it was warranted. There was no real need for me to read most of the stuff written about us because it was blatantly obvious we were poor and none of us, least of all me, needed reminding. All the same, I do follow what's written and said about the team and myself, and it wasn't nice to cop it in the way we did. But it comes with the territory and if we are happy to accept the praise and the accolades when things are going well then, equally, we have to front up and accept when the opposite is true.

That criticism of me intensified when I left the tour early, following a heavy defeat in the second ODI in Colombo, with greats of the game including Jayawardene, Michael Clarke and Michael Slater all weighing in against my return home, and the fall-out from that decision and my departure taught me a valuable lesson: no matter how much the team management or anyone else wants me to take a break of that sort in the future, I won't do it again.

The issue of me returning home to rest had actually been raised by team management ahead of the opening Test, just after we arrived in Sri Lanka. The thinking was that with a busy summer ahead, starting with the one-day matches in South Africa, followed by the home Tests and ODIs, a Chappell-Hadlee ODI series in New Zealand and a tour of India, time away from the game and the pressures of captaincy would do me some good. And the plan for me to leave after the first couple of one-day games in Colombo made sense as, after that, the squad would be going up-country and so getting back to Colombo to fly out would have been taxing. The arguments certainly had some sense behind them, although part of the thinking was based on us doing rather better than we did in the Test series, allowing me to slip away with what we all hoped was a Test series win in my kitbag.

You could argue that because we'd done so poorly in the Test series, bringing with it extra pressure on me as captain, a break was actually more necessary than it would have been had everything gone well, but the fact we didn't announce it beforehand—with the benefit of hindsight, we should have done—left me open to accusations of being a captain leaving a sinking ship, especially as my departure was confirmed after a thumping loss by 82 runs.

It meant I left Colombo with a heavy heart and strong feelings of guilt, feelings that weren't really altered by the way we bounced back under David Warner to secure a convincing 4–1 win in the one-day matches before two more wins in the T20I rounded off the tour.

I arrived home to plenty of negative publicity, not only surrounding our displays on the tour, but also because I had left the trip early, and it wasn't great to read, hear and see all that negativity. It got under my skin and I didn't like it, but the decision had been taken and I just had to live with it.

I had taken a bit of persuading to buy into the idea and there was no doubt I was worn down and tired by what had gone on in the Test series. But although I did get some downtime back in Sydney, I also watched every ball of the remaining matches, wishing I was out there playing.

The bigger picture was, of course, that it gave David the chance to lead the side and gain experience of the role so that if I were to suffer an injury, or was deemed to be past my shelf-life as a captain in the future, it meant the selectors and the Directors of Cricket Australia, who approve any decision on who captains the side, had the option of turning to a player who had done the job already. That was another positive that came from something that didn't feel very positive to me at the time.

At least the successes in the limited-overs matches meant the tour ended on a winning note, although that feel-good factor didn't last very long thanks to the thumping we copped in South Africa.

It was a tough tour as we let ourselves down with the bat, and our attack, without not only the rested Mitchell Starc and Josh Hazlewood, but also the injured quartet of Nathan Coulter-Nile, James Pattinson, Patrick Cummins and all-rounder James Faulkner, simply didn't have the firepower to trouble the home side's impressive batting line-up on very good, flat pitches.

You could argue that the batsmen failed—David Warner being the exception—because we were always aware that with our inexperienced bowling line-up we needed to go hard to build a large score to defend, or we were chasing a big total having bowled first. But that would be unfair. If you are a batsman then all you need to do is to concentrate on doing your job without worrying about other factors and that is something we failed to do all too often on the trip. We were pretty much at full-strength in the batting department on the trip—Shaun Marsh pulled out because of a broken finger he suffered in Sri Lanka, to be replaced by Usman Khawaja—and the surfaces were for the most part excellent, so we had no excuse for the failure to post substantial scores on a regular basis.

David really gave us a lesson in what was needed, taking advantage of the batsman-friendly conditions to be the leading run-scorer on either side with 386 runs, including two hundreds. For my part, although I scored 108 in Durban, I managed only 43 runs in the other four matches and that was not good enough. I was fresh after my break but I just did not stand up.

We missed Mitchell and Josh massively. The seam bowlers on the trip—Chris Tremain, Daniel Worrall, Joe Mennie and Scott Boland—did not have Mitchell's extra pace or Josh's control and South Africa's batsmen revelled in the situation. I remember one occasion among many when Faf du Plessis hit one of our seamers over mid-off for four when I was feeling pretty helpless as a captain. I wanted to have mid-off back to protect against that shot but that would have meant bringing fine leg up to ensure I had the required number of men inside the fielding circle. And if I'd done that, then I knew the South African batsmen would start lap-sweeping safe in the knowledge the ball would be full in length and they could get down and play that shot without the risk of getting a 150 kilometre-per-hour ball in the helmet grille. Having proper pace in any form of the game is vital, but in limited-overs action it is essential because it stops batsmen taking liberties.

In an ideal world, of course, you pick your best players in every match and I know the public sometimes feel short-changed. After all, they are encouraged to buy their tickets early for matches and expect to see the very best players in action, only to find out just beforehand that certain players won't be featuring after all. But the reality is that in the modern era of almost constant cricket, with the demands on players in terms of athleticism and the changes between the three formats, avoiding rotation simply isn't possible, especially when it comes to the faster bowlers. They put so much strain on their bodies that injury is an occupational hazard—as one look at that list of players missing from the trip tells you—and so you have to balance the desire to play them with the need for them to rest. And you also need to bear in mind that when players like that have a break, they don't simply go and sit on a couch or stay in bed. They actually have weights and fitness programs that allow them to build up the muscles that deteriorate when they do nothing but bowl without the opportunity to work on their strength as well.

It can be hard if you get caught in the moment and there were times during that trip to South Africa where I thought about how good it would be to have Mitchell and Josh in harness, especially given how effective they had been against the same opposition in the Caribbean only a couple of months earlier, but ultimately the sense in the strategy was obvious from how both men made it through the six home Tests against South Africa and Pakistan that followed. I hate to think what we would have done if either of them had broken down at any point in those series given we were already without the other pace bowlers I've already mentioned.

I felt for Joe, Chris, Daniel and Scott as it meant they were thrown in at the deep end and for them it was just about as tough as it can get in one-day cricket. The wickets, for the most part, were flat, the South African batting was of a high quality and the crowds were partisan. When you add to that mix our failings as a batting side then you have a recipe for a losing tour. My hope at the end of the trip was that the punishment they suffered would act as a spur to improve rather than make them fearful of making the step up again in the future.

All the same, despite my disappointment at the way things had gone both personally and for the team, I was still feeling positive that our fortunes would turn around once we got back home in conditions we knew well. I wasn't to know at the time that things would get worse before they got better.

CHAPTER 16

Hobart 2016—Learning what captaincy is all about

'*'m embarrassed to be sitting here, to be perfectly honest with you.*'

With those words I began to answer the media's questions following what was, perhaps, the most humiliating loss of my international career, the innings defeat to South Africa in Hobart in November 2016.

My openness, and the unvarnished way I tried to answer those questions, reflected the combination of anger and frustration I was feeling after our fifth successive Test loss. All of those reverses—three in Sri Lanka and the first Test against South Africa in Perth ahead of the Hobart debacle—hurt, but this one hurt just a little bit more than the others.

Put simply, we had been thrashed. Had it not been for bad weather that pushed the match into a fourth day, we would have been beaten inside seven sessions, a return to the type of loss we suffered in successive matches on the Ashes tour of 2015 at Edgbaston and Trent Bridge.

But while we consoled ourselves then that we had been turned over in conditions far too heavily weighted in favour of the home side, there were no such excuses this time around, either in Perth or in Hobart.

What hurt me the most was that in both of those matches we'd shown a distinct lack of fight and as soon as the heat got turned up we went missing.

In Perth we were in a position to totally own the match. Having bowled out South Africa for 242 on the first day, we were 0–158 before lunch on day two, only to fall in a heap against a side missing a frontline bowler for much of the time after Dale Steyn went off with a shoulder injury.

My own dismissal as part of the first innings collapse was something of a turning point as I was given out lbw despite advancing down the pitch to left-arm spinner Keshav Maharaj. But although I felt hard done by with that decision, I could not feel hard done by at the result at the WACA Ground. The South Africans showed fight, desire and determination in a way that proved beyond us, and the bowlers left after Steyn's injury deserved immense credit for the way they performed. Vernon Philander and Kagiso Rabada were magnificent with the way they took up the slack and, with Maharaj tying up an end effectively, we were well beaten in the end.

But that loss was also an illustration of the fact that we seized up when the pressure was on, just as we had in the Test series in Sri Lanka earlier in the year. And when it happened again in Hobart, only this time to a far greater degree, then it was clear that something had to give.

The pitch for the second Test of the series, at the Blundstone Arena, was by no means an easy one to bat on and Philander and Kyle Abbott—Steyn's replacement—were two of the best in the world to exploit the conditions that offered both seam movement and swing.

But all the same, I reckon, with the benefit of hindsight, that 180 to 200 would have been a decent par score, not the 85 all out that we delivered. And to go, in the second innings, from 2–129 to 161 all out was simply not acceptable for any side, let alone one with as long and as proud a history as Australia.

What I said after the match, both to the media and afterwards to the players and support staff was unscripted and from the heart. The team's media manager, Kate Hutchison, made sure I had a briefing note of likely questions and my manager, Warren Craig, spoke to me briefly beforehand— on Kate's phone—and suggested I say what I wanted to say rather than what anyone might tell me to say. Warren also told me to avoid trotting out any clichés about doing our best and fighting back, but to be honest and call it for what it was—another terrible performance off the back of several others. And so I opted for the media conference equivalent of 'see ball, hit ball', simply responding as truthfully as I could to everything that was put to me.

'Too many times we have lost wickets in clumps, 8 for 40 today, 10 for 85 in the first innings, and you are not winning any games of cricket when are you doing that. And it is happening way too consistently for my liking,' I said.

'We are not being resilient, we are not willing to tough it out and get through tough periods and the longer you spend out there, things get easier, albeit the wicket was doing quite a bit and it was hard. The boys have got to start being a bit tougher and getting in a grind and getting in a contest and try to build a few partnerships because right now it is not good enough.

'If there is anything in the wicket—spin, swing, seam— at the moment we are not adapting well enough, we are not willing to grind it out and spend enough time out in the middle to be positive.

'It comes down to that resilience and having a good defence; at the moment our defence is being challenged and it hasn't been good enough.'

That idea of not being good enough was something of a recurring theme that day in Hobart because the Cricket Australia Chief Executive Officer James Sutherland and Pat Howard, CA's General Manager of Team Performance, said as much when they visited the dressing room to speak with the players and support staff after the match. If you get a dressing-down from what you could describe as 'suits'—and one that none of us could disagree with, either—then you know things have gone badly off the rails but I don't think we had any room to query the timing of this particular message. It's not something I'd ever experienced before in my career and I hope it's not something I'll ever experience again.

James said that off the back of five losses in a row the selectors had been mandated to make changes, something designed to take the side in a new direction. Given how we'd been performing, you could hardly say that message was a surprise, but it meant that by the time it was my turn to speak the mood in the room was even more sombre than it had been before, because there was a realisation that several people in attendance wouldn't be part of the group assembling in Adelaide for the next Test. When I spoke I did so to pin-drop silence.

'If we lose and we fight until the end, then I think we can all deal with that,' I said. 'But what we've delivered here has not been acceptable and it's not been acceptable for five Tests in a row now.'

I sought to be brutally honest and I think it was the first time my teammates and the team management had seen— and heard—me, not only speak my mind to that extent, but also get a little emotional.

I was fortunate that I'd batted reasonably well in the match—certainly in comparison to most of the rest of the team—in making an unbeaten 48 in the first innings and 31 in just over two-and-a-half hours in the second and so that gave me some extra credibility and authority to have a go at the rest of the players. 'I realise I'm the captain and also one of the team's frontline batsmen,' I said. 'But I can't do everything and it needs everyone in this room to take more responsibility and not leave it to others to deliver what's required. Yes, as a captain, I am ultimately responsible but everyone here, as players, has to be responsible too.'

My words may have been critical but the idea behind them was not just to deliver a rocket, but also to press everyone to get the best out of themselves and each other. We owed that much to ourselves, the support staff and also the many followers of our fortunes across the country and around the world. It was time to draw a line under being serial losers.

One thing I was clear about, both to the media and privately in the dressing room too, was that there was no question of pressure being heaped onto coach Darren Lehmann and his staff as a result of our losses. It's true that the coach and his assistants have the responsibility to prepare us properly to produce results on the field, but as far as I was concerned they were doing that perfectly well. What they couldn't do was bat, bowl and field, for us and that was where the problems lay, not with anything that was going on in the practice nets or the dressing room.

The coach's future had suddenly become a little bit of a focus with the media, because the downturn in results had followed him signing a new deal with Cricket Australia taking him through to the end of the winter of 2019, a winter due to include our defence of the ICC CWC and an Ashes series in the UK off the back of that. One report I read suggested that the type of run we were on would be enough to end some people's careers, but that was never something that entered my head in relation to him. Darren had fostered an excellent environment and assembled some wonderful coaches and experts alongside him to provide us with everything we needed to succeed. He wasn't the problem; it was the players and the way we were performing that was the issue that needed to be sorted out.

Did I feel under pressure as captain? Not at all is the simple answer. Yes, I was under pressure to deliver wins as the head of the team, but I never felt like I should resign. After all, what would that have achieved? We would simply have been back to square one, this time with a new captain who, unlike me when I took over on a full-time basis in late 2015, hadn't had the Test job before. There was one website that put together a graphic comparing our run of losses to the one that brought about the resignation of Kim Hughes as Australia captain in 1984, but that didn't really register with me. I wasn't born when that had taken place and, in any case, my focus was on the here and now, rather than something that happened more than 30 years earlier.

I was embarrassed by our results and I was also determined to ensure I did everything possible, both as a captain and a batsman, to get us out of the rut we found ourselves in. But once I had completed my duties at the ground, my overriding feeling was one of excitement. That might seem odd given the circumstances, but I was genuinely enthused about what lay ahead. After all, we were pretty much at rock bottom; we couldn't get any lower. Players were obviously going to make way, new ones would come in and that would give us the opportunity to create something different and hopefully better. We were being weighed down by failure and it was time for an injection of fresh blood, players not scarred by what had gone on over the previous few months.

I was not a selector—something I'm comfortable with given the limited amount of domestic cricket I get the chance to watch—but as the man charged with the responsibility of leading the players over the boundary rope it was right that I was consulted on the thinking of that group and, to their credit, I always have been. I had several chats with the selectors in Hobart when the opportunity presented itself, and during the Sheffield Shield match at the SCG that followed, when New South Wales played Victoria, I spent much of my time off the field high up in the stands at the Paddington End of the ground discussing scenarios with Mark Waugh, the selector on duty for that match.

By that stage the chairman of the panel, Rodney Marsh, had resigned and I'll forever be grateful to him for making that gesture. Not grateful in the sense of wanting him to vacate the role as, from a personal point of view, I had a great relationship with him and he was someone who I found read the game really well, but grateful because by stepping down when he did he took a lot of the pressure off the rest of us. As is often the case when things go wrong, there always seems to be the need to find a scapegoat, someone who can be blamed for the failings rather than looking for solutions. Rodney was the lightning rod on this occasion and his exit was another means by which we could draw a line under what had gone before and look to forge something new, starting with the day-night Test match at the Adelaide Oval.

The selectors—with Trevor Hohns taking over as chairman in place of Rodney, while Greg Chappell joined to supplement Mark Waugh and Darren Lehmann—eventually decided upon six changes to the squad with batsmen Peter Handscomb, Matthew Renshaw and Nic Maddinson, wicketkeeper Matthew Wade and seamers Chadd Sayers and Jackson Bird all included. It was tough on those left out, especially Joe Mennie and Callum Ferguson, both of whom had only had one match in Hobart to try and prove they were worthy of a longer run, but the selectors had to be bold in the wake of what had gone before, and they were.

I got a first-hand look at Peter Handscomb during the New South Wales–Victoria match as he batted for 120 overs to score 215 in his side's victory and I was impressed. His technique was different with minimal movement forward, but during that innings and subsequently he showed an ability to play the ball late and also to know his scoring areas of strength, and I liked that. He handled the quality spin of Nathan Lyon and Stephen O'Keefe impressively, both using his feet and sweeping, and it was a mature innings. He knew there were positions in the Australian line-up there for the taking. He also knew he was in the selectors' thoughts given he had spent the previous winter with the Australia A squad, so to then go ahead and deliver left me with a positive feeling about him ahead of the Adelaide Test.

I had played with Chadd Sayers, Jackson Bird and Nic Maddinson previously, the latter at state level for New South Wales, and so I knew what they could do, but Matthew Renshaw was an unknown quantity to me. In fact, when the squad assembled at the team hotel in Adelaide, I asked a few of those players I knew to tip me off if he walked past me as I'd never set eyes on him before. What I saw as soon as I had the chance to watch Matthew in action, first in the nets and then in the middle, was that he had a very calm temperament and also a clear game plan that he did not deviate from. He knew his area of strength, through the on-side, and he was happy to wait for the bowlers to lose patience bowling in the corridor outside his off-stump and attack the stumps so he could score in that area. And I remember when we were chasing our victory target in the second innings and his outside edge was beaten he simply laughed, knowing the ball had been too good for him. He took his elevation to the national side in his stride and fitted in straight away. And the bonus was that he showed that he had great hands as a close catcher, something the bowlers appreciated.

I was delighted to have Matthew Wade alongside me in the team. Matthew is someone I've known since the Australian Institute of Sport tour to India in 2007 and we have always got on well. A journalist once told me he regarded Matthew as the cricketing equivalent of a stone in your shoe and although that might not sound all that flattering, in terms of the impact he has on the opposition I think it is an accurate and positive portrayal of what he brings to the table. I like his grittiness, his energy both on and off the field. I like the fact he's vocal on the field and I like the feisty way he's willing to get stuck in. Matthew likes to be involved in the sticky situations on the ground, something he's done already on several occasions with success in limited-overs cricket, and although he had a modest time with the bat in the Test summer of 2016–17, I think of him as someone who will get more success the more he plays in the longest form of the game. He's good to have around the group as he reads the game well and I have found him to be an excellent sounding board for ideas out on the field. He is certainly a player I enjoy having in my team.

I felt for all the players who were dropped following the Hobart loss—Joe Burns, Adam Voges, Callum Ferguson, Peter Nevill and Joe Mennie, plus the injured Mitchell Marsh—but the selectors needed to make a statement in the wake of that defeat and they did so, successfully as it turned out. We were simply not standing up to be counted at the pressure moments in matches and on that basis change was inevitable. I wonder if, given their time again, the selectors might think they could have gone down the path of playing the newcomers eventually selected for Adelaide a little earlier. I suspect they would do but, as ever, hindsight is a great thing.

I would love to be able to bottle the energy we had around the playing group during the week of the Adelaide Test and dispense it before every game we play, because it was the best atmosphere I have experienced within an Australian squad in my time in international cricket. How it came about, I don't know, but it was a terrific thing to be a part of.

From my perspective I took that excitement I felt in the aftermath of Hobart and tried to bring it to the new group. My thinking was that this was my chance to make my mark with my team. There was no baggage and with so many fresh faces it was an opportunity to build a positive culture around the group.

At our first team meeting I put into words what I was feeling: 'There are lots of you here who can be a part of the Australian team for the next 10 to 15 years. We are a predominantly young group and this is a great opportunity. The chance to play in this team is what all of us have strived for our whole lives, so let's make sure we do it to the best of our ability—and enjoy what we're doing.'

The overwhelming feeling I got back from the group was positivity. Yes, we were 2–0 down in the series but there was no anxiety; it was just a bunch of blokes who wanted to play the game they loved. It was a terrific feeling.

There were other storylines around the Adelaide Test, of course. The fact it was a day-night match was one, as there was a great deal of interest in seeing how the concept worked after it had been perceived to be a success when tried against New Zealand the previous summer. And there was also the saga of South African captain Faf du Plessis and the ball tampering charge laid against him in the wake of the Hobart Test. Both of those issues helped to deflect attention from us and that was something I was grateful for.

I am actually a big fan of day-night Tests—as long as they are played in suitable conditions, and what we found at Adelaide for that South Africa Test was just spot-on. The pitch wasn't like concrete and it had a slight covering of grass too, so those factors ensured the ball stayed hard. It meant there was enough in it throughout the match for the faster bowlers while, as a batsman, if you were prepared to work hard then there were runs to be scored too. And with the ball actually spinning off the grass cover for Nathan Lyon, I thought it was just about the perfect pitch.

Fast-forward to the following month at The Gabba when we played Pakistan in a Test under lights and I had my reservations about conditions there. Yes, I dropped a couple of catches in the fourth innings that, had I held them, would have made our victory a lot more convincing than the 39-run margin it was in the final analysis. But I believe that had that Test been played in daytime with a red ball then Pakistan would have scored no more than 250 chasing the fourth innings target of 490. As it was, with the pink ball going soft, I reckon you had maybe 20 or 25 overs of hardness in that ball for the seamers to try and exploit, but if they failed to make the breakthrough then the pitch was so flat that there would simply be no reason for batsmen to get out, which the Pakistan lower order, together with hundred-maker Asad Shafiq, demonstrated very clearly. For that reason I finished that match regarding day-night Tests at The Gabba as very much a work in progress. At the same time I was willing to accept that at both venues the crowd figures were excellent. I would love conditions to be perfect everywhere, but at the same time I know there are other factors to consider as well.

After the losses in the Perth and Hobart Tests, as well as the lead-up to those defeats, in Sri Lanka and the ODI series in South Africa, I could not have asked for a better or more impressive turnaround than the one we produced in the second half of the home Test summer of 2016–17. You could suggest the Adelaide Test match was a dead game given South Africa had already won the series, but they wanted to beat us with a clean sweep, make no mistake about that, and we were good enough to outplay them in every department.

And although we were favourites to beat Pakistan in our own conditions, our 3–0 series win did us enormous credit. After all, as recently as three months before the first Test, Misbah-ul-Haq's side had been ranked number one in the world, and although they lacked a quality third seamer, they had Wahab Riaz, one of the world's leading fast bowlers; Mohammad Amir, a left-armer with an incredible skillset; and Yasir Shah, a leg-spinner with one of the best strike rates in the game. With the bat, they had Azhar Ali, whose record spoke for itself, as well as Misbah and Younis Khan, and so to paint them as easy-beats does our efforts no justice at all.

My emotions between the times I walked into the media conference that followed the Hobart Test match and the end of the series against Pakistan in Sydney could not have been more contrasting. They were chalk and cheese. The way the new players—and the established ones, too—stood up and turned around the fortunes of the side was gratifying and the fact I'd been able to perform with the bat, with hundreds in Brisbane and Melbourne, was just the icing on the cake.

I've never been a great one for milestones and I certainly don't play the game for such things, but the fact my form meant I finished my 50th Test, which took place at my home ground in Sydney, with an average in excess of 60 *(4752 runs at 60.15)*, was something that gave me a huge amount of pride. To join Donald Bradman *(6790 runs at 99.85)* and the English duo of Jack Hobbs *(4596 runs at 61.28)* and Herbert Sutcliffe *(4247 runs at 61.55)* as the only players to have achieved the feat was something that still makes me smile to think of, but the bottom line was it helped us to four successive wins to end the home Test summer on a high.

Statistics might not be a key driver for me, but I do set myself goals. As players we all fill out individual performance plans and mine tend to be annual rather than specific to a match or series. My goal at the start of 2016 was to remain as the number-one-ranked Test batsman for the year and I achieved that. I reason that as long as I'm number one then it means that both myself and, hopefully, the team are doing well.

One of my mentors, Brad Haddin, told a reporter after the home Test summer was wrapped up, that he thought the Hobart loss was actually the making of me as a captain and I think he was right. How things pan out in the long term remains to be seen and there will be plenty of other highs and lows before my career is over. But as hard as it was to take at the time, that defeat—coming off the back of losses in Sri Lanka and South Africa—helped me realise that captaincy was not just about making bowling changes and turning up for the toss. It was also about showing leadership with the bat and underlining to my teammates what was expected of them. It taught me to be more vocal about my feelings, and the way I handled the public scrutiny and the transition we went through gave me confidence to know I was capable of dealing with whatever the job could throw at me.

CHAPTER 17
India 2017

'*I set myself high standards and I wanted to lead from the front with my performances. I've sort of been very intense in my own little bubble and at times I've let my emotions and actions just falter a little bit throughout this series and I apologise for that. That's a big stride for me moving forward and something I can really learn from and continue to grow as an individual and as a leader.*'

At the end of a hugely significant series for me, both as a batsman and a captain, the words at the top of this page weren't the ideal ones for me to be saying at the post-match media interaction but I felt they needed to be said.

I'd led by example in scoring 499 runs at 71.28, more than any other player on either side, and scored three hundreds, and also had proved to myself and others that Australian teams could be competitive in Asia.

But, I knew my job as captain was to lead from the front not only through the runs I scored, but also through the way I conducted myself and I thought, at times, I'd forgotten that, and got carried away with the drama and the intensity of the action.

The two incidents I was thinking about when I said those words during my post-match interview at the end of the series were the Decision Review System (DRS) controversy in the second Test in Bengaluru, and my reaction, captured on camera, when India's Murali Vijay claimed a catch that replays showed he hadn't managed to take cleanly during the final Test in Dharamsala.

On both occasions I was in the wrong and although I know they were out of character for me, I still thought it was right to put the record straight and confirm they weren't things I was proud of, or would ever seek to condone. I'm glad I did it too, as I wanted to draw a line under those incidents and instead focus on what had been a terrifically fought series in which there was plenty besides those controversies that reflected extremely well on both sides and, in particular, my team.

The DRS situation was bizarre, not only for how it happened, but also for the fall-out that resulted. As for how it came about, well, the best way to sum it up was that it was a bit of a perfect storm in my own mind, or a 'brain fade' as I called it when asked by the media to explain the issue. We'd owned the match for long periods on a very poor pitch— the worst of the series, by far, although it produced some incredible cricket—and found ourselves chasing a tough but attainable score in the fourth innings, something that, if we achieved it, would take us 2–0 ahead with just two Tests remaining and ensure we retained the Border-Gavaskar Trophy.

The noise and the pressure was intense. I was out in the middle with Peter Handscomb, we were three wickets down, still needing more than 100 to win and I knew that my presence for the majority of the chase was vital if we were going to have a decent chance of getting across the line. In the face of all that, I managed to receive an absolute grubber from Umesh Yadav, bowled at over 140 kilometres an hour and pretty much on line, which hit me on the left shin.

My heart sank as I saw umpire Nigel Llong's finger go up but I was hoping—and it wasn't much of a hope, I'll admit—I may just have got outside the line of off-stump at the point of impact, something that would have led to the decision being overturned on review. I looked back at my stumps just to check where I was on the crease and then I went up the pitch to ask Peter what he thought.

That was the context as I walked up the pitch to speak with Peter after I'd been struck on the shin, and all I was looking for from him was even a suggestion that I'd got outside the line of off-stump and I was prepared to make the signal to review.

Unfortunately, Peter, playing in just his sixth Test, wasn't properly aware of the DRS protocols, that the decision on whether or not to review lies in the hands of the striking batsman and that he's only allowed to consult with his partner and no one else. His first reaction was: 'See what they reckon in the dressing room', and as a reflex, without thinking and with all the things I've already mentioned going through my head, I immediately turned in that direction. There was a television at the front of the team's viewing area, watched in conjunction with the live action on the field by the various players and support staff sitting there, and also Dene Hills, one of the assistant coaches and the team's performance analyst. Dene sits logging every delivery off the screen and recording it on a hard drive in case we want to go over any footage at a later time.

As soon as I'd done it I realised it was a no-no and I think everyone else out on the field and the dressing room, apart from Peter, knew too. There wasn't even time for me to get any signal from off the field—even if anyone there had been inclined to give me one—before umpire Llong was quickly on his way down the pitch shouting that I couldn't do that and that I had to make my way off the ground. My opposite number Virat Kohli was in almost as quickly to protest about what had happened, but by that time I was on my way and I missed the aftermath of Kohli's chat with both umpires.

After calming down once I'd got back to the dressing room, the incident slipped away from the front of my mind, crowded out by our late-order collapse as we lost our last six wickets for 11 runs to slide to a 75-run loss that levelled the series, and it wasn't until afterwards that I realised what a talking point it had become, fuelled by Kohli's post-match claims that we'd called on off-field assistance twice earlier in the match to help our on-field deliberations over whether or not to review decisions.

To say I was shocked by that comment is an understatement as I'm not sure where it came from in his mind or what basis he had for making it. As far as I was concerned, we'd never tried to consult with the dressing room beforehand and although he said he'd brought those previous occasions to the notice of the umpires, I can say categorically that we were never spoken to by either those umpires or match referee Chris Broad about any such breaches in protocol.

Virat has always been a player who's thrived in the most intense of environments and, like me, he loves a battle and I can only think that it was his way of raising the temperature in the series in an attempt to get the best out of himself. The idea of getting messages from the sidelines for that purpose was not a tactic we as a team ever spoke about and, even now, as I write these words with the series disappearing in the rear-view mirror, I can't work out what he was referring to in his remarks. There was never anything further on the matter from the International Cricket Council and Virat never detailed the incidents he was referring to. And during any brief interactions we had—including at the captain's briefing for the IPL as that tournament followed the series—he was friendly and it was as if any ill-feeling he may have had over the incident had disappeared. It was and still is all a big mystery to me.

What Virat's comments and the fall-out did was to ensure I stayed off social media for several days after the Bengaluru Test match. I'm a fairly regular Twitter, Instagram and Facebook user and I've never been one who's been all that sensitive to criticism because, on the contrary, I tend to read comments and use them as one of my motivations for doing well, but following the final day of that Test some of the comments got personal and nasty and I thought it was the right thing to do to try and switch off from the issue and start afresh in Ranchi when the third match of the series got underway nine days later. I even used the time for a short break, taking a trip to my bat manufacturer in Jalandhar and so let my love for my equipment become my main focus instead of any controversy doing the rounds.

The other incident I wasn't proud of, my reaction to Murali Vijay claiming a catch to dismiss our last man Josh Hazlewood in Dharamsala, was an example of allowing frustration to get the better of me.

In the final match of the series, with everything locked up at 1–1 and almost nothing to choose between the two sides on first innings, we had the chance to post a decent second innings total and put India under real pressure with the series at stake. But instead, on what was probably the best pitch of the tour, we succumbed to pressure and produced our most disappointing batting of the trip.

Our innings was already a write-off, nine wickets down, but with Matthew Wade still in at one end and with the knowledge we had added what turned out to be a crucial 55 runs for the final wicket in our first effort of the series in

Pune, I was still hoping we could scramble a few more runs to give us a little bit more to bowl at in the fourth innings.

Josh edged the ball from spinner Ravichandran Ashwin to Murali Vijay, standing close-in on the off side, and the fielder claimed the catch. And although the umpires Marais Erasmus and Ian Gould came together to chat about it rather than send Josh on his way without hesitation, their initial impression was that it was out.

I wasn't so sure, although I was 100 metres away, and when it was reviewed my reservations were proved to be correct as television replays suggested he hadn't got his fingers properly under the ball.

When I saw the relevant replay all the frustration of our failure to drive home our position of promise came out of me and I shouted out my anger and what I thought of Murali Vijay for claiming the catch. My mistake was three-fold: to appear to accuse a player of cheating when I knew that sometimes as a fielder you believe you've caught the ball when replays suggest otherwise; to do it in front of my teammates; and to do it in our viewing area in front of our dressing room, a place accessible to camera lenses, something that meant I was captured doing it by the host television broadcaster. Any viewer wouldn't have to be a lip-reader to know or have a decent guess at what I was shouting and it wasn't something that, in retrospect, I was proud of, hence my apology after the match was over. It was a case of two lessons for me in one—that as leader of the group I had a duty to remain calm and set an example, as if I couldn't remain cool then I couldn't expect my players to do likewise; and if I ever felt so frustrated in future that I had to let my feelings out, then the best place to do it was the sanctuary and privacy of the dressing room and not in a place where I could be observed and judged.

Despite those controversies and a few others besides that didn't involve me directly, I didn't feel it was an especially bad-tempered series. Yes, there was the odd flashpoint but that was always going to happen. There was a lot of passion on show and plenty of on-field words were exchanged as two of the leading sides in the world went toe-to-toe, but my own perspective was that players didn't overstep the line. And I think that was pretty well shown by the fact that there wasn't a long queue to the match referee's room as a result of players being sanctioned by the umpires.

I know there is a view that has us as the ugly Aussies and that although, when we are on top, we are all nice as pie on the field, when the opposition gets success against us then we are quick to get into them verbally, but I don't see it like that. It's simply that, as a group of players, we don't like backing down in a contest and the greater the intensity of the action on the field the more we all back each other up. If that's through the odd word with our opponents then so be it. The umpires are there to step in if anything is out of order and I don't think there was much, if anything, that fitted that bill through the series.

There was one incident, from day three of the Dharamsala Test where the Board of Control for Cricket in India (BCCI) released some footage on social media including audio from the stump microphones of an exchange between Matthew Wade and Ravindra Jadeja and I thought that was pretty ordinary. It was an example of the banter that took place on the field, but it gave a very one-sided view of what was happening as there would have been plenty of examples that could have been released of Indian players engaging with me and my team, such as when they were constantly in the ears of Matthew Renshaw when he resumed his first innings in Pune having had to retire ill because of diarrhoea. Ian Gould asked Matthew and Ravindra to cut it out in Dharamsala and that was where it ended, handled by the on-field umpires to the satisfaction of all those involved. So to rake it up in the way that it was benefited no one.

What was overlooked in the minor controversy that followed was that, under ICC guidelines, the broadcaster shouldn't have been broadcasting audio from the stump microphones, except for instances when the ball was in play and it certainly wasn't when Matthew and Ravindra were having their discussions. But whatever the rights and wrongs of the situation, it was a timely reminder to players of both sides that the old adage of what happens on the field, stays on the field, no longer applies.

It was disappointing that the glow of such a terrific series was overshadowed to a degree not only by that issue but also, to a greater extent, by Virat's post-series comments that he no longer regarded some of my squad as friends as well as opponents. I'm not sure who he was referring to when he said that, although I can guess one player he had in mind was Glenn Maxwell, who when running back to the in-field after chasing a ball to the boundary in Ranchi, appeared to grab his shoulder in mock pain. Given Virat had landed on his shoulder earlier in the match while trying to stop a four and damaged it to the extent that he was unable to play in the final match of the series, or take his place for the Bangalore Royal Challengers at the start of the IPL that followed, I thought that wasn't a very sensible thing to do, and I certainly didn't condone it.

The Indian squad declined to have a post-series get-together with us in the dressing rooms after the match in Dharamsala was wrapped up, and I would hope that was simply a case, as their captain in that match Ajikya Rahane said, of that type of gathering not being part of their culture rather than the legacy of any bitterness any of the Indian players may have been feeling as a result of what happened on the field. Even if there was anything they were unhappy about, I've always found the best way to put things to bed is to share a drink afterwards, but that didn't happen and it was a shame. I certainly didn't think the series was any more or less bad-tempered than any other series I'd played against India. There are flashpoints in any contest, but there was nothing out of the ordinary as far as I could recall. From my perspective I tend to block out most if not all that's said to me out on the field. It goes in one ear and out the other and all I focus on is the little red ball that's sent down at me.

I can still look back on the series with an enormous amount of pride in both my team's performances and also my own efforts with the bat. After all, let's be honest, to come out of the series losing 2–1, although disappointing given some of the positions we got ourselves into, was a fantastic effort and something few people had expected of us beforehand.

To put things into context, when we arrived in India, the home side had already played nine home Tests that season, against New Zealand, England and Bangladesh, and had won eight of them, drawing the other one. And in almost 13 years since Australia, under Adam Gilchrist and Ricky Ponting, won 2–1 there in 2004, India had lost just one (of 20) series on its own turf, against England in 2012. It was a formidable home record to come up against.

In the face of that, our chances didn't appear to most observers to be all that promising, especially given our recent record in Asia. We'd lost our last nine Tests in a row in the region, a 4–0 defeat against India in early 2013, a 2–0 reverse against Pakistan in the UAE in late 2014 and the 3–0 loss in Sri Lanka in mid-2016. There weren't too many people backing us to put a halt to that run this time around and, in fact, one friend said to me that, given our record and India's impressive home form over a long period, if we managed to come away with a 2–0 series loss then we deserved open-top bus parades around Melbourne and Sydney to celebrate.

I looked at things a bit differently, partly because when you are in my position, you have to. There's no point going into any contest believing you are going to get beaten up. If you do then you might as well not bother. Don't get me wrong: I knew it was going to be incredibly tough but I honestly believed we could compete. I knew we had two good spin bowlers, batsmen who could play the turning ball and fast bowlers who could do well whatever the nature of the conditions, so I thought we had a reasonable chance of doing something good. If you could have read my mind beforehand then you wouldn't have said I was confident, but I was certainly optimistic, and that optimism only grew after our breakout victory in the first Test in Pune.

My optimism came from the build-up to the tour, which was everything our build-up to the series in Sri Lanka hadn't been. This time, rather than acclimatise at our destination well ahead of the series, but have to put up with whatever conditions were presented to us, we opted to do the majority of our preparatory work at the ICC Academy in Dubai, about a three-hour flight from Mumbai. By doing that it allowed us to get over our jetlag there, so that when we arrived in India we were in a position to get down to work straight away, and it also meant we were in control of the practice conditions we had ahead of the tour starting in earnest.

The ICC facility at Dubai Sports City really is an oasis in the desert. About half an hour's drive along a 12-lane highway from Dubai's international airport, it is hidden away within a series of gradually rising tower blocks. But when you get there you can't fail to be impressed with what it has to offer. There are something like 30 outdoor practice nets, both turf and artificial, as well as two full-sized floodlit ovals and the pitches are made of soil from all over the world, something that allows the skilled curators to tailor-make pitches depending on the requirement of the players training there. And indoors there are more net pitches, each with their own characteristics, some of them spin-friendly and others offering extra pace and bounce, as well as a whole variety of bowling machines and even something called Pro Batter, that features a giant video screen where a bowler would normally bowl from. It has footage of most of the world's leading bowlers filmed from almost behind the wicketkeeper and it means that you can actually as good as replicate facing any of those it features, as the machine can even swing and spin the ball too.

I headed to Dubai ahead of several of the squad as, having rolled my ankle in the final ODI of the home summer against Pakistan in Adelaide, I was ruled out of the ODI series in New Zealand that followed. By going to Dubai earlier than I'd originally planned, it meant I was able to continue my treatment for the injury, given the support staff for the India tour were also present. It also allowed me to work with players not in the ODI squad, men such as spinners Nathan Lyon and Stephen O'Keefe, and start to formulate plans for how we could score runs against India's bowlers, dismiss their batsmen and all in conditions that we felt we were likely to face once we arrived.

The pitches we had in Dubai offered turn and were a little variable in bounce too, exactly what we wanted, and against that backdrop we got to work. The communication between batsmen and bowlers throughout the week I was there was terrific and exactly what we'd hoped for. A bowler would bowl to me saying, for example, 'The way you're set up to face me, I think I can get you out in this way' and that would allow me to tweak my approach accordingly. At the same time, I would look to disrupt the bowlers and present problems they might face in India and it was up to them to try and combat those tactics.

My own work with the bat involved trying to get my pad out of the way of the line of the ball against spin to reduce the threat of falling lbw as so many of us did in Sri Lanka. The reality is that it's extremely difficult to alter the habits that you've formed over many years and it is a case of almost re-training your brain and your muscle memory to do things differently. I think I managed it pretty well in the end.

Players were really in an excellent groove by the time we flew out—Nathan Lyon, for example, told me he'd bowled something like 1200 deliveries over the course of the training camp and he was absolutely ready for the action to start—and it was, without doubt, the best preparation for a tour I've ever experienced. And while it might not work as a prelude for every trip in the future—the schedules we work to these days often don't allow for a period of almost four weeks between the time we leave home to a Test series getting underway, which is what we had in this instance and, in any case, going to Dubai ahead of a series in Sri Lanka in the middle of the year as an example wouldn't work because at that time the outside temperature there is usually around 50 degrees Celsius—it's certainly something I'd be happy to do again in the future where circumstances allow.

It wasn't just a case of getting our own batting and bowling game plans in place in Dubai but I also had to work out, in conjunction with the coaching staff and team-mates, how we should go about our work. Our usual way of playing, when we were at home, was to attack as much as possible, but it was an approach that simply wasn't an option on the slow, spinning surfaces we were likely to come across in India. In recent series I'd been a part of in Asia we had often been guilty of over-attacking, either with the ball by placing too many catching fielders, or with the bat by looking to be too aggressive too early in our innings. The former allowed opponents to get away from us quite quickly while the latter gifted them wickets rather than making them work hard in conditions that were usually hot and unforgiving. It was time to do things differently and I think we got the balance pretty much right in the series, often setting a boundary fielder deep on the off side to ensure that when the Indian batsmen pierced the in-field they got one rather than four. One thing I've learnt is that India's batsmen love hitting boundaries—a look at the way they played in the series against England in late 2016 when they won 4–0 showed that—and so cutting off that outlet and hence slowing down their rate of scoring was a decent way to try and play on their egos and force an error.

One of the other things we discussed in Dubai was that we would make the tour a 'no whinge' trip. We had allowed ourselves to slip all too easily into a negative mindset in Sri Lanka the previous year and with more than one billion Indians keen to see us lose this time around, the temptation to feel sorry for ourselves if anything went wrong, was an easy trap to slip into. I didn't want that mentality this time, though, and when everyone bought into the idea when I floated it, it was exactly the response I was after. We managed, for the most part, to stick to the approach too, with everyone seeing the glass as half full rather than half empty and I'm sure it contributed to our achievements.

I think few people would have banked on us keeping Virat Kohli as quiet as we did during the series, restricting him to just 46 runs in five innings before injury struck him down in Ranchi, especially given the form he was in ahead of our arrival. In those nine home Tests he had scored an incredible 1206 runs at 86.14, with four hundreds, three of them doubles, and I think there was an expectation outside our group that it would be a case of more of the same from him during the series against us.

Our plans for him were pretty simple. The role of our spinners was to attack the stumps so that any mistake he made would be fatal while, for our quicker bowlers, the idea was to operate just outside his off-stump and look for him to edge behind the wicket. The added advantage of that approach was that it allowed me to post the majority of fielders on one side of the pitch, another way of keeping the scoring rate in check, and thankfully, he kept getting out. Maybe, given the form he was in, Virat just put too much pressure on himself to deliver again, and he also found uncharacteristic ways of falling, twice in a row dismissed offering no shot to our spinners, first bowled by Stephen O'Keefe in Pune and then leg before wicket to Nathan Lyon in Bengaluru.

As for the pitches, they were all a little different to what we were expecting, but thanks to the work we'd done in Dubai they weren't quite as much of a culture shock as might otherwise have been the case.

Pune, the scene of the opening match, did represent the biggest surprise to me personally as I'd played there less than 12 months earlier for the Rising Pune Supergiants in the 2016 IPL and back then the venue was a super batting surface. What we got for the Test was a surface that turned significantly, but that meant it helped our slow bowlers as much as India's. It played into our hands because as India had shown when it beat New Zealand, England and Bangladesh so comfortably before playing us, on decent surfaces that only deteriorated to help spin late in the match, its slow bowlers were better than any members of the opposition attacks. On a pitch that was a bit more of a lottery, that gap between India's spinners and ours was removed and it was Nathan and Stephen who reaped the benefit.

Bengaluru was the worst pitch of the series, which surprised me. I'd known it to be a terrific surface in my previous years playing in and watching the IPL but it had apparently been re-laid and the issue now was not so much any spin it offered, but the fact that the bounce was so variable—and more down than up, as I found out when I was dismissed lbw by that shooter in the second innings. Ranchi, where the third Test was played, looked the worst of the four Test pitches but actually played pretty well and Dharamsala, although it helped the slower bowlers when we'd played there during the ICC WT20 in 2016, actually had some pace and bounce this time and was the best pitch of the lot.

For my part, I was pretty satisfied with my own contribution as a batsman, although doing well when we didn't get the result we were looking for meant that personal success was always tinged with a bittersweet feeling.

The innings in Pune where I got 109 on a deteriorating surface in our second innings to cement our position in the match was my most satisfying of the series because I felt it was so important to set the tone in that first Test, and the fact I was able to do it with a big score was just what I wanted. I was desperate to lead by example and having secured a big first innings advantage of 155 on a pitch that would only get harder to bat on, it was great to be the one to ensure we kept our foot on India's throat.

The innings showed off everything I think I'm about through my ability to adapt to the circumstances in front of me. I scored virtually no runs at all down the ground as I knew that pushing at the ball to try and get it there was something fraught with risk given the ball was gripping in the surface. There was always a chance the ball wouldn't come on to the bat and all I would end up doing would be chipping the ball in the air to a waiting fielder, so instead I looked to limit myself to working the ball with the spin through the on-side and waiting for the ball to be either very full or very short before trying to pierce the off-side field. Also, and this was complete instinct, I played a few sweep shots, something that I never normally attempted. It was a case of thinking on my feet and I felt that was the best way to combat the bowling and conditions I was faced with.

With the ball turning as much as it was, it was important not to get too hung up when I was beaten, and that clear thinking, a legacy of the series in Sri Lanka in 2016,

certainly helped my mindset. And given the context—
India's home record, our own poor record in Asia, the
tough conditions and the fact it was the first Test of the
series—it will go down as my best effort of the tour. It won't
go down as one of my all-time favourites because I'm the
first to admit it was far from flawless and by kindest count
I was dropped three times. All the same, it was very gratifying to get a handshake from former India spinner Harbha-
jan Singh when we met up during the IPL. He came up to
me ahead of a group match for Pune against Mumbai and
said: 'That's the best hundred I've ever seen by a visiting
batsman in India.' To receive praise like that from a player
who's watched and played in plenty of cricket in the past
20 years—as well as someone who predicted before the
series started that we'd lose 4–0!—was special.

My second hundred of the series, 178 not out of 451 in
the first innings of the third Test in Ranchi, was a completely
different innings because, unlike that effort in Pune, this
time I was batting on a surface when it was at its best. The
pitch was flat, there was no spin to speak of and although
there was a little bit of reverse swing for the faster bowlers
when the ball was old, it wasn't something that couldn't be
dealt with. Always in the forefront of my mind was the fact
that we should be getting 600 on a pitch like that—it was a
great toss to win—and the fact we didn't, left us fighting for
our lives for the second half of the match. The fact we were
able to bat throughout the final day for a draw, especially
as we were four wickets down before lunch, showed me we
were learning the lessons of previous tours. There haven't

been too many teams, especially Australian ones from the recent past, who could have done that. By that last afternoon there was a significant amount of rough forming, especially outside the off-stump of the left-handed Shaun Marsh, but he and Peter Handscomb kept it simple, didn't get flustered when they weren't scoring and did a terrific job to draw the match and keep us in the series.

The 111 I scored in the first innings of the final Test in Dharamsala was my most aggressive innings of the series. I'm not quite sure why, but it was just one of those innings you have every so often where you are seeing the ball early, your feet are moving really well right from the outset, and the only danger I felt I faced was overconfidence. It was one of those occasions that sports psychologists love, when I could say with certainty that I was in the zone, completely relaxed and in control of what I was doing. All the same, when I'm in good form—and I think the same is true for any player—it is still always important to remember that every innings starts on zero with the resultant need to adjust to conditions and the bowlers. In this instance, though, I think my approach may also have had something to do with the fact I was feeling a bit fatigued by that stage of the tour. I'd batted for long periods, spent a long time in the field and I think I may have been worried about whether I could sustain my energy levels for another innings like the one I played in Ranchi, where I batted for over eight-and-a-half hours. So, on that basis, I thought that if I was going to get a decent score, then I was going to get it relatively quickly. The 111 came off 173 balls in 224 minutes, whereas the 178 came off 361 balls in 512 minutes.

What were the positives of the tour? Even in defeat there were still plenty of stand-out performances from our players. There was Matthew Renshaw's double of 68 and 31 in Pune despite feeling unwell, followed by Stephen O'Keefe's incredible match figures of 12–70 to bowl us to victory; Nathan Lyon's 8–50 and Josh Hazlewood's 6–67 in Bengaluru, the latter part of a superb fourth morning fight-back by our bowlers that saw us take the last six Indian second innings wickets for 36 runs; Glenn Maxwell's maiden Test hundred, 104, in Ranchi as part of a fifth-wicket of 191 with me; that stand between Peter Handscomb and Shaun Marsh to save the same Test; and the outstanding return of Patrick Cummins to Test action, full of pace and hostility, over five years after his previous appearance.

I knew what Stephen O'Keefe could do better than most. He lived with me as a tenant for a couple of years soon after I moved out of home and into an apartment of my own in Coogee, and having seen him over a number of years bowl outstandingly well for New South Wales, I had a feeling he could be a big player for us on the tour, although I couldn't foresee the impact he would have in that first Test.

In Sri Lanka before he had suffered his hamstring injury, I'd liked the look of him and his ability to change his angle of delivery by adjusting the height of his arm and also the position of the seam in his hand. It marked him out as a real threat if conditions were in his favour and they certainly were in Pune. Before lunch on day two he got his length and, more importantly, his pace wrong for the surface, but after the break he pushed the ball through a bit more, attacked the stumps and the collapse he helped provoke, with India losing its last seven wickets for just 11 runs, was like nothing I'd ever seen when I'd been in the field. The only situation I could liken it to was our collapse on day one of the Trent Bridge Test in 2015 when we were bowled out for 60 in just over 90 minutes.

Stephen was less effective as the series went on, but I believe that had more to do with India's batsmen becoming used to facing him and the threats he posed rather than any significant dip in the quality of bowling he was producing. He was, after all, something of an unknown factor to them before the series. And the fact he went at just 2.46 runs per over throughout the four Tests ensured I had a decent degree of control in the field whenever he was operating. Much the same was true of Nathan Lyon too, as he learnt his lessons from the Sri Lankan series, and with the two of them taking 19 wickets apiece at averages under 26 runs each (*O'Keefe 23.26, Lyon 25.26*) it meant they could be rightly pleased with their efforts.

When Glenn Maxwell was called up for the Ranchi Test in place of the injured seam-bowling all-rounder Mitchell Marsh, there was the odd murmur in the media as he wasn't the only option we had. We could have gone for a like-for-like replacement in Marcus Stoinis, who had flown in to replace Mitchell in the squad. We could have opted for a specialist batsman, Usman Khawaja, to bolster our middle order; or we could have gone for Glenn, and I felt he was the best fit.

We thought it would be a tough surface to score on and so we wanted someone who had the potential to take the game away from the opposition, but as it turned out the surface played well—and so did Glenn. I think everyone who's seen him bat knew he could play an innings like that, but it was just a case of him knuckling down and doing it. For the most part he put away his desire to be flashy and simply got on with the job of batting properly. There was just one occasion when I had to speak with him, when he played a reverse sweep. It simply wasn't a percentage shot and brought on more risk than reward. 'What are you doing?' I said to him when we met mid-pitch. 'You're batting well, so just keep playing sensibly', and to his credit he did. As it was we didn't get as many runs as we should have in that first innings, but without Glenn's effort—and remember he came to the crease with the score at 4–140 and a real chance of us squandering the advantage of winning the toss—we would have lost the match.

One area where I've come in for some criticism is my failure to bowl him more during the series, as Glenn only got through six overs in the two matches he played. In hindsight that criticism is probably justified, but my feeling at the time was that I had two quality spinners at my disposal and I thought it was the right thing to do to back them to get the job done. That's one of the beauties of cricket— for every problem there's always more than one solution. I went one way and maybe in this instance I could and perhaps should have tried something different.

Losing Mitchell Starc to a foot injury after the second Test was a serious blow given his skills in Asian conditions, shown most clearly on the tour of Sri Lanka in 2016, but the fact it gave us the opportunity to welcome back Patrick Cummins was a delight. The selectors and I were all in agreement that it had to be him that was called up, even though he'd played just one first-class match after returning from another debilitating back injury. It was tough on Jackson Bird, our reserve seam bowler on the trip, but what Patrick offered was speed through the air in much the same way that Mitchell Starc had done and on surfaces offering little in the way of pace that was a priceless commodity. He showed his strength too through his ability to ruffle and dismiss Indian batsmen with short balls in Ranchi on a lifeless surface, and the fact he got through 77 overs without a drama in the two Tests he played was a tribute to the hard work he put in to get back to peak fitness, and also to the way he was managed by the Cricket Australia medical staff as he made his way back to action. Patrick is a superstar in my eyes and if he stays fit then Australian cricket has an absolute diamond on its hands for the next decade.

At the end of the tour I had a whole range of feelings running through my mind. There was disappointment that we'd come so close to doing something remarkable, mingled with satisfaction that we'd defied almost all expectations by being so competitive. There was the knowledge too, that with the nucleus of the squad still relatively young, we had the potential to keep improving, and that is all you can ever ask of anyone.

CHAPTER 18
The Indian Premier League

If there is one subject that's guaranteed to divide opinion among cricket fans, especially those outside India, then it's the Indian Premier League (IPL).

On the one hand there's the colour, the noise, the glamour and the back-to-back natures of matches spread over almost two months that make it serious appointment-to-view action.

But on the other side of the coin there's the criticism that it's just the cricketing equivalent of fast food compared to the gourmet diet of Test matches, that the back-to-back schedule means matches are here today and forgotten tomorrow, and that the tournament is all about razza-matazz, commercialism and money rather than the sport. To many it is Vegemite—you either love it or you hate it, with very little in between.

From my point of view, even before I was drafted, I always viewed it as a pretty cool concept—and I'm not just saying that because I've been involved on a regular basis for several years. It was the first Twenty20 franchise tournament and I loved the idea of players from all over the world coming together in a team to try and gel in a short space of time in order to get success. The fact that it took place in front of packed houses was an added attraction as that's the sort of environment that any ambitious player wants to be part of.

Short form cricket, when I was starting out as a profes-sional cricketer, was a pretty good fit for me because I was a reasonably attractive package in that context. Leg-spin was, and still is, a big weapon in Twenty20 because of its wicket-taking potential, and the fact I was well thought of in the early stages of my career stood me in good stead. When you threw in my ability with the bat and in the field, too, then I can see now why I was the type of player that appealed to teams looking for personnel.

Test cricket was always my ultimate driver and that remains the case to the extent that success in that format has always been my number one priority. But rather than Twenty20 competing in my mind and in my training against that ambition, I always thought of it—and still do—as just a different goal rather than a competing one. And I believe that my ability to adapt and be successful in the two formats shows that a player can do well in both without compromising either.

Of course, it's impossible to talk about the IPL, certainly from an Australian perspective, without the twin issues of money and rest being brought up, so there's no point in beating around the bush on either topic. Yes, it's true, the money is excellent for a season that in terms of a calendar year is very short. But with that good money comes the pressure to deliver, especially as an overseas player and definitely as a captain. If you fail as a low-profile player then that is tough enough in that environment, but if you do so as Australian captain then that is headline news all over the world. I believe the players involved earn every cent.

But more than the money, I believe the best thing the IPL offers me—and any other player, for that matter—is the ability to learn on the job in high-pressure situations. We play so much, every third day or so, that certainly for me, I get to learn on the job. As an example, as a batsman I can be in a situation where, facing a target, I might push the accelerator too early, target the wrong bowler or look for the wrong option and get out as a consequence. In a tournament like the IPL the chances are that I'll find myself in the same or a similar situation in the next match or one soon afterwards and, armed with that experience, I can put into practice what I've learnt and ensure I don't make the same mistake again.

As far as I'm concerned, all I'm doing by riding that learning curve is something that generations of Australian players did before me when they played county cricket—players like Michael Bevan, Matthew Hayden, Darren Lehmann and Michael Hussey as just four examples out of many who trod that path. Back when they played in the UK there was no IPL, but what they were doing served a similar, if not identical, purpose: they were batting two or three times a week, maybe more, in different conditions against different bowlers and were learning all the time about what worked for them and what didn't, all the while playing with the pressure of being their county's overseas star, with the responsibility resting on their shoulders.

Nowadays, with international schedules the way they are, there's no chance for an Australian player of my generation to take the same route by playing a season of county cricket—although it's something I'd love to do when my international career is winding down, a bit like David Boon when he played at Durham. And so on that basis, the IPL has to serve as my finishing school, even for a player with my experience.

The tournament takes place during Cricket Australia's designated rest period for players and there is a view that players like myself should be taking advantage of that break to recharge batteries. The argument goes that I can't complain of being tired during a season or on a tour if I've already used up my leave time playing cricket elsewhere, and for very good money too.

I can understand that point of view and the money is great, but anyone that knows me, knows I don't play cricket for money. Yes, it's my job and, like anyone else, I expect to get paid for doing my job, but my view is that if I do well then the benefits will follow, and for me the be-all-and-end-all is that success and enjoyment are my motivations, not financial reward. The way I see it, if I wasn't playing in the IPL then I'd just be at home watching it anyway, so the chance to be mixing with the best players in the world and see what they do first-hand, how they bat, bowl and field under pressure, is as good a way to be spending my time as any other I can think of.

Seeing the way players deal with pressure and what their go-to options are is invaluable as a captain. For example, my IPL experience has taught me that Indian swing bowler Bhuvneshwar Kumar will look to bowl wide yorkers at the death, while his fellow international Jasprit Bumrah will bowl either a slower ball or a yorker. Knowledge like that—and facing it in pressure situations—can only stand me in good stead when it comes to dealing with those players on the international stage in similarly tense situations, and although the trade-off is that players I'll face in international cricket will be gathering similar intelligence about me, that is a price worth paying as far as I'm concerned.

Rivalries with international players from other countries is one thing, of course, but there is no such thing as a rivalry for me if a player happens to be on my team, and one such example of that was when I helped Ben Stokes, the England all-rounder, during the 2017 edition of the IPL.

Ben, like me, played for the Rising Pune Supergiant, and was practising some big hitting during a training session at our home venue in Pune relatively early in the tournament.

The practice pitches weren't the best and he was getting frustrated at his inability to time the ball. I watched him, spotted what I thought the problem might be and went up and chatted to him. I reckoned he was opening up his hips and that meant he was losing his shape as he tried to hit the ball. The way I explained it to him was that if he was playing golf he would stay side-on as that was one way to assist in gaining power. He took in what I said, tried a few more hits with that slight adjustment to his technique and seemed to middle the ball nicely from then on in the session. And even better was the fact that in his next match, against the Gujarat Lions, he scored a spectacular hundred *(103 off 63 balls)* to help us win the game—including six sixes.

Fast forward just over a month and Ben did something similar for England against us in the Champions Trophy, an innings of 102 not out, that ultimately played a big part in sending us packing early from the tournament. On that basis, did I regret helping him during the IPL, given my advice probably contributed to his big score? Not at all is the simple answer. I like helping others and the fact we were on the same team at the time only added to my desire to do so. In any case, no matter how well Ben played that day against us at Edgbaston, we didn't help ourselves as we didn't bowl as well as we could. And I'm pretty sure given there were the likes of Mahendra Singh Dhoni and coach Stephen Fleming also watching practice in Pune that day, if I hadn't said anything, then there were plenty of well-qualified and intelligent cricket people watching on who would surely have picked up on what I saw. There may also have been those who were surprised at my readiness to assist Ben given there was history between us. In 2015, as Australia's ODI captain, I insisted on an appeal against him for obstructing the field when he blocked a throw from Mitchell Starc during a match at Lord's. It provoked bad feeling in the media and among the UK public at the time but I was convinced he'd prevented a run-out opportunity and I still feel that way today. Ben was given out after the matter was referred to the third umpire and that was the end of it as far as I was concerned and, although he didn't agree with the decision, I think Ben moved on pretty quickly too, so there was nothing lingering between us when we linked up at Pune. He was actually a player I told the team's owners they had to try and get for the 2017 season. They did so, and I think his performances more than justified my belief in his ability.

Working with Fleming and Dhoni was a fascinating experience for me and one that almost brought the ultimate reward in 2017 as we fell agonisingly close to winning the IPL, which would have been an incredible achievement for a franchise in just its second season. But having got ourselves into an excellent position to win the final, reducing Mumbai Indians to 7–79 before restricting it to 8–129 and then reaching 1–71 in reply, we lost our way and lost by a solitary run.

I blame myself to a large extent for my side's failure to get across the line. Although I made 51 off 50 balls, the top score of the match, I scored too slowly in the middle of the innings, albeit on a tricky surface to accelerate, thinking that if I was there towards the end then we would win. We would have done too, if I hadn't picked out Ambati Rayudu on the cover fence when we wanted seven for victory from four balls.

It was a full ball from Mitchell Johnson, outside the off-stump, and it's a delivery I've replayed in my head countless times since. I couldn't have made any better contact and the ball went like a rocket out to deep cover. A couple of metres either side of the fielder and it would have been six and the scores would have been tied, but I picked out Rayudu perfectly, he held on and with Mitchell bowling a pretty nerveless final few balls we couldn't quite get over the line.

When I've replayed the ball I keep asking myself why I didn't just try to use a bit more bottom hand to get a fraction more elevation on the shot. It's in the past now, of course, and we all move on, but it's still an irritant that having gone as far as we did we couldn't quite get across the line just when it mattered most.

Being given the captaincy was an interesting experience as I took over from Dhoni. Out of the blue I got a call from the owner, Sanjiv Goenka, and the Chief Executive Officer, Raghu Iyer, asking if I was willing to take on the leadership role and my first reaction was: 'Has MS retired?'

Dhoni is a legend of Indian cricket, a man who'd captained his country to the inaugural ICC WT20 in 2007, a tournament that really marked the point at which the format went from a bit of fun to something far more highly regarded, and he followed that with doing the same in the

ICC CWC of 2011 when his side defied a massive weight of expectation by winning the tournament on home soil.

On that basis, and given the success he'd enjoyed captaining Chennai Super Kings in previous IPLs before joining Pune when Chennai was banned for two years, I'd just assumed he would carry on being in charge, but Sanjiv and Raghu both said they wanted a change. I was happy to go along with it, I told them, as long as they squared it off first with Dhoni. I was aware that there was the potential for me to become a serious fall guy given Dhoni's huge popularity within India and the last thing I wanted was to spend the tournament being public enemy number one, especially as I'd just experienced that for six weeks as Australian captain in the Test series. I'd seen what happened to John Buchanan a few years earlier when, as coach of the Kolkata Knight Riders, he'd tried to move on Sourav Ganguly, another Indian legend, while Greg Chappell had experienced a tough time as India's coach when he'd sought change within the national side. Issues like that highlighted that big players commanded enormous loyalty among the public in India and it was foolish to try and row against the tide in matters surrounding them, so I wanted to be on very solid ground if I took on Dhoni's mantle.

As it turned out, Dhoni was fine with the switch and although, initially at least—especially when we started off poorly—my Twitter feed was full of Dhoni fans abusing me, as things turned around for us so did the feedback I received on social media. I read all the comments, good and bad, as once again I sought to use the negative remarks as motivation, and by the end of the tournament I hope I went some way to showing the Indian public that I was actually a decent bloke when they got to know me.

Dhoni was terrific to work with on the field. I noticed a few comments on social media that suggested he was still captain in all but name, as occasionally there'd be television shots of him directing a fielder here or there, but that was exactly what I wanted from him. The wicketkeeper is in the perfect spot, by the stumps, to be able to see the angles where batsmen are hitting the ball and it means he's well placed to move a fielder a few metres one way or the other to make sure exactly the right place is covered. I thoroughly enjoyed working with and playing alongside him and I think we made a pretty decent team, along with Stephen Fleming.

Fleming and Dhoni had worked together for a number of years already, not just at Pune in 2016 but also before that at Chennai, and Fleming was someone else I really enjoyed interacting with. He's a good guy, as anyone who's ever met him will testify, and he understands the game brilliantly, as you might expect from someone who was an international captain for a decade. His skill is to have a light touch in that he doesn't go around badgering players and getting in their ears over every little detail. He credits you with being mature enough to know your own game and what your ideal preparation should be. What Fleming did well was make the odd observation about the opposition, whether it's a player or a tactic that's likely to be employed against us, and he also proved to be a great communicator with the different elements and nationalities within the dressing room. He helped me to ensure that a diverse bunch of blokes gelled together extremely well in a relatively short space of time.

The 2017 edition wasn't the first time I'd captained in the IPL as I took over from Shane Watson at Rajasthan Royals midway through the 2015 season. But the season in charge at Pune really was a terrific experience in captaincy and all that it involved. I felt, at the end of it, I came out of the tournament a better leader, so that was another plus point in taking part from my perspective.

It made me take a lot more responsibility for the team than I had done in past IPLs. Previously, especially as an overseas player with other commitments before the tournament, it was commonplace to arrive just a few days before the first match, have a few practice sessions and try to gel as best I could with quite a few players who I was meeting for the first time, some of them with English as their second language.

That wasn't such an issue when I wasn't in charge, but as captain I knew I had to be more proactive and more involved in the way the team was set up and the way it came together. So, on that basis, although I could have gone back to Australia for a few days ahead of the tournament just to get away and recharge my batteries after the Test tour of India, I opted instead to head straight to Pune, link up with Fleming and start running the rule over the squad ahead of the action commencing.

That proved to be a very useful exercise. At the outset we'd planned to open the innings with Ajinkya Rahane, with Mayank Agarwal as his opening partner. But during the centre-wicket internal practice matches we held I got the chance to see Rahul Tripathi too, and straight away he made an impression on me. He was running at the quicker bowlers, hitting the ball hard through point and he scored runs at a very healthy rate. We actually decided to persevere with our original plan of opening with Agarwal but when he didn't come off in that role then I was able to remember what I'd seen of Tripathi, push him up to the top of the list and he had a terrific tournament in that role, scoring more runs for the side *(391)* than anyone else apart from me *(472)*. I wouldn't have had that background knowledge on Tripathi to draw upon if I'd just pitched up a few days beforehand.

The Tripathi inclusion was something of a light bulb moment for us as a side as we had started off slowly. We won our first match only to lose our next three, but then we got on a tremendous roll, winning eight of our next 10 on our way to a play-off place, and we booked our spot in the grand final by beating Mumbai, ironic given we lost to Mumbai when it really mattered five days later.

What was satisfying for me was actually making it through a complete edition of the IPL without having to cry off injured, something I had to do in 2011, 2013 and 2016 when I had niggles. I could have gone on in each case but my aim was to be right for my next Australian commitment and so I pulled the pin and went home early to seek treatment to ensure I was fit and ready to go.

My IPL career has actually been a rather checkered one in the sense that I've been on the books for five different franchises—Royal Challengers Bangalore, Kochi Tuskers Kerala, Pune Warriors, Rajasthan Royals and Rising Pune Supergiants (or Supergiant as it was changed to in 2017)—but have only played for three of them as I didn't make it on the field for either Bangalore or Kochi.

With all that chopping and changing, the issue of gelling with a team was always an issue for me in the IPL because, unlike some players who've always been involved with just one or perhaps two franchises, and so get to know many of the players and staff over time, I've had to form new friendships multiple times, something far from ideal, because, familiarity with teammates and roles within a side is something that I believe is a key to success in Twenty20 cricket. One look at a side like Chennai that finished as either winner or runner-up in six of the first eight editions of the IPL is all the evidence needed to back up that theory. That franchise had a settled spine for much of that time with the likes of Dhoni, Dwayne Smith, Dwayne Bravo, Ravichandran Ashwin, Suresh Raina, Michael Hussey and Albie Morkel, and the results spoke for themselves.

In 2010 I was contracted to Bangalore, but I got a call from the team manager before the tournament to say that the overseas roster they had was more than sufficient to see the squad through and on that basis, rather than dragging me around India without much prospect of playing, I should stay at home, keep training and remain fit. If I was needed then I'd be called. I didn't get that call so that was the beginning and end of my time with that franchise. I contented myself instead with some time playing

Twenty20 cricket for English county side Worcestershire, something I thoroughly enjoyed.

The following year, 2011, I was all ready to play for Kochi after being picked up in the draft and was actually very excited at the prospect of finally featuring after my failure to make it as far as India 12 months earlier. Although I knew there was a strong chance I'd be dropped from the Test side after the Ashes series of 2010–11—even though that bad news was still to come at that stage—I was still very much a feature of Australia's limited-overs squads, but on international duty in Bangladesh, in April, I realised that something was wrong with my left ankle.

I felt out of rhythm when I was batting and although I've never been a big bender of my front leg at the best of times when playing forward, at that time I was struggling to put any weight at all on my ankle. It meant when I was batting, my right side was coming around to help balance me and compensate for my inability to put weight through my left ankle and that was getting me into some very awkward positions at the crease. And when I was bowling I just couldn't drive over my front leg as I wanted, something that helped me get good pace and revolutions on the ball.

The clincher that something serious was wrong came with my inability to complete the knee to wall test, something that's usually checked as part of regular medical screenings whenever the Australian squad is together. The test involves a ruler against a wall with the player balancing on one foot, which is flat to the ground. On that foot the player then bends his knee to hit the wall, with the amount of bend measured by the ruler. A player with a strong ankle and knee can bend a long way down, but I couldn't bend at all—not one centimetre. It was agreed that I should get the problem checked out and when it was, what was revealed was a significant bone spur that was causing the issue. I had no idea what had caused the problem—there was no moment that I could recall, like a twisting movement in a foot hole or a yorker striking the ankle—and once it was removed I very quickly found myself getting back to full fitness, but that injury cost me the chance to play for Kochi.

After two false starts, my appearance for New South Wales in the Champions League in India at the start of the 2011–12 season was especially important for me to keep my name in the IPL shop window, and I made sure that I took advantage of that opportunity. We had a decent side that included David Warner, Moisés Henriques, Simon Katich, Mitchell Starc, Patrick Cummins, Stephen O'Keefe and Stuart Clark among others, and we reached the semi-finals before losing out to Royal Challengers Bangalore in a run-fest in which both sides topped 200. I got a few runs here and there, including 45 not out in a low-scoring win against Mumbai, and that helped get me a gig with the Pune Warriors.

I was with the Warriors for two years, in 2012 and 2013, and it's fair to say those editions weren't the most enjoyable experience of my cricketing career. To put it bluntly, in both seasons we ended up as a bit of a rabble. In 2012 there were some strong characters in the dressing room, players like Ganguly and Marlon Samuels, and although we started off by winning three of our first four matches, we managed only one more win in our next 12 games. As results nose-dived there was more and more chopping and changing of personnel, we lacked a consistent starting 11, players didn't really know their roles and we ended up using 23 players. I had the consolation of playing well, scoring 362 runs with a strike rate close to 140 runs per hundred balls, but that was one of the few bright spots in a miserable campaign.

Things didn't improve much the following season either, and we actually ended up using 26 players then, including a real game of musical chairs with the leadership. Michael Clarke was a likely captain, but had to pull out through injury and Angelo Mathews was given the role but then wasn't able to lead the side in Chennai as there was an issue with the safety of Sri Lankan players playing in that part of India. Ross Taylor took charge and then Aaron Finch led the side for the second half of the edition but once again results were poor—we conceded 263 against Royal Challengers Bangalore, including 175 not out off 66 balls from Chris Gayle—and everyone was left once again searching for answers and a successful combination. My frustration was only heightened by the fact I only played seven matches as other players got picked in the overseas slots ahead of me and had it not been for Delhi Daredevils having an even more disastrous season than us, we would have finished bottom of the log in successive seasons.

That was the year—2013—when I was actually contracted to play in the inaugural season of the Caribbean Premier League for the Antigua Hawksbills. That would have been an interesting experience, and a bit of history too as the tournament saw Ricky Ponting play his last professional cricket for that franchise, and it would have been wonderful to be a part of that. But by that stage I had been called up for the Ashes series in the UK and so the CPL had to drop off the radar.

I moved franchises for the 2014 season, picked up by Rajasthan Royals in the draft that took place on the opening day of the Centurion Test against South Africa where I scored one of my best international hundreds, and although we missed out on a place in the play-offs on net run-rate, and I only played 10 matches in my first season with that side, it was still a far more positive experience.

That net run-rate failure was all down to one of the more bizarre matches I've ever played in, against Mumbai Indians in Mumbai when the opposition chased down our 189 in 14.4 overs to just edge ahead of us. Corey Anderson blitzed us with 95 from 44 balls and we lost the plot in the face of that incredible onslaught.

The confusion we felt in the field was best summed up when one of our reserve players ran on at the climax of the run chase to tell James Faulkner to bowl a wide as he said that would put us through. I had no idea how that would have helped and I don't think James did either, but it scrambled his mind to the extent that he bowled a leg-side full-toss that Aditya Tare, the Mumbai wicketkeeper, clipped over long leg for six to knock us out.

Shane Watson was our captain that night, and a hard task it was. The following year he approached me after the season had begun and asked me if I'd take over the leadership role. He said he found trying to focus on the captaincy very taxing, especially in the field when he was also expected to make a telling contribution with the ball. By that stage I'd led Australia at Test and one-day international level and my approach had always been that I tried to think like a captain on the field anyway, rather than just drift along, so it suited me fine and gave me a bit more experience in charge of a side.

This time we made the play-offs only to lose to the Royal Challengers Bangalore in the eliminator, but I thoroughly enjoyed the captaincy and wanted more of it, although initially that wasn't possible when I moved to Rising Pune Supergiants for the 2016 season with Dhoni in charge.

That season, which wasn't a great one for the side as injuries crippled our campaign, ended in a bizarre manner for me, thanks to a minor hand injury. The IPL took place shortly after the ICC WT20 had finished and between tournaments I'd gone to Dubai for a break. At the end of my stay there I went to shake the hotel manager's hand and felt an intense pain in the back of my right hand. The handshake wasn't the cause of the problem—it must have happened when a ball hit me during the ICC event, although I couldn't remember any incident—but it didn't get any better during the IPL.

As the pain increased I spoke with Pat Howard, Cricket Australia's Executive General Manager of Team Performance, and we agreed that I should return home to get the issue checked out, but I didn't want to leave Pune in the lurch, especially as the franchise had already lost Kevin

Pietersen, Faf du Plessis and Mitchell Marsh to injury, so I said I'd go after a match against the Gujarat Lions. In that match I actually made my maiden Twenty20 hundred, 101 from 54 balls batting at number three, but we still lost off the last ball, which summed up our season.

That hundred was, to an extent, a monkey off my back as many of the world's leading players had scored three figures in the format before me, so it was another tick in the box from that point of view. But, honestly, scoring hundreds in Twenty20 cricket was not something I ever thought about before I actually achieved one. The bottom line is that with so few balls on offer it's rare to get the chance to face the 50 or 60 you need to reach that mark so the focus, with me at least, has always been about working out what a good team total is for whatever side I'm playing for and then batting accordingly. The hundred came in that instance, but the fact we didn't even win the game meant it didn't count for very much in the end anyway, and that's the point I always tend to remember.

There was a view that I couldn't have been too badly injured to have scored that hundred, but the problem was hampering me and was diagnosed as bone bruising, which eventually settled down ahead of our limited-overs tour of the Caribbean against the West Indies and South Africa in June 2016. It was just a confirmation that whatever the riches on offer at the IPL, and despite the fact that when I was on duty in India I was always full-on for whatever side I played for, Australia remained my toast and Vegemite.

CHAPTER 19

Frustration—World Twenty20 2016 and Champions Trophy 2017

One of the best lessons I've learnt as a cricketer is to enjoy the highs because you soon realise they don't come along all that often.

It's true that I have a great life. I do something for a living that I love and which pays me well and I get to travel the world doing it.

But at the same time, like any ambitious person, I want to be successful at what I do and when success doesn't follow, for whatever reason, it's a bitter pill to swallow.

I've mentioned already that the ICC CWC win in 2015, far from satisfying me, actually served as a major motivation in my career. I enjoyed the experience of winning a global event so much that I wanted to do it again.

And so when it came to me, captaining Australia at both the ICC WT20 in India in 2016 and the ICC Champions Trophy in the UK just over 12 months later, I was determined to add more silverware to the sideboard.

The fact we weren't able to do so on both occasions, actually failing to reach the semi-finals each time, was a major source of frustration for me, especially as I knew that we had squads that, had things turned out just a little differently, could have gone on to win those events.

But, for a variety of reasons that didn't happen, and all we were ultimately left with was to look on from the outside as other teams lifted those trophies.

Certainly, if I had my time again in the 2016 WT20 then David Warner and Aaron Finch would be the opening pair. The fact they weren't during the tournament when they were both chosen in the starting eleven was down to me, as the captain determines the batting order once the side is selected, and I opted to go down a different route—and the wrong one as it turned out.

On the face of it, having the two of them at the top of the order would appear to have been a no-brainer. Aaron was the top-ranked T20I batsman in the world at the time and had forged his reputation in that format as an opener, while David's reputation as a destructive player in that position in the shortest form of the game was and is well known. Straight after the WT20 he went on to lead the Sunrisers Hyderabad to the IPL title and enjoyed an outstanding tournament.

But the problem that confronted us as we contemplated the WT20 was that we had an embarrassment of top-order riches, and it was a question of trying to find a way to fit them all in to best suit the side.

Also in the squad was Usman Khawaja, who was off the back of a superb Big Bash League season at home, which included two hundreds for the Sydney Thunder, while Shane Watson had scored an outstanding hundred against India when he opened the batting in the final T20I of our home summer, in Sydney.

We had a three-match series in South Africa ahead of the WT20 and looked at combinations there, with Usman and Aaron opening in game one, Aaron and Shane in game two and Usman and Shane in game three. Now you could be critical here and say we should have just picked one pairing and given them a chance to bed in together, and India used that strategy in the three-match T20I series in early 2016 when it named the same 11 players for every game—and won 3-0. And nothing boosts confidence in a side like winning.

But each of the three openers we used in that series in South Africa, plus David, had outstanding claims on an opening berth, so we wanted to give them the opportunity to press their claims. It was a case, from a management point of view, of being damned if we did and damned if we didn't.

David didn't open in any of those matches in South Africa and was actually very successful at three and four in the order, scoring more runs than anyone else in the squad, including helping us chase down 205 in game two in Johannesburg with 77 off 40 balls. But although that seemed to make our lives easier, as by doing so well in those positions he made them his own and so took himself out of the battle for opening berths. In retrospect, it was the worst thing that could have happened. If David had failed at three or four then we would have been forced to revisit the idea of him opening, and that would have been the best result for us all. Hindsight, though, is a wonderful thing, isn't it?

You see, going into the WT20 and being mindful of how many good—and proven—players we had for a limited number of top-order positions, all I could think about was David's ability to be flexible as he showed in those matches against South Africa. But, by thinking along those lines, I lost sight of something else, that he was perhaps our most destructive player, was used to opening in Twenty20 cricket and, in a format where above all else you want your best players facing most deliveries, he needed to be walking out at the start of the innings.

I really shouldn't have paid as much attention as I did to what happened in South Africa, because, although it was excellent to get the whole squad together ahead of the WT20, the conditions we encountered were nothing like those we then faced in India. The ball came on to the bat to a far greater degree in South Africa, and the emphasis was on faster bowling with limited use of spin by both sides.

I eventually settled on Usman and Shane as openers for our first match of the tournament against New Zealand in

Dharamsala and the two opened again against Bangladesh in Bengaluru before Aaron Finch came back into the side to open against Pakistan and India in Mohali alongside Usman, while Shane dropped down the order as Mitchell Marsh made way for Aaron's recall.

The fact that Aaron was left out of those first two matches was a tough one for the selectors, given his excellence in the shortest form of the game and his experience of Indian conditions through time in the IPL, and it must have been even tougher for him—not that he showed it—given that less than two months earlier he had been captain of the T20I side.

Aaron had first taken on that role for a match against Pakistan in Dubai in late 2014 when George Bailey stepped down at a time when Michael Clarke, the Test and ODI captain, wasn't playing in the shortest format. At that time no one batted an eyelid at the leadership role being split between players.

But once I took over the Test and ODI sides, then there was an argument for saying I should do the T20I role too for the sake of continuity, and that was what happened for the WT20 and the tour of South Africa beforehand.

It was tough on Aaron as the schedule had meant he'd barely had a chance to stamp his mark on the role with just four matches in charge in late 2014, a solitary game that he missed against England in August 2015 because he was recovering from injury and then three matches against India at home in early 2016, during the second of which he damaged his hamstring and missed the third.

I found it a little awkward taking charge on that basis but, in truth, the issue of T20I scheduling was one that left me a bit bewildered. To play just the one on that tour of the UK in 2015 made no sense to me at all—if you are going to play a format, then at least make it a decent series of three matches—and I think it made even less sense to Cameron Boyce, the leg-spinner who was flown over from Australia for that one encounter.

With two of England's left-handers, Moeen Ali and Eoin Morgan, involved in a long partnership during that game, I had a huge dilemma about when to use him. Having flown him 16,000 kilometres I knew I had to bowl him but tactically, I wouldn't have normally considered bringing him on against two players well-suited to leg-spin and the ball turning into their pads. In the end I threw him the ball, his one over cost 19 and that was a key factor in us losing the match—we eventually lost by five runs—but it was no fault of Cameron's and more an issue of scheduling.

Leaving aside any awkwardness I may have felt about how I got the role from Aaron—not that it lingered for very long—I had no concern about taking over the captaincy in all three formats. There was a case for me to return to the ranks for T20Is to take a break from the pressures of leadership, but it wasn't an argument I ever had much time for. I was someone who tried to think like a captain out on the field, whether or not I was actually leading the side, so doing the job wasn't a great leap for me from that position, and I was at the stage of my career where I just wanted to play every match I could. I regarded myself as a good

Twenty20 player and so bringing the captaincy together across the formats made perfect sense to me.

Having said that, the tournament as a whole was certainly a steep learning curve for me as captain, and the lack of T20Is I'd played in the run-up to the tour of South Africa beforehand, was something that registered with me straight away. Fans of the game may not have realised it at the time, but the 2016 event was actually the first ICC WT20 I'd played in since 2010 when I was part of the side that reached the final. I'd missed the 2012 and 2014 events in Sri Lanka and Bangladesh as I transitioned from a bowling all-rounder to a batsman, and so getting up to speed again in tournament play took me a while to adjust to. In the IPL or the Big Bash League when I played that back home, there was usually a bowler or two within a side that, as a batsman, you could target—a weak link. Those weak links were a lot less common at international level, and so runs were a lot harder to come by.

The decision to bat David down the order in the WT20 didn't work, it was as simple as that. He faced just 35 balls, for 38 runs, across the four matches we played and that wasn't enough for a player of his ability to make the impact we needed from him. We did shift him up from four to three after the first two matches against New Zealand and Bangladesh, swapping places in the order with me, but we should have gone all the way and put him and Aaron back together. We will know better next time.

My other major regret from that tournament was not bowling Adam Zampa for enough overs in our do-or-die match against India. We'd scrambled to 6–160 in a game where the loser would drop out while the winner would go on to the semi-final, and Adam had bowled his first two overs very tidily, conceding just 11 runs. I could have gone with him again later in the innings, but I was mindful of how well Yuvraj Singh and Mahendra Singh Dhoni played against spin and so I opted instead for my faster bowlers. It proved to be the wrong call as that duo, together with Virat Kohli, just took the game away from us. Virat actually played so well in the end that it may well not have mattered which bowlers I'd used, but it was something that caused a gnawing in the back of my mind after the match.

Of course, it might all have been irrelevant if we'd had Mitchell Starc to call upon, but he was still recovering from surgery he'd had on his right foot and ankle during the previous home summer. Mitchell had established himself as one of the very best Twenty20 bowlers in the world through his ability to bowl fast, full-length deliveries to order, even getting the ball to reverse-swing late in the innings, and his knowledge of Indian conditions through playing in the IPL with the Bangalore Royal Challengers would have made him an invaluable member of the squad. But he wasn't there and we had to make the best of things in his absence and, in all fairness, we still had sufficient bowling quality—and quality across all disciplines—to have gone on and won the tournament. The majority of our players would walk into most other teams in the world, but as a collective we just weren't good enough at crucial times, and suffered a couple of self-inflicted wounds I've already owned up to, and that was enough to cost us the chance to progress and ultimately lift the trophy.

If the WT20 wasn't satisfactory, then the 2017 Champions Trophy was even less so. We didn't get to finish a single match and went home with one defeat against England when rain intervened during its chase, plus wash-outs against New Zealand and Bangladesh.

Against New Zealand we were definitely behind in the game. We bowled poorly to allow them to get to 291 and by the time the rain came we were already three wickets down for not many. I was still there and confident I could engineer a turnaround but, as I said in my post-match media conference, I would rather have been in New Zealand's position than ours when the match was called off.

The boot was on the other foot against Bangladesh; all we needed was to have batted for another four overs to complete 20 in our innings and therefore pick up the two points on offer, because by that stage we were already 1–83 chasing 183 for victory. It was frustrating but that is the game, unfortunately.

We knew at that point we had to beat England to progress, but frankly we got blown away on the day. Having scored 9–277, we were definitely in the game even though we should have gone past 300, as several players including myself got out when well set. We reduced England to 3–35 in reply but then got well beaten by a brilliant and brutal hundred by Ben Stokes, in partnership with Eoin Morgan. I had got to know Ben pretty well by playing alongside him for Rising Pune Supergiant in the 2017 IPL and it was interesting speaking with him after the match, as he told me that when England walked off at the end of our innings, its players regarded our total as well below average and that the chase would be a walk in the park for them. I think that is an indication of the way one-day cricket has now gone. Now that sides are so full of aggressive players, and Twenty20 cricket has shown batsmen what is possible, a score that used to appear tricky is now considered run-of-the-mill.

It means more and more sides in 2017 prefer to chase rather than set targets, as setting targets can be fraught with danger. With the knowledge that an opposition has players capable of scoring rapidly over long periods, and with players now more relaxed about chasing than may have been the case in years gone by, sides batting first are feeling duty-bound to go hard right from the off to try and give themselves larger and larger scores to defend. When that approach comes off then it's thrilling, but equally it can be something that has the potential to leave a team with egg on its face if things go wrong. Just look at what happened to England in a ODI against South Africa on the eve of the Champions Trophy, slipping to 6–20.

Our loss to England at Edgbaston was galling because having taken those three early wickets, Stokes *(102 off 109 balls, 2 sixes, 13 fours)* and Morgan went hard at us *(87 off 81 balls, 5 sixes, 8 fours)* and we simply didn't have an answer. *(They added 159 in 26.1 overs.)* Taken as a whole, our bowling in the first power play wasn't good enough but that, unfortunately, was a regular theme for us over the first two years of my time as ODI captain. The plea to start better with the ball was a constant one made in team meetings on numerous occasions, but for whatever reason we failed to do it on a regular basis. It was not for want of trying—and perhaps sometimes the bowlers were guilty of trying too hard—and we retained a happy knack of quite often being able to claw things back after the opposition got away to a flying start. But rarely did we start well with the ball and then continue to inflict damage. All too often sides were 0–60 or 1–60 rather than 2–40 against us after the opening 10 overs.

Whether we got the balance of our side right was something that was debated, and I could understand that. The selectors went with Moisés Henriques at number four in the order after Aaron Finch, David Warner and me, but there was a case for us playing an extra specialist batsman instead with Chris Lynn in the squad.

My own view was that I was happy with the balance of our line-up as after Moisés we had Glenn Maxwell and Travis Head—a player capable of batting anywhere in the top six—followed by Matthew Wade, and I tended to see Chris as an opener who could go hard in the first 10 overs. Including him in that role would have meant breaking up the Warner-Finch partnership that had served us well for a number of years, and perhaps after we made the mistake of doing that in the WT20 it was a case of once bitten and twice shy. But on the basis of us failing to progress beyond the group stages, it was a point that was an obvious subject of discussion and debate.

Aaron enjoyed success away from the opener's role for the Gujarat Lions in the IPL, and so perhaps, in the future, a top order of Warner, Lynn, Finch and Smith would be an option, but for Champions Trophy 2017 the selectors opted to go down a different path and it didn't work out.

Batting depth was certainly something that was a topic of discussions in the media during the tournament and England showed against us how important it was. Despite losing those three early wickets, Stokes and Morgan still had the confidence to continue to attack our bowlers, safe in the knowledge they had capable players down the list, with a player as dangerous as Moeen Ali set to bat at seven. In the first global 50-over tournament after our World Cup win of 2015, it was certainly an aspect of the game that had moved forward, and it gave us a jolt two years before the time came to defend our title in the same location.

It was tough to find too many positives from a tournament in which we failed to win a match and with rain an almost constant companion, but something I took away from the trip was that, given the age and quality of our squad, I reckoned most, if not all, of them were strong contenders to be around for the 2019 World Cup. Experience of conditions, venues and situations is always vital, and if we can use our failure in 2017 as a springboard to plan and execute a winning tournament in 2019, then some good will come from bad.

The elephant in the room both before and during the Champions Trophy was the dispute over the new Memorandum of Understanding between Cricket Australia and the Australian Cricketers' Association. There were plenty of suggestions I heard that the issue was a distraction for the players, and there is no doubt the fact the issue played out in public rather than in private, did no one any favours at all. But I can say hand on heart that it played no part in our failure to go beyond the group stage of the tournament.

I was actually quite clear with the players at the first team meeting we had after we got together. 'This is a big tournament, an ICC event and the second biggest one-day competition after the World Cup, and if we want to achieve anything here, then we can't afford to be thinking about or talking about pay,' I said. And in all fairness, it was never an issue that I heard raised when we got together as a group.

In any case, to blame the impasse for our failures with bat, ball and in the field would be a nonsense, because I can say without fear of contradiction that when I attended practice sessions or walked out to the middle, then the last thing on my mind was how much I was getting paid, and I'm certain the same was true of everyone else that was in our squad. If that sort of thought ever entered a player's head, then that player wouldn't be playing international cricket for very long. It's a tough enough profession without allowing things that are beyond your control to distract you. As a player, all you focus on is what's in front of you, whether as a bowler you're at the end of your mark and thinking about what you're about to deliver, whether you're a batsman contemplating facing and trying to work out where you'll score your next run, whether you're a fielder or wicketkeeper trying to make sure you stop or catch a ball if it comes your way, or whether you're a captain trying to determine how to control a game.

Fatigue was another possible explanation for our failure, and it was a question I fielded at the post-match media conference after our defeat to England but, again, there was no way we could use that as an excuse. It was true that several of the squad had been involved in the IPL and I joined up with the squad straight off the back of the final of that tournament. But to say I was therefore tired and not in the right condition to play, and to suggest that of any other member of the side, would be nonsense.

From my perspective, the IPL was excellent preparation for the Champions Trophy because it gave me a sustained period of white-ball cricket in pressure situations and so I felt absolutely ready when I landed in the UK. And as for fatigue, while the IPL was a testing event over a long period of time, I made sure I got some downtime when there were breaks in the schedule. I actually headed to Dubai twice to get away from cricket for a few days, switch off and relax, and so tiredness was nowhere near a factor for me in our early departure and I'm sure the same was true of the rest of the squad too.

And even if players had been tired or burnt out, I wouldn't have regarded that as a valid excuse anyway. The Champions Trophy is a big event, you're playing for your country and you're a professional, so it's part of your job to motivate yourself to perform in situations like that. You just get on with it.

The issue of terrorism was one that loomed large during our stay at the event, but that, too, was no distraction for the squad. A couple of days before I arrived in the UK a suicide bomber claimed 22 lives and inflicted injuries on dozens more at an Ariana Grande concert in Manchester, about 320 kilometres north-west of London, and then on 3 June there were a further eight deaths at London Bridge when attackers drove a van into members of the public and then attacked passers-by with knives. That followed on from an earlier attack near the Houses of Parliament, also in London, in March when five people were killed by an attacker and over 50 were injured.

The attack on 3 June coincided with a surprise birthday party for me that Dani had arranged at a restaurant in central London with players and support staff also in attendance. Dani and I had just got back to the team hotel in Kensington when I saw the news of the incident unfolding on Twitter and I turned on the television for further information. There was a period of concern in my mind for the wellbeing of the rest of the squad, but our security manager Frank Dimasi was able to account for everyone within 20 minutes and the hotel went into lockdown to ensure we were safe in case of any further incidents.

That was unnerving, especially with our next match against Bangladesh just 36 hours away, but although I can't speak for the rest of the squad, I can't say I ever felt in danger. Knowing London well, having been there on many occasions in the past, I was comfortable with the advice the team received from the tournament organisers and our own security personnel, that the arrangements put in place were sufficient to allow the tournament to continue unaffected. We were simply reminded to be vigilant at all times and to ensure we avoided built-up areas, but the thought of being threatened wasn't something that ever entered my head as I was playing or training.

In the current climate, the issue of security is only going to become more significant, not only for cricket, but for all sports to deal with. My first instinct is always to play cricket because that is what I am, a professional cricketer, and that's what I love doing. I also recognise that cricket, and sport in general, gives a great deal of pleasure to billions of people, and in this day and age, that is more important than ever.

At the same time, I know that as part of a high-profile sporting team we are potential targets, and terrorists in the past have shown they are willing to go after cricketers, as was the case in Lahore in 2009 when the Sri Lankan squad and match officials were attacked on their way to the Gaddafi Stadium in Lahore during a Test match.

It makes the issue of how to decide on the validity of threats and whether or not to play in a particular country more and more difficult to judge. A whole industry within cricket has now developed around threat assessment and although I recognise that it's a necessity, that doesn't make it any more palatable. I'm just glad I'm not the one who has to make those decisions.

CHAPTER 20
The future

I've captained my country, hit the winning runs in a World Cup final on home soil, been an Ashes winner, been part of the number-one-ranked Test and ODI sides and topped the individual Test batting rankings. On that basis you could ask what more there is to achieve in the game—and if you did, then my answer would be 'Plenty'.

As I write these words I'm only 28 and, I like to think, still nearer the beginning of my international career than the end. That decision might not necessarily be up to me, of course, as form, injury or the decision of the selectors may play their roles in bringing the curtain down on that part of my life, but at the moment I still feel there are plenty of cricketing ambitions left for me to aim for.

There are four principal goals on my cricketing bucket list and to be part of an Ashes-winning squad in the UK is certainly one of them. It's amazing that an Australian side hasn't actually won a series there since 2001, an eternity in cricketing terms, particularly when you think about some of the outstanding players we've had in the intervening years. We've had our chances since then but haven't been good enough to take them, but hopefully, come 2019, I'll still be in charge and will be able to help put that particular record straight.

That northern summer will be a significant one for Australian cricket due to more than just the Ashes, as it will also feature the CWC, and it would be fantastic to retain the trophy we won so emphatically in 2015. The last time the tournament took place in the UK, in 1999, Steve Waugh's side lifted the title, the first of three successive Australian wins, and the ideal for me would obviously be for history to repeat itself, although the Champions Trophy in 2017 left me under no illusions about how tough a task it will be. There'll be an added element of uncertainty to the quest too, as 2019 is set to involve just ten teams in a round-robin format ahead of the semi-finals, so there are unlikely to be any easy matches and we know from the Australian side's efforts the last time the format was tried, in 1992, that being a pre-event favourite doesn't necessarily count for anything at all.

What fills me with optimism for that date with destiny is that our early exit from the Champions Trophy gave us pointers about what we need to do and how we need to play in 2019, as well as showing us the same conditions at the same time of year that we'll face at the World Cup. We didn't adapt well enough to circumstances in our 2017 campaign, but our players will be two years further down the line in terms of experience by the time we get to 2019. And although we won't have quite as much experience as was the case within the 2015 squad, I would still fancy us, if we play to our potential, to go very close to securing the ultimate prize.

A year later will see the next edition of the ICC WT20 take place at home in Australia, at the start of the 2020–21 season, and I would dearly love to be involved in helping us lift the one global trophy that's eluded us. The fact the tournament is in familiar conditions should give us an advantage, but as it's due to take place at the start of the summer, that throws up a potential challenge as it may mean the pitches aren't as batsman-friendly as would be the case if it took place after Christmas. Knowing the public's love for Twenty20, as shown through the support of the Big Bash League, and knowing what a wonderful feeling it was to be involved in winning a home World Cup, it would be a dream come true to be on the winner's stage again for that event. We've always had the players capable of winning a global Twenty20 event, but have never quite achieved it in the past; I hope 2020 will be different.

Last, but by no means least on my list of remaining ambitions, would be a Test series win in Asia. We came mighty close against India in 2017, but until we actually get over the line, we will have the accusation that we are poor players in that part of the world hanging over us every time we travel. When I think of the progress we made from the Sri Lanka series in 2016 to that India series less than 12 months later, I am filled with optimism, but optimism is one thing and actually delivering on it is quite another.

None of these ambitions holds any more importance than any other, but if I can be part of sides that achieve them then that will be hugely rewarding. And as for individual goals, I like to think that if I've been involved in the line-ups that secure these successes then that would be satisfaction enough for me.

As for how much longer I'll continue as captain or how much longer I'll continue to play professionally, I can honestly say that neither thought has crossed my mind.

With the captaincy, I look at those who've gone before me in the recent past and the shelf life for the role seems to be between four and five years, certainly of the Test team. Mark Taylor did the job for just over four years, the same as Steve Waugh, and while Ricky Ponting lasted longer, managing almost seven years, Michael Clarke packed in after just over four years too. As I write these words, I've been permanent Test captain for two years.

My advantage when it comes to the potential for sticking in the role is that I took on the job relatively early, certainly in comparison to those I've just mentioned. I was 25 when I stood in for Michael in three Tests against India, and 26 when I took on the Test role full-time, whereas Mark, Ricky and Michael were all 29 and Steve was 33. That should hopefully ensure that if I stay fit and in form I have a chance at retaining the captaincy for a few years yet.

Would a few more years in the ranks, like all of the above players, have been beneficial for me ahead of taking on the captaincy? My simple answer would be no, as I didn't see it that way when I took the job and I still don't. I felt ready, the selectors and Cricket Australia's Board of Directors agreed, and on that basis it was a case of getting stuck in.

I certainly wouldn't like to make myself a hostage to fortune by saying 'I'll pack in the role by this time or that time', or 'I'll retire as a player in this year or that year' as all that does is start a discussion that's simply not necessary. I still have a total love of playing the game in all its forms and a love of being captain and as long as that continues then why would I entertain thoughts of it all finishing?

The captaincy has been pretty much as I expected in terms of what it demands of me both on and off the field. Although I was relatively young when I took on the job, I had been captain at lower levels, had the opportunity to observe others doing it and, as I mentioned earlier, had always tried to think like a captain in the field even when I wasn't one, so that helped to prepare me for the time when I stepped up full-time.

I still had a decent amount of experience as an international cricketer when the time came for me to captain the side as the Brisbane Test of 2014 was my twenty-fourth, while the New Zealand Test at the same venue 11 months later, when I officially became Michael's successor was my thirty-fourth. And in one-day cricket, when I led the side in Hobart in 2015, it was my forty-eighth one-day international, and the match against Ireland in Belfast when I took on that role on a permanent basis was my fifty-ninth. I certainly wasn't a novice.

The off-field demands of leadership, although I knew they were coming, did take some adjusting to, whether it's meeting with Cricket Australia officials or selectors or dealing with the media, as I'm now the face of the national team. It all consumes a great deal of time that, when I was just a player, I used to call my own, but with an excellent support network around the squad, plus decent time management, it's not impossible to come to terms with it by any stretch of the imagination.

Captaining the side across all three formats is a challenge, but at this stage of my life and my career I don't think of it as one that's beyond me. I've seen players pack in playing one of the formats to give themselves the best chance of success in one of the others and before I took charge we had different captains in different formats for several years, but that's not something that's entered my thinking. To start with, we play so little T20I cricket anyway that there's little point in giving that away as it would make little or no difference to my schedule.

But the bigger picture for me is that I love playing the game so much and want to be involved all the time, that I'm not sure I could stomach watching on from the sidelines while there was a game going on, thinking 'I should be there'. I had that feeling during the latter part of the Sri Lanka tour after I'd gone home to rest and I don't want it again anytime soon. My attitude may change over time as my body starts to get older and my life outside cricket starts to take on a greater importance, but at the moment I want to play as much as I can. After all, the way I look at it, I'll be a long time retired.

For all the initial success I enjoyed in my career as a short-form player and despite the enjoyment I derived from captaining Rising Pune Supergiant at the IPL in 2017, Test cricket remains my favourite format and I hope it retains its primacy within the game at international level. I know a lot has been written about the fact that the international schedule is cluttered and that five-day cricket is from a different era and should be modified or even abandoned, but as far as I'm concerned it's still the ultimate. There is no greater satisfaction for me than walking off at the end of play having batted throughout a day or through an especially tough period in a Test. There is no better sensation in the game than the first morning of a series and no better feeling than relaxing and enjoying the company of teammates after victory over five hard-fought days.

I'm probably from the last generation of players who grew up before Twenty20 took serious root all over the world, and for me the baggy green has always been something to be cherished. I realise that youngsters now, especially as they sit and watch the Big Bash League during their summer holidays, might see things a bit differently, and with the sizeable pay packets available to players tripping around the world from Twenty20 league to Twenty20 league, that is understandable, but I am determined to do all I can personally to ensure that I'm not part of the player group on duty if Test cricket goes down the plughole. That is something I hope will never happen in my lifetime. If that means more day-night Tests then so be it, and I'm encouraged by the talk of a properly constituted Test championship with a climax in order to give the format greater context. I accept that Test crowds are poor in certain countries around the world, but we have enough smart people within the game to address issues like that if there really is the will to do something about it. Test cricket is what I still judge myself on and I want it to be that way for as long as I'm still involved in the game and beyond. The Boxing Day Test in Melbourne and the New Year's Test in Sydney, for two, are in my mind iconic events and the numbers of people that turn up to watch, as well as the people following on television, radio and the internet are testament to that. I know sometimes change can be good but I'd like to think that certain things, like those matches, won't fall victims to any desire to bring it about, however well-meaning the motives.

I know the current schedule is like trying to fit a quart into a pint pot, especially for the higher profile international sides like Australia, but I'd also hope that all three formats—Tests, ODIs and T20Is—can and will remain part of the landscape at international level. I think they all offer something different and on that basis I'd love to see them all continue to play a part in cricket at the highest level during my career. ODIs are the format that's been spoken of as being most under pressure because of the rise of Twenty20, but it's a format I love. I guess I'm biased because of the 2015 World Cup but to me, 50 overs per side offers something for everyone: the chance for a person who only has the odd day to watch cricket can see both sides bat and bowl in a day and at the same time do so over a number of overs that allows for ebbs and flows that aren't possible in the faster pace of Twenty20 cricket.

Our schedule over the coming years might be enough to cause some people to shudder given the volume of cricket we have in front of us. In 2018–19, for example, from the start of that summer, we have pencilled in ODIs and T20Is against Pakistan and South Africa, four Tests against India, two more Tests against Sri Lanka plus a ODI series, then limited-overs matches against India, three more Tests against Pakistan and all that before the IPL, if any of us are able to take part, followed by the CWC and then a five-Test Ashes series. There's certainly plenty on but, rather than being daunted by it, I'm excited. I'd like to hope I'm still close to the top of my game by then and if I am then what could be better than facing up to the best players in the world and getting paid, and paid well, to do it in some special places around the world? As players we always have to remember how fortunate we are to be doing what we love and doing something millions of people would love to be doing in our places.

Again, I may be biased, but I reckon I'm playing in a terrific era for the game. When I look at the line-ups of some of the other teams we come up against, it's easy to see that there are plenty who feature who will go down as all-time greats. It's flattering to be mentioned alongside Virat Kohli, Joe Root and Kane Williamson, and the fact all four of us are part of the same era and seen as going up against each other to be considered the world's best batsman can only be good for the sport.

Do I regard them as rivals? Not as such and I don't set out every time I play against them to simply better their performances in some personal points-scoring duel. At the same time I'd be lying if I said I didn't keep an eye out for their scores. If it is a rivalry then I'd call it a healthy one. The others are all fantastic players. I have huge respect for all of them and the fact that we all have different styles as batsmen only adds to the potential for interest. One journalist said to me he saw the four of us at the top end of the batting rankings and thought of it as the modern equivalent of the rivalry between the four great all-rounders of the 1970s and 1980s: Ian Botham, Kapil Dev, Richard Hadlee and Imran Khan. If we're able to have as positive an effect on the game as that quartet then we will be leaving a pretty decent legacy.

I realise I've been in a fantastic run of form with barely a blip now since the start of the 2014–15 season and there will be those who will wonder how I'll cope, both as a batsman and a captain, if I suffer a downturn in that form. But, hand on heart, I can say the thought hasn't crossed my mind. You could argue I should have a plan in place to deal with such a situation but my attitude is that I'll cross that bridge if and when I come to it. I like to think of my approach as looking at the glass as half-full rather than half-empty. I'd rather focus on continuing to do well than preparing for a time when I might fail.

I know my time as an international cricketer will have to end at some time and when it does, as things stand at the moment, I'd still like to keep playing if I was able. Whether that's as a jobbing Twenty20 gun for hire or through a season or two in county cricket I can't say, although as I mentioned earlier the idea of county cricket does appeal. I can't see myself being able to do both, given the length of the county season and how it overlaps with other cricket around the world, but I think that will become clearer to me in the future—and hopefully it's quite a few years away yet.

As for the time when I won't be able to play any more, I have no idea what I'll be doing yet, although I think I'd want to stay involved with the game. I know from speaking with Warren Craig that attitudes and thought processes can change over time as he has given me the example of another of his clients, Glenn McGrath. Warren said Glenn always told him when he was still playing that the two things he could never see himself doing were commentary and coaching, and yet he's now doing both and loving them. That makes me realise that there's no point in being too set in my ways about the future at this stage of my life.

I had a spell in the Network Ten commentary box during the Big Bash League in 2016–17 and thoroughly enjoyed the experience, and although it could be argued that I should have been relaxing on a rare day off, my attitude was that the match was at the SCG, which is only 10 minutes' drive from my home, and I would have been watching it on television anyway, so why shouldn't I take up the chance to experience something different? I'm not sure it's necessarily something I would think about doing full-time, but at least if my thoughts ever headed down that road in the future and an opportunity presented itself, then I'll have a bit more information in order to make an informed decision.

My love of the game and the technique that's involved in playing it and playing it well might lend itself to coaching, but I'm not sure I could get on the same relentless treadmill as many of the current international coaches without experiencing the enjoyment that comes from playing. Perhaps a compromise would be some short-term consultancy roles, the sort of thing that Ricky Ponting has been doing for the past couple of years. I look at him and think he has the balance about right post-play.

All of that's in the future though. For now all I'm focused on is playing well and continuing to enjoy what is the best job in the world.

ACKNOWLEDGEMENTS

There are so many people who deserve thanks and gratitude for helping me achieve my dream of playing cricket for Australia and going on to captain my country.

That dream wouldn't have become a reality without the love and support of my family, and especially my dad Peter, mum Gillian and sister Kristie, as well as my fiancée Danielle. All of you have sacrificed so much to get me to where I am today. I owe you everything.

Cricket is a team sport full of individuals, and the players, coaches, team management and selectors within the teams I've lined up for have been instrumental in my success too.

317

It goes right back to the Sutherland Junior District Cricket Association and on to Menai High School, New South Wales juniors, the Sutherland and District Cricket Club, Sevenoaks Vine Cricket Club in England, the Australian Institute of Sport, Kent and Surrey's second teams and then the sides I've represented professionally: New South Wales, the Sydney Sixers, Worcestershire, the three IPL sides I've taken the field for—Pune Warriors, Rajasthan Royals and Rising Pune Supergiant—and, of course, Australia. I've made many friends and learnt many things about the game through my time with all these sides, it's been a pleasure to play for each one and I owe each of them a big debt of thanks.

The same applies to my manager Warren Craig, who's helped guide my career since the age of 18. Warren's been full of sound advice and wisdom and he's been someone who's always kept any success I've had very much in perspective. Thanks to you, Warren, for your invaluable assistance.

To Cricket Australia, your faith in me, both as a cricketer and a captain, have been much appreciated and I hope I've repaid that faith. I'm proud to have joined a select group of people to lead my country onto the cricket field. And to the Australian Cricketers' Association: thanks for continuing to support the lifeblood of the sport—the players.

To my sponsors: Sanitarium, Fox Sports, New Balance and the Commonwealth Bank, thanks for backing my career in the way you have. And to the fans, both at home in Australia and all over the world, your support allows people like me to earn a living playing the game and so, without you, I have no idea what I'd be doing for a job! Hopefully my performances on the field have served as some form of repayment for that support.

To Brian Murgatroyd, thanks so much for your hard work and assistance in helping to put my life and thoughts down on paper. The idea behind the book was that, rather than produce a blow-by-blow account of my life, in chronological order, I've looked at key passages and aspects of my life, how they affected me and how I developed as a result of them. The process has been a new and fascinating experience to be involved in and I've enjoyed it as you've helped to make it stress-free. Thanks, too, to Brian's wife Aarti and their daughter Aariana, his father Walter and his in-laws Jaswant and Reena Singh Dabas for putting up with his long hours chatting and working with me. I'm delighted with the end result.

To Allen and Unwin, the publishers of this book, and in particular Publishing Director Tom Gilliatt and Senior Editor Siobhán Cantrill, thanks for your faith in the project, your commitment to it, and your dedication in helping it come to fruition. I hope you're as happy with the result as I am.

To Colin Clowes, Clive and Lesley Upton; John, Jennifer, Jack, Jemima and Pippi Gayleard; Olympia Walker Galt; Jessica, Charlie and Matilda Crane; Garry Rainford; Padam, Pooja, Praniti and Prapti Singh Janghu; David Richardson; Jacqueline Pompeus; Agnelo Fernandes; Ben Leaver; Holly Colvin; Sami Burney; Tariq Khan; Jonathan Rose; Tim Whittaker; Alex Kountouris; Stephen Gray of Queensland Cricket; Brad Haddin; Phil Jaques; Mark Taylor; Stephen

O'Keefe; Trent Woodhill; Gavan Burden; and the Catho Bowlo Club at Catherine Hill Bay, you all played a pivotal role in this book reaching the shelves. Thanks to all of you.

My overriding feeling as I've put together this book has been that I've had a wonderful life to this point. I fell in love with cricket at an early age and I still feel the same about it all these years later. I'm so fortunate to play the game for a living and I want to keep doing it for many years to come. Hopefully this book is just the first chapter of my story.

INDEX